KT-195-637

26950

262

JOHN STUART MILL'S

AUTOBIOGRAPHY

Oxford University Press, Ely House, London W. 1

GLASGOW NEW YORK TORONTO MELBOURNE WELLINGTON
CAPE TOWN SALISBURY IBADAN NAIROBI LUSAKA ADDIS ABABA
BOMBAY CALCUTTA MADRAS KARACHI LAHORE DACCA
KUALA LUMPUR SINGAPORE HONG KONG TOKYO

JOHN STUART MILL

AUTOBIOGRAPHY

*With an Appendix of
hitherto unpublished speeches
and an introduction by*
HAROLD J. LASKI

LONDON
OXFORD UNIVERSITY PRESS

JOHN STUART MILL

Born: **13** Rodney Street, Pentonville   20 May 1806
Died: Avignon   8 May 1873

Mill's Autobiography *was first published* in 1873. In
The World's Classics *it was first published, together
with six hitherto unpublished speeches, in* 1924 *and
reprinted in* 1928, 1931, 1935, 1940, 1944, 1949, 1952
1955, 1958, 1963, *and* 1969

PRINTED IN GREAT BRITAIN

TO AUGUSTINE BIRRELL

WHOSE LOVE OF BOOKS IS AN ASSURANCE **THAT**

THESE PAGES WILL HAVE ONE READER

H. J. L.

16 *April* 1924

CONTENTS

INTRODUCTION

SIR LESLIE STEPHEN has complained that Mill's
Autobiography is almost wholly lacking in the
qualities which give charm to that class of literature. Certainly it is far more completely an intellectual exercise than any comparable work.
Save for the few pages which deal with his wife,[1]
there is almost no reference to the human emotions
of love or friendship. Even his most intimate
friends are judged much as a writer would judge
a person whose obituary estimate he had been
charged to compile. The Mill who was a tender
and lovable human being, anxious, as in the case
of Lord Morley, to do all he could to further the
prospects of a young man on the threshold of
a career, hardly emerges in these pages. The book
is essentially a record of the development of convictions. It has nothing of that magic which
makes Newman's *cri de cœur* so irresistible. It is
not, like Gibbon's *Autobiography*, a living picture
of its creator. It does not, like Trollope's portrait
of himself, move us more than we care to admit by
its humble simplicity.

But Mill's *Autobiography* is, nevertheless, a
document of the first importance in the intellectual
history of the nineteenth century. It is, in the first

[1] On this much discussed question see L. Stephen, *The
English Utilitarians*, iii. 56–60.

place, a careful record, by the subject himself, of a great educational experiment; and though, to most, the experiment will read like a record of medieval torture, no one can deny the value of its details. It is, in the second place, an account of the influence and creed of the Benthamite School by one who, Bentham himself apart, was probably its most distinguished member. It explains better than any other record why Benthamism failed to satisfy the England of the later nineteenth century, and why, after 1870, T. H. Green took the place of Mill as the most influential writer on matters of social philosophy. It paints a convincing, and, I think, a not unattractive picture of the way in which a body of ardent young men set out to convert a dubious generation to the acceptance of ideas which are only commonplaces now because they were occupied, with full minds and full hearts, in making them commonplaces. It reveals a devotion to the public good which is, it may be urged, without parallel in English history when the width of its achievement and the period of its effort are taken into account. It shows how that life on the heights which Plato commended can be combined with essential happiness. It displays a catholicity of outlook which is, I think, rarely achieved by men engaged in the promotion of a particular doctrine. It lacks, obviously, that power of self-analysis which makes the great autobiography, above all, for instance, the *Confessions* of Saint Augustine, a part of the essential literature of the world. But no man can afford to neglect it, who desires to understand the forces which make for the success of great movements.

The *Autobiography* was written within the last

five years of Mill's life, after his defeat at Westminster in 1868; most of it dating, as appears from the book itself, from 1870. We do not possess the manuscript in its complete form. Mill bequeathed it, with all his papers, to his stepdaughter Helen Taylor, who published it shortly after his death. Her own excisions from the complete manuscript are obvious in the printed text. But in 1922 there were sold at Messrs. Sotheby's all Mill's papers, the manuscript of the *Autobiography* being included. From an examination of it then made, I concluded that the printed text is some half-dozen pages shorter than the form in which Mill left it. The omissions principally related to Mill's relations with his father and his wife. I have been unable to obtain permission from the present owner of the complete text to reproduce it verbatim. The present edition is, therefore, simply a reprint of the ordinary edition as published by Helen Taylor.

At the sale above mentioned, however, there were sold a large number of Mill's speeches, none of which had previously seen the light. All of them were written out by him in full. With two exceptions, they date from the years 1825–30, which was, as the *Autobiography* explains, a period of intense intellectual activity on Mill's part. He had co-operated with Bentham in editing the *Rationale of Judicial Evidence*, and with his father in the latter's *Elements of Political Economy*, the basis of which, as he tells us, were the *comptes rendus* he provided of their daily talks upon the subject. His own first independent writings date from 1822; his first considerable essay from 1825, being an article in the *Parliamentary History and Review*

on the Commercial Crisis of 1825 and the Currency
Debates. These speeches, therefore, represent the
Mill who was beginning to feel his powers, and
attempting the expression of independent opinion.
I have selected for reproduction here six of these
speeches. All, except the first and the last, were
delivered by Mill at the meetings of the London
Debating Society founded at the instance of
J. R. McCulloch, the economist, of which men so
various as Praed, Macaulay, Thirlwall, Samuel
Wilberforce, and Mill himself were members. They
were carefully preserved by Mill; and each bears
on it his endorsement of the year and occasion of
its delivery.

From the materials in my possession, it is clear
that these debates aroused an intense interest in
Mill. He has referred in the *Autobiography* to the
'considerable part' they played in his life. He
acted as the Secretary of the Society. He was
accustomed to write out his remarks in full before-
hand. He kept careful notes of the substance of
the discussion; and he seems fairly constantly to
have exercised his right of reply. Not seldom the
interest of a discussion was so great that Grote or
Charles Austin would pass over to him a note to
suggest further dissection of the problem at Grote's
house at Blackheath on the following Sunday;
and some of Mill's notes of the discussions are
written on the backs of these invitations. The
range of the discussion was very wide. The state
of literature, the disastrous nature of Byron's
influence (on which subject Mill took the affirma-
tive side), the problem of population, the use of
history, university education, and government by
coalition, are typical of the subjects considered.

It has seemed worth while to print some fragments of debates of which Mill himself retained such happy memories.

The preservation of these speeches, moreover, is interesting evidence of Mill's zeal in preserving all possible documents which throw light upon his life and opinions. Mr. Hugh Elliott has printed two ample volumes of his letters; [1] but these constitute only a fragment of those Mill considered sufficiently important to preserve. There are in existence several diaries of his journeys to Yorkshire and the Lake Country, full of minute, and, as I am informed, accurate botanical information. He kept a most detailed diary, in his early years, of the way in which his days were passed; and any one who reads the extracts given by Alexander Bain will obtain an admirable index to Mill's way of life in the early period.[2] He will also learn, what is sometimes forgotten, that Mill as a young man did not fail to take lessons in music and dancing. It may perhaps also be mentioned, since Mill omits to notice it, that he was a great reader of novels. I was told by Lord Morley that few people enjoyed more, or read more often, *Pickwick Papers* and *David Copperfield*; and, like every true admirer of Dickens, he was devoted to Mrs. Nickleby.

In the fifty years that have passed since Mill's death, no teacher has arisen whose influence upon the mind of his generation has been so beneficent or so far-reaching. Green did, indeed, gather about him a band of earnest souls; but his voice did not

[1] *Letters of John Stuart Mill.* Edited by Hugh Elliott, 2 vols., 1910.
[2] *John Stuart Mill.* By Alexander Bain (1882), p. 18.

penetrate far beyond the walls of the university. Our own day boasts a multitude of competing prophets; but they do not play so universal a part as Mill. Accessibility to new ideas, indignation against injustice, catholicity of temper, and an infinite patience—these were the qualities that made him the mirror of all that was best in his age. He transcended an environment as difficult and as compelling as any from which a great thinker has had to escape. Bentham and the Utilitarians did their best to destroy in him that individuality of mind which he estimated later as the best quality of man. The theories of their antagonists were set in a system as mean and narrow as ever disgraced a great people. Those who desire to evaluate the worth of Mill must remember that when he began to do his work the franchise was still unreformed, there was no popular education, the universities were still the jealously guarded preserve of the Church, and trade unions were enmeshed within the categories of a selfish law of conspiracy. Most of these things have been either wholly or in part revised. The rights of the people have assumed a new dignity in political discourse. The iniquities of our social system are confronted by a challenge at once defiant and decisive. It is not untrue to say that the evolution which has occurred was in large part foreseen by Mill, and that, Darwin apart, he was more responsible for its coming than any other thinker.

No one can appreciate Mill who does not realize how wide are the influences which went to the formation of his thought. Not merely Bentham and James Mill, but Coleridge and Saint-Simon,

Comte, and Tocqueville, were streams that emptied themselves into the central ocean. The result is that in a period of narrow dogma he is distinguished by that instinct for eclecticism which is always characteristic of the most influential minds. He was a democrat, but no one was more critical of the evils of democracy. He was an individualist, but no one was more hostile to the excesses of *laissez-faire*. As Carlyle well saw, he was ultimately a mystic, but no one exposed more ruthlessly than he the dangers and illogic of ecclesiasticism. The ultimate thing for which he was concerned was the elevation of the mind of man. That was, at bottom, the root of all he wrote. It lends a quiet passion to his economic discussion as to his examination of the foundations of logic. It was the explanation alike of his zeal for popular education and of his defence of femininism. It was the motive behind his every attack upon injustice, whether of the American slave or the Irish peasant. Indignant pity, indeed, was with Mill, as with Burke, one of the noblest elements in his composition. That quality, with the power to be optimistic even when progress was heartbreakingly slow, informed all that he said and wrote. It lends, in the aftermath of fifty years, something of a prophetic quality to much of his speculation. It serves almost as much to encourage as to warn. It meant, as he once somewhere remarked, that if you can inform the passion of the multitude against the self-interest of a few, you have the right to await the outcome with confidence. But it meant also that the outcome is not a matter of some single person's lifetime. The great changes of history are the result of a gradual and imperceptible accumulation of minute changes; and the adjustment of man's nature to new demands is, in matters of ultimate social constitution, the slowest of all efforts. But the adjustment can be made; and it was therein that Mill discovered our right to hope.

He is not the author of a system. His mind, unlike that of his father or Bentham, responded too quickly to new ideas to acquire the vigour of outline that system-making demands. But there are certain points of emphasis in his work that are unmistakable. Like all the Utilitarians, he realized the vast importance of institutions to the society which lived under them. He saw that institutions are built by human effort, and he did not, therefore, fail to emphasize the importance of legislation. There is nothing of the administrative nihilist about Mill. He was for compulsory education, legal limitation of the hours of labour, State endowment of research, the control by Government of public works, Government assistance to the poor. His individualism, that is, was tempered by the lesson from experience that the unfettered competition of private interests cannot produce a well-ordered commonwealth. The State was for Mill, as it was also for Bentham, the great reserve force of society which interferes to prevent the capture of the engines of social power by sinister interests. Nor must we miss the significance in this context of his continuous emphasis upon co-operation. The student of Saint-Simon did not fail to remark that the wage-earning relationship is, in its simplest terms, a form of slavery. He believed that it was possible—more, that it was imperative—to reorganize the industries of the nation upon co-operative lines. The workers could govern themselves industrially not less than politically upon the supreme condition that they were educated as citizens.

That was the fact of urgency to which Mill never failed to return. His oft-expressed contempt for the intellectual standards of English life lay in his unwearied insistence that education ' is not the principal but the sole remedy, if understood in its proper sense '. That sense was the realization that ' the main branch of the education of human beings is their habitual employment '; and, like Adam Smith, he understood that the more complex the industrial system, the more impossible for most is a creative citizenship unless the total environment is itself a moral and mental discipline. He realized that no such claim could be made for the industrial atmosphere of the mid-nineteenth century. Men who were made in their daily lives the mere tenders of machines could never have full access to the riches of civilization. Mill's plea was for the conferring of that full and stimulating responsibility to which, at least ultimately, enduring civic strength is traceable. The private must feel that the platoon is an expression of himself if it is to do its duty on the field of battle; and he can never gain that sense if he is condemned for life to be the unheeded recipient of orders it is his duty unthinkingly to obey. We, doubtless, should state his problem in different terms; for half a century's further experience of capitalism has, on the one hand, raised new problems of international scope, and, on the other, intensified our perception that the qualities of democratic citizenship cannot be made manifest while autocracy presides over the industrial sphere. Yet the limitations of private enterprise were never long absent from Mill's mind; and the posthumous essays on Socialism are, even in their fragmentary form, evidence that he found its more extreme theses incompatible with social good.

It is in this economic background that Mill's individualism needs to be placed. And it is essential to its understanding to realize that it is not an automatic individualism. The thing for which Mill was concerned was that the citizen should be given the full chance to be himself at his best. That, at bottom, is the meaning alike of his emphasis upon the importance of diversity and upon the fact that there are reserves within the human mind into which organization cannot, and ought not to, enter. It was for that end that he built the social fabric upon a toleration so wide as to seem to not a few the coronation of eccentricity. To that end, also, he gave an earnest adherence to schemes like that of Hare, which aim at protecting minorities from the paralyzing effect of custom and numerical power. The object he had in view was the great object that individual vigour of mind should fructify the varied interests which it is the purpose of the democratic State to bring to the door of its humblest citizen. We should, perhaps, state Mill's problem differently; and the experience of half a century would make us emphasize more firmly the degree to which the preservation of individuality depends upon the positive character of social control. But the ideal of Mill is still as noble an ideal as a man may desire: the perception that the eminent worth of human personality is too precious to be degraded by institutions. Mill's method may, as Burke once put it, turn duties into doubts; but the common welfare depends, more surely than we are apt to realize, upon the extent to which men can be persuaded not to confound our wonted institutions with the ultimate principles of social organization.

Mill, of course, was no more free than others from the doubts of the time-spirit. It has been easy to show that the concessions he made to the critics of Benthamism have been destructive of its foundations. He thought that the theory of economic value was complete; and Jevons and Menger arose to demonstrate the instability of scientific hypothesis. His psychology reads a little pathetically now; for Hartley and the Associationists do not hold the proud place that was theirs in his day. Clearly, too, his pattern of representative government is more simple than the facts would warrant; and Fitzjames Stephen was able to make the theory of toleration seem to Conservatives an exercise in bad logic. Certainly, it must be admitted that none of Mill's construction has the permanence which belongs to work of the first literary rank. The corroding hand of Time lays its fingers more surely on political writing than upon any other kind. Fashions change; men answer problems in new ways. Yet it is essential to bear in mind that the difficulties Mill's critics have found are in large part the result of his own sense of the complexity of life, in part also of the fact that they inherit the consequences of his work. The modern economist may use a technique more refined than that of Mill; he rarely conveys the same sense of generous insight into his material. The modern logician has an apparatus incomparably more delicate and subtle; but those very qualities make his work less accessible, and, therefore, less educative than Mill's. The tradition is different because he wrote; and that, after all, is the final answer to critical analysis.

For the truest word about Mill has been spoken, as is fitting, by the most loved of all his disciples. 'Respect for him', says Lord Morley, 'became an element of men's own self-respect.' No one, on any final estimate, can doubt that Mill, as no other figure of his time, raised the moral stature of his generation. He ceaselessly directed its attention to the problems that are fundamental; he always made those problems intelligible and interesting. The *Autobiography*, in the end the most imperishable of his writings, is a record as noble as any in our literature of consistent devotion to the public good. Whatever he touched he did not fail to clarify. Few men have been more rigorous in their standards, and no man more zealous in the pursuit of justice. Certain defects, of course, he had; beside Rousseau, for instance, the fires of his emotion seem pallid and thin. But where Rousseau appealed to men's hearts, Mill elevated their minds. He held as high as any man the lamp of reason, and it burned the more brightly because he lived. There are men in the record of English thought, like Hobbes and Hume, whose work has been more universal; there have been men also, like Bentham, whose immediate influence has been more profound. But there are few who have better illuminated the tradition of their age, and none whose contribution was more honourable or more nearly stainless.

HAROLD J. LASKI.

THE LONDON SCHOOL OF ECONOMICS
    AND POLITICAL SCIENCE.

CHAPTER I

CHILDHOOD AND EARLY EDUCATION.

IT seems proper that I should prefix to the following biographical sketch, some mention of the reasons which have made me think it desirable that I should leave behind me such a memorial of so uneventful a life as mine. I do not for a moment imagine that any part of what I have to relate, can be interesting to the public as a narrative, or as being connected with myself. But I have thought that in an age in which education, and its improvement, are the subject of more, if not of profounder study than at any former period of English history, it may be useful that there should be some record of an education which was unusual and remarkable, and which, whatever else it may have done, has proved how much more than is commonly supposed may be taught, and well taught, in those early years which, in the common modes of what is called instruction, are little better than wasted. It has also seemed to me that in an age of transition in opinions, there may be somewhat both of interest and of benefit in noting the successive phases of any mind which was always pressing forward, equally ready to learn and to unlearn either from its own thoughts or from those of others. But a motive which weighs more with me than either of these, is a desire to make acknowledgment of the debts which my intellectual and moral develop-

B

ment owes to other persons ; some of them of recognised eminence, others less known than they deserve to be, and the one to whom most of all is due, one whom the world had no opportunity of knowing. The reader whom these things do not interest, has only himself to blame if he reads farther, and I do not desire any other indulgence from him than that of bearing in mind, that for him these pages were not written.

I was born in London, on the 20th of May, 1806, and was the eldest son of James Mill, the author of the History of British India. My father, the son of a petty tradesman and (I believe) small farmer, at Northwater Bridge, in the county of Angus, was, when a boy, recommended by his abilities to the notice of Sir John Stuart, of Fettercairn, one of the Barons of the Exchequer in Scotland, and was, in consequence, sent to the University of Edinburgh, at the expense of a fund established by Lady Jane Stuart (the wife of Sir John Stuart) and some other ladies for educating young men for the Scottish Church. He there went through the usual course of study, and was licensed as a Preacher, but never followed the profession ; having satisfied himself that he could not believe the doctrines of that or any other Church. For a few years he was a private tutor in various families in Scotland, among others that of the Marquis of Tweeddale, but ended by taking up his residence in London, and devoting himself to authorship. Nor had he any other means of support until 1819, when he obtained an appointment in the India House.

In this period of my father's life there are two things which it is impossible not to be struck with :

one of them unfortunately a very common circumstance, the other a most uncommon one. The first is, that in his position, with no resource but the precarious one of writing in periodicals, he married and had a large family; conduct than which nothing could be more opposed, both as a matter of good sense and of duty, to the opinions which, at least at a later period of life, he strenuously upheld. The other circumstance, is the extraordinary energy which was required to lead the life he led, with the disadvantages under which he laboured from the first, and with those which he brought upon himself by his marriage. It would have been no small thing, had he done no more than to support himself and his family during so many years by writing, without ever being in debt, or in any pecuniary difficulty; holding, as he did, opinions, both in politics and in religion, which were more odious to all persons of influence, and to the common run of prosperous Englishmen in that generation than either before or since; and being not only a man whom nothing would have induced to write against his convictions, but one who invariably threw into everything he wrote, as much of his convictions as he thought the circumstances would in any way permit: being, it must also be said, one who never did anything negligently; never undertook any task, literary or other, on which he did not conscientiously bestow all the labour necessary for performing it adequately. But he, with these burdens on him, planned, commenced, and completed, the History of India; and this in the course of about ten years, a shorter time than has been occupied (even by writers who had no other employment) in the production of almost any other historical work of equal bulk, and of anything approaching to the same amount of reading and research. And to this is to be added, that during the whole period, a considerable part of almost every day was employed in the instruction of his children : in the case of one of whom, myself, he exerted an amount of labour, care, and perseverance rarely, if ever, employed for a similar purpose, in endeavouring to give, according to his own conception, the highest order of intellectual education.

A man who, in his own practice, so vigorously acted up to the principle of losing no time, was likely to adhere to the same rule in the instruction of his pupil. I have no remembrance of the time when I began to learn Greek, I have been told that it was when I was three years old. My earliest recollection on the subject, is that of committing to memory what my father termed vocables, being lists of common Greek words, with their signification in English, which he wrote out for me on cards. Of grammar, until some years later, I learnt no more than the inflexions of the nouns and verbs, but, after a course of vocables, proceeded at once to translation ; and I faintly remember going through Æsop's Fables, the first Greek book which I read. The Anabasis, which I remember better, was the second. I learnt no Latin until my eighth year. At that time I had read, under my father's tuition, a number of Greek prose authors, among whom I remember the whole of Herodotus, and of Xenophon's Cyropædia and Memorials of Socrates ; some of the lives of the philosophers by Diogenes Laertius ; part of Lucian, and Isocrates ad Demonicum and Ad Nicoclem. I also read, in

1813, the first six dialogues (in the common arrangement) of Plato, from the Euthyphron to the Theoctetus inclusive: which last dialogue, I venture to think, would have been better omitted, as it was totally impossible I should understand it. But my father, in all his teaching, demanded of me not only the utmost that I could do, but much that I could by no possibility have done. What he was himself willing to undergo for the sake of my instruction, may be judged from the fact, that I went through the whole process of preparing my Greek lessons in the same room and at the same table at which he was writing: and as in those days Greek and English lexicons were not, and I could make no more use of a Greek and Latin lexicon than could be made without having yet begun to learn Latin, I was forced to have recourse to him for the meaning of every word which I did not know. This incessant interruption, he, one of the most impatient of men, submitted to, and wrote under that interruption several volumes of his History and all else that he had to write during those years.

The only thing besides Greek, that I learnt as a lesson in this part of my childhood, was arithmetic: this also my father taught me: it was the task of the evenings, and I well remember its disagreeableness. But the lessons were only a part of the daily instruction I received. Much of it consisted in the books I read by myself, and my father's discourses to me, chiefly during our walks. From 1810 to the end of 1813 we were living in Newington Green, then an almost rustic neighbourhood. My father's health required considerable and constant exercise, and he walked habitually before breakfast, generally in the green lanes towards Hornsey. In these walks I always accompanied him, and with my earliest recollections of green fields and wild flowers, is mingled that of the account I gave him daily of what I had read the day before. To the best of my remembrance, this was a voluntary rather than a prescribed exercise. I made notes on slips of paper while reading, and from these in the morning walks, I told the story to him; for the books were chiefly histories, of which I read in this manner a great number: Robertson's histories, Hume, Gibbon; but my greatest delight, then and for long afterwards, was Watson's Philip the Second and Third. The heroic defence of the Knights of Malta against the Turks, and of the revolted Provinces of the Netherlands against Spain, excited in me an intense and lasting interest. Next to Watson, my favourite historical reading was Hooke's History of Rome. Of Greece I had seen at that time no regular history, except school abridgments and the last two or three volumes of a translation of Rollin's Ancient History, beginning with Philip of Macedon. But I read with great delight Langhorne's translation of Plutarch. In English history, beyond the time at which Hume leaves off, I remember reading Burnet's History of his Own Time, though I cared little for anything in it except the wars and battles; and the historical part of the 'Annual Register,' from the beginning to about 1788, where the volumes my father borrowed for me from Mr. Bentham left off. I felt a lively interest in Frederic of Prussia during his difficulties, and in Paoli, the Corsican patriot; but when I came to the American war, I took my

part, like a child as I was (until set right by my
father) on the wrong side, because it was called the
English side. In these frequent talks about the
books I read, he used, as opportunity offered, to
give me explanations and ideas respecting civilization, government, morality, mental cultivation,
which he required me afterwards to restate to him
in my own words. He also made me read, and
give him a verbal account of, many books which
would not have interested me sufficiently to induce
me to read them of myself: among others, Millar's
Historical View of the English Government, a book
of great merit for its time, and which he highly
valued; Mosheim's Ecclesiastical History, McCrie's
Life of John Knox, and even Sewell and Rutty's
Histories of the Quakers. He was fond of putting
into my hands books which exhibited men of
energy and resource in unusual circumstances,
struggling against difficulties and overcoming
them: of such works I remember Beaver's
African Memoranda, and Collins's Account of the
First Settlement of New South Wales. Two books
which I never wearied of reading were Anson's
Voyages, so delightful to most young persons, and
a collection (Hawkesworth's, I believe) of Voyages
round the World, in four volumes, beginning with
Drake and ending with Cook and Bougainville.
Of children's books, any more than of playthings,
I had scarcely any, except an occasional gift from
a relation or acquaintance: among those I had,
Robinson Crusoe was pre-eminent, and continued
to delight me through all my boyhood. It was no
part, however, of my father's system to exclude
books of amusement, though he allowed them very
sparingly. Of such books he possessed at that

time next to none, but he borrowed several for me; those which I remember are the Arabian Nights, Cazotte's Arabian Tales, Don Quixote, Miss Edgeworth's Popular Tales, and a book of some reputation in its day, Brooke's Fool of Quality.

In my eighth year I commenced learning Latin, in conjunction with a younger sister, to whom I taught it as I went on, and who afterwards repeated the lessons to my father: and from this time, other sisters and brothers being successively added as pupils, a considerable part of my day's work consisted of this preparatory teaching. It was a part which I greatly disliked; the more so, as I was held responsible for the lessons of my pupils, in almost as full a sense as for my own: I, however, derived from this discipline the great advantage, of learning more thoroughly and retaining more lastingly the things which I was set to teach: perhaps, too, the practice it afforded in explaining difficulties to others, may even at that age have been useful. In other respects, the experience of my boyhood is not favourable to the plan of teaching children by means of one another. The teaching, I am sure, is very inefficient as teaching, and I well know that the relation between teacher and taught is not a good moral discipline to either. I went in this manner through the Latin grammar, and a considerable part of Cornelius Nepos and Cæsar's Commentaries, but afterwards added to the superintendence of these lessons, much longer ones of my own.

In the same year in which I began Latin, I made my first commencement in the Greek poets with the Iliad. After I had made some progress in this, my father put Pope's translation into my hands. It was the first English verse I had cared to read, and it became one of the books in which for many years I most delighted : I think I must have read it from twenty to thirty times through. I should not have thought it worth while to mention a taste apparently so natural to boyhood, if I had not, as I think, observed that the keen enjoyment of this brilliant specimen of narrative and versification is not so universal with boys, as I should have expected both *à priori* and from my individual experience. Soon after this time I commenced Euclid, and somewhat later, Algebra, still under my father's tuition.

From my eighth to my twelfth year, the Latin books which I remember reading were, the Bucolics of Virgil, and the first six books of the Æneid ; all Horace, except the Epodes ; the Fables of Phædrus ; the first five books of Livy (to which from my love of the subject I voluntarily added, in my hours of leisure, the remainder of the first decade) ; all Sallust ; a considerable part of Ovid's Metamorphoses ; some plays of Terence ; two or three books of Lucretius ; several of the Orations of Cicero, and of his writings on oratory ; also his letters to Atticus, my father taking the trouble to translate to me from the French the historical explanations in Mingault's notes. In Greek I read the Iliad and Odyssey through ; one or two plays of Sophocles, Euripides, and Aristophanes, though by these I profited little ; all Thucydides ; the Hellenics of Xenophon ; a great part of Demosthenes, Æschines, and Lysias ; Theocritus ; Anacreon ; part of the Anthology ; a little of Dionysius ; several books of Polybius; and lastly Aristotle's Rhetoric, which, as the first expressly scientific treatise on any moral or psychological subject which I had read, and containing many of the best observations of the ancients on human nature and life, my father made me study with peculiar care, and throw the matter of it into synoptic tables. During the same years I learnt elementary geometry and algebra thoroughly, the differential calculus, and other portions of the higher mathematics far from thoroughly: for my father, not having kept up this part of his early acquired knowledge, could not spare time to qualify himself for removing my difficulties, and left me to deal with them, with little other aid than that of books: while I was continually incurring his displeasure by my inability to solve difficult problems for which he did not see that I had not the necessary previous knowledge.

As to my private reading, I can only speak of what I remember. History continued to be my strongest predilection, and most of all ancient history. Mitford's Greece I read continually; my father had put me on my guard against the Tory prejudices of this writer, and his perversions of facts for the whitewashing of despots, and blackening of popular institutions. These points he discoursed on, exemplifying them from the Greek orators and historians, with such effect that in reading Mitford my sympathies were always on the contrary side to those of the author, and I could, to some extent, have argued the point against him: yet this did not diminish the ever new pleasure with which I read the book. Roman history, both in my old favourite, Hooke, and in

Ferguson, continued to delight me. A book which, in spite of what is called the dryness of its style, I took great pleasure in, was the Ancient Universal History, through the incessant reading of which, I had my head full of historical details concerning the obscurest ancient people, while about modern history, except detached passages, such as the Dutch War of Independence, I knew and cared comparatively little. A voluntary exercise, to which throughout my boyhood I was much addicted, was what I called writing histories. I successively composed a Roman History, picked out of Hooke; an Abridgment of the Ancient Universal History; a History of Holland, from my favourite Watson and from an anonymous compilation; and in my eleventh and twelfth year I occupied myself with writing what I flattered myself was something serious. This was no less than a History of the Roman Government, compiled (with the assistance of Hooke) from Livy and Dionysius: of which I wrote as much as would have made an octavo volume, extending to the epoch of the Licinian Laws. It was, in fact, an account of the struggles between the patricians and plebeians, which now engrossed all the interest in my mind which I had previously felt in the mere wars and conquests of the Romans. I discussed all the constitutional points as they arose: though quite ignorant of Niebuhr's researches, I, by such lights as my father had given me, vindicated the Agrarian Laws on the evidence of Livy, and upheld, to the best of my ability, the Roman Democratic party. A few years later, in my contempt of my childish efforts, I destroyed all these papers, not then anticipating that I could ever feel any curiosity about my first attempts at writing and reasoning. My father encouraged me in this useful amusement, though, as I think judiciously, he never asked to see what I wrote ; so that I did not feel that in writing it I was accountable to any one, nor had the chilling sensation of being under a critical eye.

But though these exercises in history were never a compulsory lesson, there was another kind of composition which was so, namely, writing verses, and it was one of the most disagreeable of my tasks. Greek and Latin verses I did not write, nor learnt the prosody of those languages. My father, thinking this not worth the time it required, contented himself with making me read aloud to him, and correcting false quantities. I never composed at all in Greek, even in prose, and but little in Latin. Not that my father could be indifferent to the value of this practice, in giving a thorough knowledge of these languages, but because there really was not time for it. The verses I was required to write were English. When I first read Pope's Homer, I ambitiously attempted to compose something of the same kind, and achieved as much as one book of a continuation of the Iliad. There probably, the spontaneous promptings of my poetical ambition would have stopped ; but the exercise, begun from choice, was continued by command. Conformably to my father's usual practice of explaining to me, as far as possible, the reasons for what he required me to do, he gave me, for this, as I well remember, two reasons highly characteristic of him : one was, that some things could be expressed better and more forcibly in verse than in prose : this, he said, was a real advantage. The other was, that people in general attached more value to verse than it deserved, and the power of writing it, was, on this account, worth acquiring. He generally left me to choose my own subjects, which, as far as I remember, were mostly addresses to some mythological personage or allegorical abstraction ; but he made me translate into English verse many of Horace's shorter poems : I also remember his giving me Thomson's 'Winter' to read, and afterwards making me attempt (without book) to write something myself on the same subject. The verses I wrote were, of course, the merest rubbish, nor did I ever attain any facility of versification, but the practice may have been useful in making it easier for me, at a later period, to acquire readiness of expression.[1] I had read, up to this time, very little English poetry. Shakspeare my father had put into my hands, chiefly for the sake of the historical plays, from which, however, I went on to the others. My father never was a great admirer of Shakspeare, the English idolatry of whom he used to attack with some severity. He cared little for any English poetry except Milton (for whom he had the highest admiration), Goldsmith, Burns, and Gray's Bard, which he preferred to his Elegy : perhaps I may add Cowper and Beattie. He had some value for Spenser, and I remember his reading to me (unlike his usual practice of making me read to him), the

---

[1] In a subsequent stage of boyhood, when these exercises had ceased to be compulsory, like most youthful writers I wrote tragedies ; under the inspiration not so much of Shakspeare as of Joanna Baillie, whose 'Constantine Paleologus' in particular appeared to me one of the most glorious of human compositions. I still think it one of the best dramas of the last two centuries.

first book of the Fairie Queene ; but I took little pleasure in it. The poetry of the present century he saw scarcely any merit in, and I hardly became acquainted with any of it till I was grown up to manhood, except the metrical romances of Walter Scott, which I read at his recommendation and was intensely delighted with ; as I always was with animated narrative. Dryden's Poems were among my father's books, and many of these he made me read, but I never cared for any of them except Alexander's Feast, which, as well as many of the songs in Walter Scott, I used to sing internally, to a music of my own : to some of the latter, indeed, I went so far as to compose airs, which I still remember. Cowper's short poems I read with some pleasure, but never got far into the longer ones ; and nothing in the two volumes interested me like the prose account of his three hares. In my thirteenth year I met with Campbell's poems, among which Lochiel, Hohenlinden, the Exile of Erin, and some others, gave me sensations I had never before experienced from poetry. Here, too, I made nothing of the longer poems, except the striking opening of Gertrude of Wyoming, which long kept its place in my feelings as the perfection of pathos.

During this part of my childhood, one of my greatest amusements was experimental science ; in the theoretical, however, not the practical sense of the word ; not trying experiments—a kind of discipline which I have often regretted not having had—nor even seeing, but merely reading about them. I never remember being so wrapt up in any book, as I was in Joyce's Scientific Dialogues ; and I was rather recalcitrant to my father's criticisms of the bad reasoning respecting the first principles of physics, which abounds in the early part of that work. I devoured treatises on Chemistry, especially that of my father's early friend and schoolfellow, Dr. Thomson, for years before I attended a lecture or saw an experiment.

From about the age of twelve, I entered into another and more advanced stage in my course of instruction; in which the main object was no longer the aids and appliances of thought, but the thoughts themselves. This commenced with Logic, in which I began at once with the Organon, and read it to the Analytics inclusive, but profited little by the Posterior Analytics, which belong to a branch of speculation I was not yet ripe for. Contemporaneously with the Organon, my father made me read the whole or parts of several of the Latin treatises on the scholastic logic; giving each day to him, in our walks, a minute account of what I had read, and answering his numerous and searching questions. After this, I went in a similar manner, through the ' Computatio sive Logica ' of Hobbes, a work of a much higher order of thought than the books of the school logicians, and which he estimated very highly; in my own opinion beyond its merits, great as these are. It was his invariable practice, whatever studies he exacted from me, to make me as far as possible understand and feel the utility of them : and this he deemed peculiarly fitting in the case of the syllogistic logic, the usefulness of which had been impugned by so many writers of authority. I well remember how, and in what particular walk, in the neighbourhood of Bagshot Heath (where we were on a visit to his old friend Mr. Wallace, then one of the Mathematical Professors at Sandhurst) he first attempted by questions to make me think on the subject, and frame some conception of what constituted the utility of the syllogistic logic, and when I had failed in this, to make me understand it by explanations. The explanations did not make the matter at all clear to me at the time; but they were not therefore useless; they remained as a nucleus for my observations and reflections to crystallize upon; the import of his general remarks being interpreted to me, by the particular instances which came under my notice afterwards. My own consciousness and experience ultimately led me to appreciate quite as highly as he did, the value of an early practical familiarity with the school logic. I know of nothing, in my education, to which I think myself more indebted for whatever capacity of thinking I have attained. The first intellectual operation in which I arrived at any proficiency, was dissecting a bad argument, and finding in what part the fallacy lay: and though whatever capacity of this sort I attained, was due to the fact that it was an intellectual exercise in which I was most perseveringly drilled by my father, yet it is also true that the school logic, and the mental habits acquired in studying it, were among the principal instruments of this drilling. I am persuaded that nothing, in modern education, tends so much, when properly used, to form exact thinkers, who attach a precise meaning to words and propositions, and are not imposed on by vague, loose, or ambiguous terms. The boasted influ-ence of mathematical studies is nothing to it; for in mathematical processes, none of the real difficulties of correct ratiocination occur. It is also a study peculiarly adapted to an early stage in the education of philosophical students, since it does not presuppose the slow process of acquiring, by experience and reflection, valuable thoughts of their own. They may become capable of disentangling the intricacies of confused and self-contradictory thought, before their own thinking faculties are much advanced; a power which, for want of some such discipline, many otherwise able men altogether lack; and when they have to answer opponents, only endeavour, by such arguments as they can command, to support the opposite conclusion, scarcely even attempting to confute the reasonings of their antagonists; and, therefore, at the utmost, leaving the question, as far as it depends on argument, a balanced one.

During this time, the Latin and Greek books which I continued to read with my father were chiefly such as were worth studying, not for the language merely, but also for the thoughts. This included much of the orators, and especially Demosthenes, some of whose principal orations I read several times over, and wrote out, by way of exercise, a full analysis of them. My father's comments on these orations when I read them to him were very instructive to me. He not only drew my attention to the insight they afforded into Athenian institutions, and the principles of legislation and government which they often illustrated, but pointed out the skill and art of the orator—how everything important to his purpose was said at the exact moment when he had brought the minds of his audience into the state most fitted to receive it; how he made steal into their minds, gradually and by insinuation, thoughts which, if

expressed in a more direct manner would have
roused their opposition. Most of these reflections
were beyond my capacity of full comprehension
at the time; but they left seed behind, which
germinated in due season. At this time I also read
the whole of Tacitus, Juvenal, and Quintilian.
The latter, owing to his obscure style and to the
scholastic details of which many parts of his
treatise are made up, is little read, and seldom
sufficiently appreciated. His book is a kind of
encyclopædia of the thoughts of the ancients on
the whole field of education and culture; and
I have retained through life many valuable ideas
which I can distinctly trace to my reading of him,
even at that early age. It was at this period that
I read, for the first time, some of the most important dialogues of Plato, in particular the Gorgias,
the Protagoras, and the Republic. There is no
author to whom my father thought himself more
indebted for his own mental culture, than Plato,
or whom he more frequently recommended to
young students. I can bear similar testimony in
regard to myself. The Socratic method, of which
the Platonic dialogues are the chief example, is
unsurpassed as a discipline for correcting the
errors, and clearing up the confusions incident to
the *intellectus sibi permissus*, the understanding
which has made up all its bundles of associations
under the guidance of popular phraseology. The
close, searching *elenchus* by which the man of
vague generalities is constrained either to express
his meaning to himself in definite terms, or to
confess that he does not know what he is talking
about; the perpetual testing of all general statements by particular instances; the siege in form

which is laid to the meaning of large abstract terms, by fixing upon some still larger class-name which includes that and more, and dividing down to the thing sought—marking out its limits and definition by a series of accurately drawn distinctions between it and each of the cognate objects which are successively parted off from it—all this, as an education for precise thinking, is inestimable, and all this, even at that age, took such hold of me that it became part of my own mind. I have felt ever since that the title of Platonist belongs by far better right to those who have been nourished in, and have endeavoured to practise Plato's mode of investigation, than to those who are distinguished only by the adoption of certain dogmatical conclusions, drawn mostly from the least intelligible of his works, and which the character of his mind and writings makes it uncertain whether he himself regarded as anything more than poetic fancies, or philosophic conjectures.

In going through Plato and Demosthenes, since I could now read these authors, as far as the language was concerned, with perfect ease, I was not required to construe them sentence by sentence, but to read them aloud to my father, answering questions when asked : but the particular attention which he paid to elocution (in which his own excellence was remarkable) made this reading aloud to him a most painful task. Of all things which he required me to do, there was none which I did so constantly ill, or in which he so perpetually lost his temper with me. He had thought much on the principles of the art of reading, especially the most neglected part of it, the inflections of the voice, or *modulation* as writers on elocution call it (in contrast with *articulation* on the one side, and *expression* on the other), and had reduced it to rules, grounded on the logical analysis of a sentence. These rules he strongly impressed upon me, and took me severely to task for every violation of them : but I even then remarked (though I did not venture to make the remark to him) that though he reproached me when I read a sentence ill, and *told* me how I ought to have read it, he never, by reading it himself, *showed* me how it ought to be read. A defect running through his otherwise admirable modes of instruction, as it did through all his modes of thought, was that of trusting too much to the intelligibleness of the abstract, when not embodied in the concrete. It was at a much later period of my youth, when practising elocution by myself, or with companions of my own age, that I for the first time understood the object of his rules, and saw the psychological grounds of them. At that time I and others followed out the subject into its ramifications and could have composed a very useful treatise, grounded on my father's principles. He himself left those principles and rules unwritten. I regret that when my mind was full of the subject, from systematic practice, I did not put them, and our improvements of them, into a formal shape.

A book which contributed largely to my education, in the best sense of the term, was my father's History of India. It was published in the beginning of 1818. During the year previous, while it was passing through the press, I used to read the proof sheets to him ; or rather, I read the manuscript to him while he corrected the proofs. The

number of new ideas which I received from this
remarkable book, and the impulse and stimulus
as well as guidance given to my thoughts by its
criticisms and disquisitions on society and civilization in the Hindoo part, on institutions and the
acts of governments in the English part, made my
early familiarity with it eminently useful to my
subsequent progress. And though I can perceive
deficiencies in it now as compared with a perfect
standard, I still think it, if not the most, one of
the most instructive histories ever written, and
one of the books from which most benefit may be
derived by a mind in the course of making up its
opinions.

The Preface, among the most characteristic of
my father's writings, as well as the richest in
materials of thought, gives a picture which may
be entirely depended on, of the sentiments and
expectations with which he wrote the History.
Saturated as the book is with the opinions and
modes of judgment of a democratic radicalism
then regarded as extreme ; and treating with a
severity, at that time most unusual, the English
Constitution, the English law, and all parties and
classes who possessed any considerable influence
in the country ; he may have expected reputation,
but certainly not advancement in life, from its
publication ; nor could he have supposed that it
would raise up anything but enemies for him in
powerful quarters : least of all could he have
expected favour from the East India Company,
to whose commercial privileges he was unquali-
fiedly hostile, and on the acts of whose government
he had made so many severe comments : though,
in various parts of his book, he bore a testimony

in their favour, which he felt to be their just due, namely, that no Government had on the whole given so much proof, to the extent of its lights, of good intention towards its subjects ; and that if the acts of any other Government had the light of publicity as completely let in upon them, they would, in all probability, still less bear scrutiny.

On learning, however, in the spring of 1819, about a year after the publication of the History, that the East India Directors desired to strengthen the part of their home establishment which was employed in carrying on the correspondence with India, my father declared himself a candidate for that employment, and, to the credit of the Directors, successfully. He was appointed one of the Assistants of the Examiner of India Correspondence ; officers whose duty it was to prepare drafts of despatches to India, for consideration by the Directors, in the principal departments of administration. In this office, and in that of Examiner, which he subsequently attained, the influence which his talents, his reputation, and his decision of character gave him, with superiors who really desired the good government of India, enabled him to a great extent to throw into his drafts of despatches, and to carry through the ordeal of the Court of Directors and Board of Control, without having their force much weakened, his real opinions on Indian subjects. In his History he had set forth, for the first time, many of the true principles of Indian administration : and his despatches, following his History, did more than had ever been done before to promote the improvement of India, and teach Indian officials to understand their business. If a selection of them were published, they would, I am convinced, place his character as a practical statesman fully on a level with his eminence as a speculative writer.

This new employment of his time caused no relaxation in his attention to my education. It was in this same year, 1819, that he took me through a complete course of political economy. His loved and intimate friend, Ricardo, had shortly before published the book which formed so great an epoch in political economy; a book which never would have been published or written, but for the entreaty and strong encouragement of my father; for Ricardo, the most modest of men, though firmly convinced of the truth of his doctrines, deemed himself so little capable of doing them justice in exposition and expression, that he shrank from the idea of publicity. The same friendly encouragement induced Ricardo, a year or two later, to become a member of the House of Commons; where, during the few remaining years of his life, unhappily cut short in the full vigour of his intellect, he rendered so much service to his and my father's opinions both on political economy and on other subjects.

Though Ricardo's great work was already in print, no didactic treatise embodying its doctrines, in a manner fit for learners, had yet appeared. My father, therefore, commenced instructing me in the science by a sort of lectures, which he delivered to me in our walks. He expounded each day a portion of the subject, and I gave him next day a written account of it, which he made me rewrite over and over again until it was clear, precise, and tolerably complete. In this manner I went through the whole extent of the science;

and the written outline of it which resulted from my daily *compte rendu*, served him afterwards as notes from which to write his Elements of Political Economy. After this I read Ricardo, giving an account daily of what I read, and discussing, in the best manner I could, the collateral points which offered themselves in our progress.

On Money, as the most intricate part of the subject, he made me read in the same manner Ricardo's admirable pamphlets, written during what was called the Bullion controversy; to these succeeded Adam Smith; and in this reading it was one of my father's main objects to make me apply to Smith's more superficial view of political economy, the superior lights of Ricardo, and detect what was fallacious in Smith's arguments, or erroneous in any of his conclusions. Such a mode of instruction was excellently calculated to form a thinker; but it required to be worked by a thinker, as close and vigorous as my father. The path was a thorny one, even to him, and I am sure it was so to me, notwithstanding the strong interest I took in the subject. He was often, and much beyond reason, provoked by my failures in cases where success could not have been expected; but in the main his method was right, and it succeeded. I do not believe that any scientific teaching ever was more thorough, or better fitted for training the faculties, than the mode in which logic and political economy were taught to me by my father. Striving, even in an exaggerated degree, to call forth the activity of my faculties, by making me find out everything for myself, he gave his explanations not before, but after, I had felt the full force of the difficulties; and not only gave me an accurate knowledge of these two great subjects, as far as they were then understood, but made me a thinker on both. I thought for myself almost from the first, and occasionally thought differently from him, though for a long time only on minor points, and making his opinion the ultimate standard. At a later period I even occasionally convinced him, and altered his opinion on some points of detail: which I state to his honour, not my own. It at once exemplifies his perfect candour, and the real worth of his method of teaching.

At this point concluded what can properly be called my lessons: when I was about fourteen I left England for more than a year; and after my return, though my studies went on under my father's general direction, he was no longer my schoolmaster. I shall therefore pause here, and turn back to matters of a more general nature connected with the part of my life and education included in the preceding reminiscences.

In the course of instruction which I have partially retraced, the point most superficially apparent is the great effort to give, during the years of childhood an amount of knowledge in what are considered the higher branches of education, which is seldom acquired (if acquired at all) until the age of manhood. The result of the experiment shows the ease with which this may be done, and places in a strong light the wretched waste of so many precious years as are spent in acquiring the modicum of Latin and Greek commonly taught to schoolboys; a waste which has led so many educational reformers to entertain the ill-judged proposal of discarding these languages altogether from general education. If I had been by nature extremely quick of apprehension, or had possessed a very accurate and retentive memory, or were of a remarkably active and energetic character, the trial would not be conclusive; but in all these natural gifts I am rather below than above par; what I could do, could assuredly be done by any boy or girl of average capacity and healthy physical constitution: and if I have accomplished anything, I owe it, among other fortunate circumstances, to the fact that through the early training bestowed on me by my father, I started, I may fairly say, with an advantage of a quarter of a century over my contemporaries.

There was one cardinal point in this training, of which I have already given some indication, and which, more than anything else, was the cause of whatever good it effected. Most boys or youths who have had much knowledge drilled into them, have their mental capacities not strengthened, but overlaid by it. They are crammed with mere facts, and with the opinions or phrases of other people, and these are accepted as a substitute for the power to form opinions of their own: and thus the sons of eminent fathers, who have spared no pains in their education, so often grow up mere parroters of what they have learnt, incapable of using their minds except in the furrows traced for them. Mine, however, was not an education of cram. My father never permitted anything which I learnt to degenerate into a mere exercise of memory. He strove to make the understanding not only go along with every step of the teaching, but, if possible, precede it. Anything which could be found out by thinking I never was told, until

I had exhausted my efforts to find it out for myself. As far as I can trust my remembrance, I acquitted myself very lamely in this department; my recollection of such matters is almost wholly of failures, hardly ever of success. It is true the failures were often in things in which success in so early a stage of my progress, was almost impossible. I remember at some time in my thirteenth year, on my happening to use the word idea, he asked me what an idea was; and expressed some displeasure at my ineffectual efforts to define the word: I recollect also his indignation at my using the common expression that something was true in theory but required correction in practice; and how, after making me vainly strive to define the word theory, he explained its meaning, and showed the fallacy of the vulgar form of speech which I had used; leaving me fully persuaded that in being unable to give a correct definition of Theory, and in speaking of it as something which might be at variance with practice, I had shown unparalleled ignorance. In this he seems, and perhaps was, very unreasonable; but I think, only in being angry at my failure. A pupil from whom nothing is ever demanded which he cannot do, never does all he can.

One of the evils most liable to attend on any sort of early proficiency, and which often fatally blights its promise, my father most anxiously guarded against. This was self-conceit. He kept me, with extreme vigilance, out of the way of hearing myself praised, or of being led to make self-flattering comparisons between myself and others. From his own intercourse with me I could derive none but a very humble opinion of myself; and the standard of comparison he always held up to me, was not what other people did, but what a man could and ought to do. He completely succeeded in preserving me from the sort of influences he so much dreaded. I was not at all aware that my attainments were anything unusual at my age. If I accidentally had my attention drawn to the fact that some other boy knew less than myself—which happened less often than might be imagined—I concluded, not that I knew much, but that he, for some reason or other, knew little, or that his knowledge was of a different kind from mine. My state of mind was not humility, but neither was it arrogance. I never thought of saying to myself, I am, or I can do, so and so. I neither estimated myself highly nor lowly: I did not estimate myself at all. If I thought anything about myself, it was that I was rather backward in my studies, since I alwa s found myself so, in comparison with what my father expected from me. I assert this with confidence, though it was not the impression of various persons who saw me in my childhood. They, as I have since found, thought me greatly and disagreeably self-conceited ; probably because I was disputatious, and did not scruple to give direct contradictions to things which I heard said. I suppose I acquired this bad habit from having been encouraged in an unusual degree to talk on matters beyond my age, and with grown persons, while I never had inculcated on me the usual respect for them. My father did not correct this ill-breeding and impertinence, probably from not being aware of it, for I was always too much in awe of him to be otherwise than extremely subdued and quiet in his presence.

Yet with all this I had no notion of any superiority in myself; and well was it for me that I had not. I remember the very place in Hyde Park where, in my fourteenth year, on the eve of leaving my father's house for a long absence, he told me that I should find, as I got acquainted with new people, that I had been taught many things which youths of my age did not commonly know; and that many persons would be disposed to talk to me of this, and to compliment me upon it. What other things he said on this topic I remember very imperfectly; but he wound up by saying, that whatever I knew more than others, could not be ascribed to any merit in me, but to the very unusual advantage which had fallen to my lot, of having a father who was able to teach me, and willing to give the necessary trouble and time; that it was no matter of praise to me, if I knew more than those who had not had a similar advantage, but the deepest disgrace to me if I did not. I have a distinct remembrance, that the suggestion thus for the first time made to me, that I knew more than other youths who were considered well educated, was to me a piece of information, to which, as to all other things which my father told me, I gave implicit credence, but which did not at all impress me as a personal matter. I felt no disposition to glorify myself upon the circumstance that there were other persons who did not know what I knew; nor had I ever flattered myself that my acquirements, whatever they might be, were any merit of mine: but, now when my attention was called to the subject, I felt that what my father had said respecting my peculiar advantages was exactly the truth and common sense of the matter, and it fixed my opinion and feeling from that time forward.

It is evident that this, among many other of the purposes of my father's scheme of education, could not have been accomplished if he had not carefully kept me from having any great amount of intercourse with other boys. He was earnestly bent upon my escaping not only the corrupting influence which boys exercise over boys, but the contagion of vulgar modes of thought and feeling ; and for this he was willing that I should pay the price of inferiority in the accomplishments which school-boys in all countries chiefly cultivate. The deficiencies in my education were principally in the things which boys learn from being turned out to shift for themselves, and from being brought together in large numbers. From temperance and much walking, I grew up healthy and hardy, though not muscular ; but I could do no feats of skill or physical strength, and knew none of the ordinary bodily exercises. It was not that play, or time for it, was refused me. Though no holidays were allowed, lest the habit of work should be broken, and a taste for idleness acquired, I had ample leisure in every day to amuse myself ; but as I had no boy companions, and the animal need of physical activity was satisfied by walking, my amusements, which were mostly solitary, were in general, of a quiet, if not a bookish turn, and gave little stimulus to any other kind even of mental activity than that which was already called forth by my studies : I consequently remained long, and in a less degree have always remained, inexpert in anything requiring manual dexterity ; my mind, as well as my hands, did its work very lamely when it was applied, or ought to have been applied, to the practical details which, as they are the chief interest of life to the majority of men, are also the things in which whatever mental capacity they have, chiefly shows itself: I was constantly meriting reproof by inattention, inobservance, and general slackness of mind in matters of daily life. My father was the extreme opposite in these particulars: his senses and mental faculties were always on the alert; he carried decision and energy of character in his whole manner and into every action of life: and this, as much as his talents, contributed to the strong impression which he always made upon those with whom he came into personal contact. But the children of energetic parents, frequently grow up unenergetic, because they lean on their parents, and the parents are energetic for them. The education which my father gave me, was in itself much more fitted for training me to *know* than to *do*. Not that he was unaware of my deficiencies; both as a boy and as a youth I was incessantly smarting under his severe admonitions on the subject. There was anything but insensibility or tolerance on his part towards such shortcomings: but, while he saved me from the demoralizing effects of school life, he made no effort to provide me with any sufficient substitute for its practicalizing influences. Whatever qualities he himself, probably, had acquired without difficulty or special training, he seems to have supposed that I ought to acquire as easily. He had not, I think, bestowed the same amount of thought and attention on this, as on most other branches of education; and here, as well [as] in some other points of my tuition, he seems to have expected effects without causes.

CHAPTER II

MORAL INFLUENCES IN EARLY YOUTH.   MY
FATHER'S CHARACTER AND OPINIONS.

IN my education, as in that of everyone, the
moral influences, which are so much more important than all others, are also the most complicated,
and the most difficult to specify with any approach
to completeness. Without attempting the hopeless
task of detailing the circumstances by which, in
this respect, my early character may have been
shaped, I shall confine myself to a few leading
points, which form an indispensable part of any
true account of my education.

I was brought up from the first without any
religious belief, in the ordinary acceptation of the
term. My father, educated in the creed of Scotch
Presbyterianism, had by his own studies and
reflections been early led to reject not only the
belief in Revelation, but the foundations of what
is commonly called Natural Religion. I have
heard him say, that the turning point of his mind
on the subject was reading Butler's Analogy.
That work, of which he always continued to speak
with respect, kept him, as he said, for some considerable time, a believer in the divine authority
of Christianity; by proving to him, that whatever
are the difficulties in believing that the Old and
New Testament proceed from, or record the acts
of, a perfectly wise and good being, the same and
still greater difficulties stand in the way of the

belief, that a being of such a character can have
been the Maker of the universe. He considered
Butler's argument as conclusive against the only
opponents for whom it was intended. Those who
admit an omnipotent as well as perfectly just and
benevolent maker and ruler of such a world as this,
can say little against Christianity but what can,
with at least equal force, be retorted against
themselves. Finding, therefore, no halting place
in Deism, he remained in a state of perplexity,
until, doubtless after many struggles, he yielded
to the conviction, that, concerning the origin of
things nothing whatever can be known. This is
the only correct statement of his opinion ; for
dogmatic atheism he looked upon as absurd ; as
most of those, whom the world has considered
Atheists, have always done. These particulars
are important, because they show that my father's
rejection of all that is called religious belief, was
not, as many might suppose, primarily a matter
of logic and evidence : the grounds of it were
moral, still more than intellectual. He found it
impossible to believe that a world so full of evil
was the work of an Author combining infinite
power with perfect goodness and righteousness.
His intellect spurned the subtleties by which men
attempt to blind themselves to this open contradiction. The Sabæan, or Manichæan theory of
a Good and an Evil Principle, struggling against
each other for the government of the universe, he
would not have equally condemned ; and I have
heard him express surprise, that no one revived
it in our time. He would have regarded it as
a mere hypothesis ; but he would have ascribed to
it no depraving influence. As it was, his aversion

to religion, in the sense usually attached to the term, was of the same kind with that of Lucretius: he regarded it with the feelings due not to a mere mental delusion, but to a great moral evil. He looked upon it as the greatest enemy of morality: first, by setting up fictitious excellences,—belief in creeds, devotional feelings, and ceremonies, not connected with the good of human-kind,—and causing these to be accepted as substitutes for genuine virtues: but above all, by radically vitiating the standard of morals; making it consist in doing the will of a being, on whom it lavishes indeed all the phrases of adulation, but whom in sober truth it depicts as eminently hateful. I have a hundred times heard him say, that all ages and nations have represented their gods as wicked, in a constantly increasing progression, that mankind have gone on adding trait after trait till they reached the most perfect conception of wickedness which the human mind can devise, and have called this God, and prostrated themselves before it. This *ne plus ultra* of wickedness he considered to be embodied in what is commonly presented to mankind as the creed of Christianity. Think (he used to say) of a being who would make a Hell—who would create the human race with the infallible foreknowledge, and therefore with the intention, that the great majority of them were to be consigned to horrible and everlasting torment. The time, I believe, is drawing near when this dreadful conception of an object of worship will be no longer identified with Christianity; and when all persons, with any sense of moral good and evil, will look upon it with the same indignation with which my father regarded it. My father was as well aware as any one that Christians do not, in general, undergo the demoralizing consequences which seem inherent in such a creed, in the manner or to the extent which might have been expected from it. The same slovenliness of thought, and subjection of the reason to fears, wishes, and affections, which enable them to accept a theory involving a contradiction in terms, prevents them from perceiving the logical consequences of the theory. Such is the facility with which mankind believe at one and the same time things inconsistent with one another, and so few are those who draw from what they receive as truths, any consequences but those recommended to them by their feelings, that multitudes have held the undoubting belief in an Omnipotent Author of Hell, and have nevertheless identified that being with the best conception they were able to form of perfect goodness. Their worship was not paid to the demon which such a Being as they imagined would really be, but to their own ideal of excellence. The evil is, that such a belief keeps the ideal wretchedly low; and opposes the most obstinate resistance to all thought which has a tendency to raise it higher. Believers shrink from every train of ideas which would lead the mind to a clear conception and an elevated standard of excellence, because they feel (even when they do not distinctly see) that such a standard would conflict with many of the dispensations of nature, and with much of what they are accustomed to consider as the Christian creed. And thus morality continues a matter of blind tradition, with no consistent principle, nor even any consistent feeling, to guide it.

It would have been wholly inconsistent with my father's ideas of duty, to allow me to acquire impressions contrary to his convictions and feelings respecting religion : and he impressed upon me from the first, that the manner in which the world came into existence was a subject on which nothing was known : that the question, ' Who made me ? ' cannot be answered, because we have no experience or authentic information from which to answer it ; and that any answer only throws the difficulty a step further back, since the question immediately presents itself, ' Who made God ? ' He, at the same time, took care that I should be acquainted with what had been thought by mankind on these impenetrable problems. I have mentioned at how early an age he made me a reader of ecclesiastical history ; and he taught me to take the strongest interest in the Reformation, as the great and decisive contest against priestly tyranny for liberty of thought.

I am thus one of the very few examples, in this country, of one who has, not thrown off religious belief, but never had it : I grew up in a negative state with regard to it. I looked upon the modern exactly as I did upon the ancient religion, as something which in no way concerned me. It did not seem to me more strange that English people should believe what I did not, than that the men I read of in Herodotus should have done so. History had made the variety of opinions among mankind a fact familiar to me, and this was but a prolongation of that fact. This point in my early education had, however, incidentally one bad consequence deserving notice. In giving me an opinion contrary to that of the world, my father thought it necessary to give it as one which could not prudently be avowed to the world. This lesson of keeping my thoughts to myself, at that early age, was attended with some moral disadvantages; though my limited intercourse with strangers, especially such as were likely to speak to me on religion, prevented me from being placed in the alternative of avowal or hypocrisy. I remember two occasions in my boyhood, on which I felt myself in this alternative, and in both cases I avowed my disbelief and defended it. My opponents were boys, considerably older than myself: one of them I certainly staggered at the time, but the subject was never renewed between us: the other, who was surprised and somewhat shocked, did his best to convince me for some time, without effect.

The great advance in liberty of discussion, which is one of the most important differences between the present time and that of my childhood, has greatly altered the moralities of this question; and I think that few men of my father's intellect and public spirit, holding with such intensity of moral conviction as he did, unpopular opinions on religion, or on any other of the great subjects of thought, would now either practise or inculcate the withholding of them from the world, unless in the cases, becoming fewer every day, in which frankness on these subjects would either risk the loss of means of subsistence, or would amount to exclusion from some sphere of usefulness peculiarly suitable to the capacities of the individual. On religion in particular the time appears to me to have come, when it is the duty of all who being qualified in point of knowledge, have on mature consideration satisfied themselves that the current opinions are not only false but hurtful, to make their dissent known ; at least, if they are among those whose station or reputation, gives their opinion a chance of being attended to. Such an avowal would put an end, at once and for ever, to the vulgar prejudice, that what is called, very improperly, unbelief, is connected with any bad qualities either of mind or heart. The world would be astonished if it knew how great a proportion of its brightest ornaments—of those most distinguished even in popular estimation for wisdom and virtue—are complete sceptics in religion ; many of them refraining from avowal, less from personal considerations, than from a conscientious, though now in my opinion a most mistaken apprehension, lest by speaking out what would tend to weaken existing beliefs, and by consequence (as they suppose) existing restraints, they should do harm instead of good.

Of unbelievers (so called) as well as of believers, there are many species, including almost every variety of moral type. But the best among them, as no one who has had opportunities of really knowing them will hesitate to affirm, are more genuinely religious, in the best sense of the word religion, than those who exclusively arrogate to themselves the title. The liberality of the age, or in other words the weakening of the obstinate prejudice which makes men unable to see what is before their eyes because it is contrary to their expectations, has caused it to be very commonly admitted that a Deist may be truly religious : but if religion stands for any graces of character and not for mere dogma, the assertion may equally be made of many whose belief is far short of

Deism. Though they may think the proof incomplete that the universe is a work of design, and though they assuredly disbelieve that it can have an Author and Governor who is *absolute* in power as well as perfect in goodness, they have that which constitutes the principal worth of all religions whatever, an ideal conception of a Perfect Being, to which they habitually refer as the guide of their conscience; and this ideal of Good is usually far nearer to perfection than the objective Deity of those, who think themselves obliged to find absolute goodness in the author of a world so crowded with suffering and so deformed by injustice as ours.

My father's moral convictions, wholly dissevered from religion, were very much of the character of those of the Greek philosophers; and were delivered with the force and decision which characterized all that came from him. Even at the very early age at which I read with him the Memorabilia of Xenophon, I imbibed from that work and from his comments a deep respect for the character of Socrates; who stood in my mind as a model of ideal excellence: and I well remember how my father at that time impressed upon me the lesson of the ' Choice of Hercules '. At a somewhat later period the lofty moral standard exhibited in the writings of Plato operated upon me with great force. My father's moral inculcations were at all times mainly those of the ' Socratici viri ' ; justice, temperance (to which he gave a very extended application), veracity, perseverance, readiness to encounter pain and especially labour; regard for the public good; estimation of persons according to their merits,

and of things according to their intrinsic usefulness ; a life of exertion in contradiction to one of
self-indulgent ease and sloth. These and other
moralities he conveyed in brief sentences, uttered
as occasion arose, of grave exhortation, or stern
reprobation and contempt.

But though direct moral teaching does much,
indirect does more ; and the effect my father
produced on my character, did not depend solely
on what he said or did with that direct object, but
also, and still more, on what manner of man he
was.

In his views of life he partook of the character
of the Stoic, the Epicurean, and the Cynic, not in
the modern but the ancient sense of the word.
In his personal qualities the Stoic predominated.
His standard of morals was Epicurean, inasmuch
as it was utilitarian, taking as the exclusive test
of right and wrong, the tendency of actions to
produce pleasure or pain. But he had (and this
was the Cynic element) scarcely any belief in
pleasure ; at least in his later years, of which alone,
on this point, I can speak confidently. He was
not insensible to pleasures ; but he deemed very
few of them worth the price which, at least in the
present state of society, must be paid for them.
The greater number of miscarriages in life, he
considered to be attributable to the over-valuing
of pleasures. Accordingly, temperance, in the
large sense intended by the Greek philosophers—
stopping short at the point of moderation in all
indulgences—was with him, as with them, almost
the central point of educational precept. His
inculcations of this virtue fill a large place in my
childish remembrances. He thought human life

a poor thing at best, after the freshness of youth and of unsatisfied curiosity had gone by. This was a topic on which he did not often speak, especially, it may be supposed, in the presence of young persons: but when he did, it was with an air of settled and profound conviction. He would sometimes say, that if life were made what it might be, by good government and good education, it would be worth having: but he never spoke with anything like enthusiasm even of that possibility. He never varied in rating intellectual enjoyments above all others, even in value as pleasures, independently of their ulterior benefits. The pleasures of the benevolent affections he placed high in the scale; and used to say, that he had never known a happy old man, except those who were able to live over again in the pleasures of the young. For passionate emotions of all sorts, and for everything which has been said or written in exaltation of them, he professed the greatest contempt. He regarded them as a form of madness. 'The intense' was with him a bye-word of scornful disapprobation. He regarded as an aberration of the moral standard of modern times, compared with that of the ancients, the great stress laid upon feeling. Feelings, as such, he considered to be no proper subjects of praise or blame. Right and wrong, good and bad, he regarded as qualities solely of conduct—of acts and omissions; there being no feeling which may not lead, and does not frequently lead, either to good or to bad actions: conscience itself, the very desire to act right, often leading people to act wrong. Consistently carrying out the doctrine, that the object of praise and blame should be the discouragement of wrong conduct and the encouragement of right, he refused to let his praise or blame be influenced by the motive of the agent. He blamed as severely what he thought a bad action, when the motive was a feeling of duty, as if the agents had been consciously evil doers. He would not have accepted as a plea in mitigation for inquisitors, that they sincerely believed burning heretics to be an obligation of conscience. But though he did not allow honesty of purpose to soften his disapprobation of actions, it had its full effect on his estimation of characters. No one prized conscientiousness and rectitude of intention more highly, or was more incapable of valuing any person in whom he did not feel assurance of it. But he disliked people quite as much for any other deficiency, provided he thought it equally likely to make them act ill. He disliked, for instance, a fanatic in any bad cause, as much or more than one who adopted the same cause from self-interest, because he thought him even more likely to be practically mischievous. And thus, his aversion to many intellectual errors, or what he regarded as such, partook, in a certain sense, of the character of a moral feeling. All this is merely saying that he, in a degree once common, but now very unusual, threw his feelings into his opinions; which truly it is difficult to understand how any one who possesses much of both, can fail to do. None but those who do not care about opinions, will confound this with intolerance. Those, who having opinions which they hold to be immensely important, and their contraries to be prodigiously hurtful, have any deep regard for the general good, will necessarily dislike, as a class and in the abstract,

those who think wrong what they think right, and
right what they think wrong : though they need
not therefore be, nor was my father, insensible to
good qualities in an opponent, nor governed in
their estimation of individuals by one general
presumption, instead of by the whole of their
character. I grant that an earnest person, being
no more infallible than other men, is liable to
dislike people on account of opinions which do not
merit dislike ; but if he neither himself does them
any ill office, nor connives at its being done by
others, he is not intolerant : and the forbearance
which flows from a conscientious sense of the
importance to mankind of the equal freedom of
all opinions, is the only tolerance which is com-
mendable, or, to the highest moral order of minds,
possible.

It will be admitted, that a man of the opinions,
and the character, above described, was likely to
leave a strong moral impression on any mind
principally formed by him, and that his moral
teaching was not likely to err on the side of laxity
or indulgence. The element which was chiefly
deficient in his moral relation to his children was
that of tenderness. I do not believe that this
deficiency lay in his own nature. I believe him to
have had much more feeling than he habitually
showed, and much greater capacities of feeling
than were ever developed. He resembled most
Englishmen in being ashamed of the signs of
feeling, and by the absence of demonstration,
starving the feelings themselves. If we consider
further that he was in the trying position of sole
teacher, and add to this that his temper was
constitutionally irritable, it is impossible not to

feel true pity for a father who did, and strove to do, so much for his children, who would have so valued their affection, yet who must have been constantly feeling that fear of him was drying it up at its source. This was no longer the case later in life, and with his younger children. They loved him tenderly : and if I cannot say so much of myself, I was always loyally devoted to him. As regards my own education, I hesitate to pronounce whether I was more a loser or gainer by his severity. It was not such as to prevent me from having a happy childhood. And I do not believe that boys can be induced to apply themselves with vigour, and what is so much more difficult, perseverance, to dry and irksome studies, by the sole force of persuasion and soft words. Much must be done, and much must be learnt, by children, for which rigid discipline, and known liability to punishment, are indispensable as means. It is, no doubt, a very laudable effort, in modern teaching, to render as much as possible of what the young are required to learn, easy and interesting to them. But when this principle is pushed to the length of not requiring them to learn anything *but* what has been made easy and interesting, one of the chief objects of education is sacrificed. I rejoice in the decline of the old brutal and tyrannical system of teaching, which, however, did succeed in enforcing habits of application ; but the new, as it seems to me, is training up a race of men who will be incapable of doing anything which is disagreeable to them. I do not, then, believe that fear, as an element in education, can be dispensed with ; but I am sure that it ought not to be the main element ; and when it predominates so much as to preclude love and confidence on the part of the child to those who should be the unreservedly trusted advisers of after years, and perhaps to seal up the fountains of frank and spontaneous communicativeness in the child's nature, it is an evil for which a large abatement must be made from the benefits, moral and intellectual, which may flow from any other part of the education.

During this first period of my life, the habitual frequenters of my father's house were limited to a very few persons, most of them little known to the world, but whom personal worth, and more or less of congeniality with at least his political opinions (not so frequently to be met with then as since) inclined him to cultivate; and his conversations with them I listened to with interest and instruction. My being an habitual inmate of my father's study made me acquainted with the dearest of his friends, David Ricardo, who by his benevolent countenance, and kindliness of manner, was very attractive to young persons, and who after I became a student of political economy, invited me to his house and to walk with him in order to converse on the subject. I was a more frequent visitor (from about 1817 or 1818) to Mr. Hume, who, born in the same part of Scotland as my father, and having been, I rather think, a younger schoolfellow or college companion of his, had on returning from India renewed their youthful acquaintance, and who coming like many others greatly under the influence of my father's intellect and energy of character, was induced partly by that influence to go into Parliament, and there adopt the line of conduct which has

given him an honourable place in the history of
his country. Of Mr. Bentham I saw much more,
owing to the close intimacy which existed between
him and my father. I do not know how soon after
my father's first arrival in England they became
acquainted. But my father was the earliest
Englishman of any great mark, who thoroughly
understood, and in the main adopted, Bentham's
general views of ethics, government and law:
and this was a natural foundation for sympathy
between them, and made them familiar companions
in a period of Bentham's life during which he
admitted much fewer visitors than was the case
subsequently. At this time Mr. Bentham passed
some part of every year at Barrow Green House,
in a beautiful part of the Surrey Hills, a few miles
from Godstone, and there I each summer accompanied my father in a long visit. In 1813 Mr.
Bentham, my father, and I made an excursion,
which included Oxford, Bath and Bristol, Exeter,
Plymouth, and Portsmouth. In this journey I saw
many things which were instructive to me, and
acquired my first taste for natural scenery, in the
elementary form of fondness for a ' view.' In the
succeeding winter we moved into a house very near
Mr. Bentham's, which my father rented from him,
in Queen Square, Westminster. From 1814 to
1817 Mr. Bentham lived during half of each year
at Ford Abbey, in Somersetshire (or rather in a
part of Devonshire surrounded by Somersetshire),
which intervals I had the advantage of passing at
that place. This sojourn was, I think, an important circumstance in my education. Nothing
contributes more to nourish elevation of sentiments
in a people, than the large and free character of

their habitations. The middle-age architecture, the baronial hall, and the spacious and lofty rooms, of this fine old place, so unlike the mean and cramped externals of English middle class life, gave the sentiment of a larger and freer existence, and were to me a sort of poetic cultivation, aided also by the character of the grounds in which the Abbey stood; which were *riant* and secluded, umbrageous, and full of the sound of falling waters.

I owed another of the fortunate circumstances in my education, a year's residence in France, to Mr. Bentham's brother, General Sir Samuel Bentham. I had seen Sir Samuel Bentham and his family at their house near Gosport in the course of the tour already mentioned (he being then Superintendent of the Dockyard at Portsmouth), and during a stay of a few days which they made at Ford Abbey shortly after the peace, before going to live on the Continent. In 1820 they invited me for a six months' visit to them in the South of France, which their kindness ultimately prolonged to nearly a twelvemonth. Sir Samuel Bentham, though of a character of mind different from that of his illustrious brother, was a man of very considerable attainments and general powers, with a decided genius for mechanical art. His wife, a daughter of the celebrated chemist, Dr. Fordyce, was a woman of strong will and decided character, much general knowledge, and great practical good sense of the Edgeworth kind : she was the ruling spirit of the household, as she deserved, and was well qualified, to be. Their family consisted of one son (the eminent botanist) and three daughters, the youngest about two years my senior. I am indebted to them for much and various instruction,

and for an almost parental interest in my welfare.
When I first joined them, in May 1820, they
occupied the Château of Pompignan (still belonging
to a descendant of Voltaire's enemy) on the heights
overlooking the plain of the Garonne between
Montauban and Toulouse. I accompanied them
in an excursion to the Pyrenees, including a stay
of some duration at Bagnères de Bigorre, a journey
to Pau, Bayonne, and Bagnères de Luchon, and
an ascent of the Pic du Midi de Bigorre.

This first introduction to the highest order of
mountain scenery made the deepest impression on
me, and gave a colour to my tastes through life.
In October we proceeded by the beautiful mountain
route of Castres and St. Pons, from Toulouse to
Montpellier, in which last neighbourhood Sir
Samuel had just bought the estate of Restinclière,
near the foot of the singular mountain of St. Loup.
During this residence in France I acquired a
familiar knowledge of the French language, and
acquaintance with the ordinary French literature ;
I took lessons in various bodily exercises, in none
of which however I made any proficiency ; and
at Montpellier I attended the excellent winter
courses of lectures at the Faculté des Sciences,
those of M. Anglada on chemistry, of M. Provençal
on zoology, and of a very accomplished representative of the eighteenth century metaphysics,
M. Gergonne, on logic, under the name of Philosophy of the Sciences. I also went through a course
of the higher mathematics under the private
tuition of M. Lenthéric, a professor at the Lycée
of Montpellier. But the greatest, perhaps, of the
many advantages which I owed to this episode in
my education, was that of having breathed for

a whole year, the free and genial atmosphere of
Continental life. This advantage was not the less
real though I could not then estimate, nor even
consciously feel it. Having so little experience of
English life, and the few people I knew being
mostly such as had public objects, of a large and
personally disinterested kind, at heart, I was
ignorant of the low moral tone of what, in England,
is called society; the habit of, not indeed professing, but taking for granted in every mode of
implication, that conduct is of course always
directed towards low and petty objects; the
absence of high feelings which manifests itself by
sneering depreciation of all demonstrations of
them, and by general abstinence (except among
a few of the stricter religionists) from professing
any high principles of action at all, except in those
preordained cases in which such profession is put
on as part of the costume and formalities of the
occasion. I could not then know or estimate the
difference between this manner of existence, and
that of a people like the French, whose faults, if
equally real, are at all events different; among
whom sentiments, which by comparison at least
may be called elevated, are the current coin of
human intercourse, both in books and in private
life; and though often evaporating in profession,
are yet kept alive in the nation at large by constant
exercise, and stimulated by sympathy, so as to
form a living and active part of the existence of
great numbers of persons, and to be recognised and
understood by all. Neither could I then appreciate
the general culture of the understanding, which
results from the habitual exercise of the feelings,
and is thus carried down into the most uneducated

classes of several countries on the Continent, in
a degree not equalled in England among the so-
called educated, except where an unusual tenderness of conscience leads to a habitual exercise of
the intellect on questions of right and wrong.
I did not know the way in which, among the
ordinary English, the absence of interest in things
of an unselfish kind, except occasionally in a special
thing here and there, and the habit of not speaking
to others, nor much even to themselves, about the
things in which they do feel interest, causes both
their feelings and their intellectual faculties to
remain undeveloped, or to develope themselves
only in some single and very limited direction;
reducing them, considered as spiritual beings, to
a kind of negative existence. All these things I did
not perceive till long afterwards; but I even then
felt, though without stating it clearly to myself,
the contrast between the frank sociability and
amiability of French personal intercourse, and the
English mode of existence in which everybody
acts as if everybody else (with few, or no exceptions) was either an enemy or a bore. In France,
it is true, the bad as well as the good points, both
of individual and of national character, come more
to the surface, and break out more fearlessly in
ordinary intercourse, than in England: but the
general habit of the people is to show, as well as
to expect, friendly feeling in every one towards
every other, wherever there is not some positive
cause for the opposite. In England it is only of
the best bred people, in the upper or upper middle
ranks, that anything like this can be said.

In my way through Paris, both going and returning, I passed some time in the house of M. Say, the

eminent political economist, who was a friend and
correspondent of my father, having become
acquainted with him on a visit to England a year
or two after the peace. He was a man of the later
period of the French Revolution, a fine specimen
of the best kind of French Republican, one of those
who had never bent the knee to Bonaparte though
courted by him to do so; a truly upright, brave,
and enlightened man. He lived a quiet and
studious life, made happy by warm affections,
public and private. He was acquainted with
many of the chiefs of the Liberal party, and I saw
various noteworthy persons while staying at his
house; among whom I have pleasure in the
recollection of having once seen Saint-Simon, not
yet the founder either of a philosophy or a religion,
and considered only as a clever *original*. The
chief fruit which I carried away from the society
I saw, was a strong and permanent interest in
Continental Liberalism, of which I ever afterwards
kept myself *au courant*, as much as of English
politics: a thing not at all usual in those days
with Englishmen, and which had a very salutary
influence on my development, keeping me free
from the error always prevalent in England, and
from which even my father with all his superiority
to prejudice was not exempt, of judging universal
questions by a merely English standard. After
passing a few weeks at Caen with an old friend of
my father's, I returned to England in July 1821;
and my education resumed its ordinary course.

CHAPTER III

LAST STAGE OF EDUCATION, AND FIRST OF SELF-EDUCATION.

For the first year or two after my visit to France, I continued my old studies, with the addition of some new ones. When I returned, my father was just finishing for the press his Elements of Political Economy, and he made me perform an exercise on the manuscript, which Mr. Bentham practised on all his own writings, making what he called ' marginal contents '; a short abstract of every paragraph, to enable the writer more easily to judge of, and improve, the order of the ideas, and the general character of the exposition. Soon after, my father put into my hands Condillac's Traité des Sensations, and the logical and metaphysical volumes of his Cours d'Etudes; the first (notwithstanding the superficial resemblance between Condillac's psychological system and my father's) quite as much for a warning as for an example. I am not sure whether it was in this winter or the next that I first read a history of the French Revolution. I learnt with astonishment, that the principles of democracy, then apparently in so insignificant and hopeless a minority everywhere in Europe, had borne all before them in France thirty years earlier, and had been the creed of the nation. As may be supposed from this, I had previously a very vague idea of that great commotion.

I knew only that the French had thrown off the absolute monarchy of Louis XIV. and XV., had put the King and Queen to death, guillotined many persons, one of whom was Lavoisier, and had ultimately fallen under the despotism of Bonaparte. From this time, as was natural, the subject took an immense hold of my feelings. It allied itself with all my juvenile aspirations to the character of a democratic champion. What had happened so lately, seemed as if it might easily happen again : and the most transcendent glory I was capable of conceiving, was that of figuring, successful or unsuccessful, as a Girondist in an English Convention.

During the winter of 1821–2, Mr. John Austin, with whom at the time of my visit to France my father had but lately become acquainted, kindly allowed me to read Roman law with him. My father, notwithstanding his abhorrence of the chaos of barbarism called English Law, had turned his thoughts towards the bar as on the whole less ineligible for me than any other profession : and these readings with Mr. Austin, who had made Bentham's best ideas his own, and added much to them from other sources and from his own mind, were not only a valuable introduction to legal studies, but an important portion of general education. With Mr. Austin I read Heineccius on the Institutes, his Roman Antiquities, and part of his exposition of the Pandects ; to which was added a considerable portion of Blackstone. It was at the commencement of these studies that my father, as a needful accompaniment to them, put into my hands Bentham's principal speculations, as interpreted to the Continent, and indeed to all the world, by Dumont, in the Traité de Législation. The reading of this book was an epoch in my life; one of the turning points in my mental history.

My previous education had been, in a certain sense, already a course of Benthamism. The Benthamic standard of ' the greatest happiness ' was that which I had always been taught to apply; I was even familiar with an abstract discussion of it, forming an episode in an unpublished dialogue on Government, written by my father on the Platonic model. Yet in the first pages of Bentham it burst upon me with all the force of novelty. What thus impressed me was the chapter in which Bentham passed judgment on the common modes of reasoning in morals and legislation, deduced from phrases like ' law of nature,' ' right reason,' ' the moral sense,' ' natural rectitude,' and the like, and characterized them as dogmatism in disguise, imposing its sentiments upon others under cover of sounding expressions which convey no reason for the sentiment, but set up the sentiment as its own reason. It had not struck me before, that Bentham's principle put an end to all this. The feeling rushed upon me, that all previous moralists were superseded, and that here indeed was the commencement of a new era in thought. This impression was strengthened by the manner in which Bentham put into scientific form the application of the happiness principle to the morality of actions, by analysing the various classes and orders of their consequences. But what struck me at that time most of all, was the Classification of Offences, which is much more

clear, compact and imposing in Dumont's *rédaction*
than in the original work of Bentham from which
it was taken. Logic and the dialectics of Plato,
which had formed so large a part of my previous
training, had given me a strong relish for accurate
classification. This taste had been strengthened
and enlightened by the study of botany, on the
principles of what is called the Natural Method,
which I had taken up with great zeal, though
only as an amusement, during my stay in France ;
and when I found scientific classification applied
to the great and complex subject of Punishable
Acts, under the guidance of the ethical principle
of Pleasurable and Painful Consequences, followed
out in the method of detail introduced into these
subjects by Bentham, I felt taken up to an
eminence from which I could survey a vast
mental domain, and see stretching out into the
distance intellectual results beyond all computa-
tion. As I proceeded further, there seemed to
be added to this intellectual clearness, the most
inspiring prospects of practical improvement
in human affairs. To Bentham's general view
of the construction of a body of law I was not
altogether a stranger, having read with attention
that admirable compendium, my father's article
on Jurisprudence : but I had read it with little
profit, and scarcely any interest, no doubt from
its extremely general and abstract character,
and also because it concerned the form more
than the substance of the *corpus juris*, the logic
rather than the ethics of law. But Bentham's
subject was Legislation, of which Jurisprudence
is only the formal part : and at every page he
seemed to open a clearer and broader conception

of what human opinions and institutions ought to be, how they might be made what they ought to be, and how far removed from it they now are. When I laid down the last volume of the Traité, I had become a different being. The 'principle of utility' understood as Bentham understood it, and applied in the manner in which he applied it through these three volumes, fell exactly into its place as the keystone which held together the detached and fragmentary component parts of my knowledge and beliefs. It gave unity to my conceptions of things. I now had opinions; a creed, a doctrine, a philosophy; in one among the best senses of the word, a religion; the inculcation and diffusion of which could be made the principal outward purpose of a life. And I had a grand conception laid before me of changes to be effected in the condition of mankind through that doctrine. The Traité de Législation wound up with what was to me a most impressive picture of human life as it would be made by such opinions and such laws as were recommended in the treatise. The anticipations of practicable improvement were studiously moderate, deprecating and discountenancing as reveries of vague enthusiasm many things which will one day seem so natural to human beings, that injustice will probably be done to those who once thought them chimerical. But, in my state of mind, this appearance of superiority to illusion added to the effect which Bentham's doctrines produced on me, by heightening the impression of mental power, and the vista of improvement which he did open was sufficiently large and brilliant to light up my

life, as well as to give a definite shape to my
aspirations.

After this I read, from time to time, the most
important of the other works of Bentham which
had then seen the light, either as written by
himself or as edited by Dumont. This was my
private reading: while, under my father's direction,
my studies were carried into the higher branches
of analytic psychology. I now read Locke's
Essay, and wrote out an account of it, consisting
of a complete abstract of every chapter, with
such remarks as occurred to me : which was read
by, or (I think) to, my father, and discussed
throughout. I performed the same process with
Helvetius de l'Esprit, which I read of my own
choice. This preparation of abstracts, subject
to my father's censorship, was of great service
to me, by compelling precision in conceiving
and expressing psychological doctrines, whether
accepted as truths or only regarded as the opinion
of others. After Helvetius, my father made me
study what he deemed the really master-produc-
tion in the philosophy of mind, Hartley's Observations on Man. This book, though it did not,
like the Traité de Législation, give a new colour
to my existence, made a very similar impression
on me in regard to its immediate subject. Hartley's
explanation, incomplete as in many points it is,
of the more complex mental phenomena by the
law of association, commended itself to me at
once as a real analysis, and made me feel by
contrast the insufficiency of the merely verbal
generalizations of Condillac, and even of the
instructive gropings and feelings about for psychological explanations, of Locke. It was at this

very time that my father commenced writing
his Analysis of the Mind, which carried Hartley's
mode of explaining the mental phenomena to
so much greater length and depth. He could
only command the concentration of thought
necessary for this work, during the complete
leisure of his holiday of a month or six weeks
annually: and he commenced it in the summer of
1822, in the first holiday he passed at Dorking;
in which neighbourhood, from that time to the
end of his life, with the exception of two years,
he lived, as far as his official duties permitted,
for six months of every year. He worked at
the Analysis during several successive vacations,
up to the year 1829 when it was published, and
allowed me to read the manuscript, portion by
portion, as it advanced. The other principal
English writers on mental philosophy I read as
I felt inclined, particularly Berkeley, Hume's
Essays, Reid, Dugald Stewart and Brown on
Cause and Effect. Brown's Lectures I did not
read until two or three years later, nor at that
time had my father himself read them.

Among the works read in the course of this
year which contributed materially to my development, I ought to mention a book (written on the
foundation of some of Bentham's manuscripts
and published under the pseudonyme of Philip
Beauchamp) entitled ' Analysis of the Influence
of Natural Religion on the Temporal Happiness
of Mankind.' This was an examination not of
the truth, but of the usefulness of religious belief,
in the most general sense, apart from the pecu-
iarities of any special Revelation; which, of all
the parts of the discussion concerning religion,

is the most important in this age, in which real belief in any religious doctrine is feeble and precarious, but the opinion of its necessity for moral and social purposes almost universal; and when those who reject revelation, very generally take refuge in an optimistic Deism, a worship of the order of Nature, and the supposed course of Providence, at least as full of contradictions, and perverting to the moral sentiments, as any of the forms of Christianity, if only it is as completely realized. Yet, very little, with any claim to a philosophical character, has been written by sceptics against the usefulness of this form of belief. The volume bearing the name of Philip Beauchamp had this for its special object. Having been shown to my father in manuscript, it was put into my hands by him, and I made a marginal analysis of it as I had done of the Elements of Political Economy. Next to the Traité de Législation, it was one of the books which by the searching character of its analysis produced the greatest effect upon me. On reading it lately after an interval of many years, I find it to have some of the defects as well as the merits of the Benthamic modes of thought, and to contain, as I now think, many weak arguments, but with a great overbalance of sound ones, and much good material for a more completely philosophic and conclusive treatment of the subject.

I have now, I believe, mentioned all the books which had any considerable effect on my early mental development. From this point I began to carry on my intellectual cultivation by writing still more than by reading. In the summer of

1822 I wrote my first argumentative essay. I remember very little about it, except that it was an attack on what I regarded as the aristocratic prejudice, that the rich were, or were likely to be, superior in moral qualities to the poor. My performance was entirely argumentative, without any of the declamation which the subject would admit of, and might be expected to suggest to a young writer. In that department however I was, and remained, very inapt. Dry argument was the only thing I could manage, or willingly attempted; though passively I was very susceptible to the effect of all composition, whether in the form of poetry or oratory, which appealed to the feelings on any basis of reason. My father, who knew nothing of this essay until it was finished, was well satisfied, and as I learnt from others, even pleased with it; but, perhaps from a desire to promote the exercise of other mental faculties than the purely logical, he advised me to make my next exercise in composition one of the oratorical kind: on which suggestion, availing myself of my familiarity with Greek history and ideas and with the Athenian orators, I wrote two speeches, one an accusation, the other a defence of Pericles, on a supposed impeachment for not marching out to fight the Lacedemonians on their invasion of Attica. After this I continued to write papers on subjects often very much beyond my capacity, but with great benefit both from the exercise itself, and from the discussions which it led to with my father.

I had now also begun to converse, on general subjects, with the instructed men with whom I came in contact: and the opportunities of such contact naturally became more numerous. The two friends of my father from whom I derived most, and with whom I most associated, were Mr. Grote and Mr. John Austin. The acquaintance of both with my father was recent, but had ripened rapidly into intimacy. Mr. Grote was introduced to my father by Mr. Ricardo, I think in 1819, (being then about twenty-five years old), and sought assiduously his society and conversation. Already a highly instructed man, he was yet, by the side of my father, a tyro in the great subjects of human opinion ; but he rapidly seized on my father's best ideas ; and in the department of political opinion he made himself known as early as 1820, by a pamphlet in defence of Radical Reform, in reply to a celebrated article by Sir James Mackintosh, then lately published in the Edinburgh Review. Mr. Grote's father, the banker, was, I believe, a thorough Tory, and his mother intensely Evangelical ; so that for his liberal opinions he was in no way indebted to home influences. But, unlike most persons who have the prospect of being rich by inheritance, he had, though actively engaged in the business of banking, devoted a great portion of time to philosophic studies ; and his intimacy with my father did much to decide the character of the next stage in his mental progress. Him I often visited, and my conversations with him on political, moral, and philosophical subjects gave me, in addition to much valuable instruction, all the pleasure and benefit of sympathetic communion with a man of the high intellectual and moral eminence which his life and writings have since manifested to the world.

Mr. Austin, who was four or five years older than Mr. Grote, was the eldest son of a retired miller in Suffolk, who had made money by contracts during the war, and who must have been a man of remarkable qualities, as I infer from the fact that all his sons were of more than common ability and all eminently gentlemen. The one with whom we are now concerned, and whose writings on jurisprudence have made him celebrated, was for some time in the army, and served in Sicily under Lord William Bentinck. After the peace he sold his commission and studied for the bar, to which he had been called for some time before my father knew him. He was not, like Mr. Grote, to any extent, a pupil of my father, but he had attained, by reading and thought, a considerable number of the same opinions, modified by his own very decided individuality of character. He was a man of great intellectual powers which in conversation appeared at their very best; from the vigour and richness of expression with which, under the excitement of discussion, he was accustomed to maintain some view or other of most general subjects; and from an appearance of not only strong, but deliberate and collected will; mixed with a certain bitterness, partly derived from temperament, and partly from the general cast of his feelings and reflections. The dissatisfaction with life and the world, felt more or less in the present state of society and intellect by every discerning and highly conscientious mind, gave in his case a rather melancholy tinge to the character, very natural to those whose passive moral susceptibilities are more than proportioned to their active energies. For it must be said, that the strength of will of which his manner seemed to give such strong assurance, expended itself principally in manner. With great zeal for human improvement, a strong sense of duty, and capacities and acquirements the extent of which is proved by the writings he has left, he hardly ever completed any intellectual task of magnitude. He had so high a standard of what ought to be done, so exaggerated a sense of deficiencies in his own performances, and was so unable to content himself with the amount of elaboration sufficient for the occasion and the purpose, that he not only spoilt much of his work for ordinary use by overlabouring it, but spent so much time and exertion in superfluous study and thought, that when his task ought to have been completed, he had generally worked himself into an illness, without having half finished what he undertook. From this mental infirmity (of which he is not the sole example among the accomplished and able men whom I have known), combined with liability to frequent attacks of disabling though not dangerous ill-health, he accomplished, through life, little in comparison with what he seemed capable of; but what he did produce is held in the very highest estimation by the most competent judges; and, like Coleridge, he might plead as a set-off that he had been to many persons, through his conversation, a source not only of much instruction but of great elevation of character. On me his influence was most salutary. It was moral in the best sense. He took a sincere and kind interest in me, far beyond what could have been expected towards a mere youth from a man of his age, standing, and what seemed austerity of character. There was in his conversation and demeanour a tone of highmindedness which did not show itself so much, if the quality existed as much, in any of the other persons with whom at that time I associated. My intercourse with him was the more beneficial, owing to his being of a different mental type from all other intellectual men whom I frequented, and he from the first set himself decidedly against the prejudices and narrownesses which are almost sure to be found in a young man formed by a particular mode of thought or a particular social circle.

His younger brother, Charles Austin, of whom at this time and for the next year or two I saw much, had also a great effect on me, though of a very different description. He was but a few years older than myself, and had then just left the University, where he had shone with great *éclat* as a man of intellect and a brilliant orator and converser. The effect he produced on his Cambridge contemporaries deserves to be accounted an historical event; for to it may in part be traced the tendency towards Liberalism in general, and the Benthamic and politico-economic form of it in particular, which showed itself in a portion of the more active-minded young men of the higher classes from this time to 1830. The Union Debating Society, at that time at the height of its reputation, was an arena where what were then thought extreme opinions, in politics and philosophy, were weekly asserted, face to face with their opposites, before audiences consisting of the *élite* of the Cambridge youth: and though many persons afterwards of more or less note, (of whom Lord Macaulay is the most celebrated), gained their first oratorical laurels in those debates, the really influential mind among these intellectual gladiators was Charles Austin. He continued, after leaving the University, to be, by his conversation and personal ascendancy, a leader among the same class of young men who had been his associates there; and he attached me among others to his car. Through him I became acquainted with Macaulay, Hyde and Charles Villiers, Strutt (now Lord Belper), Romilly (now Lord Romilly and Master of the Rolls), and various others who subsequently figured in literature or politics, and among whom I heard discussions on many topics, as yet to a certain degree new to me. The influence of Charles Austin over me differed from that of the persons I have hitherto mentioned, in being not the influence of a man over a boy, but that of an elder contemporary. It was through him that I first felt myself, not a pupil under teachers, but a man among men. He was the first person of intellect whom I met on a ground of equality, though as yet much his inferior on that common ground. He was a man who never failed to impress greatly those with whom he came in contact, even when their opinions were the very reverse of his. The impression he gave was that of boundless strength, together with talents which, combined with such apparent force of will and character, seemed capable of dominating the world. Those who knew him, whether friendly to him or not, always anticipated that he would play a conspicuous part in public life. It is seldom that men produce so great an immediate effect by speech, unless they, in some degree, lay themselves out for it; and he did this in no ordinary degree. He loved to strike, and even to startle. He knew that decision is the greatest element of effect, and he uttered his opinions with all the decision he could throw into them, never so well pleased as when he astonished any one by their audacity. Very unlike his brother, who made war against the narrower interpretations and applications of the principles they both professed, he, on the contrary, presented the Benthamic doctrines in the most startling form of which they were susceptible, exaggerating everything in them which tended to consequences offensive to any one's preconceived feelings. All which, he defended with such verve and vivacity, and carried off by a manner so agreeable as well as forcible, that he always either came off victor, or divided the honours of the field. It is my belief that much of the notion popularly entertained of the tenets and sentiments of what are called Benthamites or Utilitarians had its origin in paradoxes thrown out by Charles Austin. It must be said, however, that his example was followed, *haud passibus æquis*, by younger proselytes, and that to *outrer* whatever was by anybody considered offensive in the doctrines and maxims of Benthamism, became at one time the badge of a small coterie of youths. All of these who had anything in them, myself among others, quickly outgrew this boyish vanity; and those who had not, became tired of differing from other people, and gave up both the good and the bad part of the heterodox opinions they had for some time professed.

It was in the winter of 1822–3 that I formed the plan of a little society, to be composed of young men agreeing in fundamental principles—acknowledging Utility as their standard in ethics and politics, and a certain number of the principal corollaries drawn from it in the philosophy I had accepted—and meeting once a fortnight to read essays and discuss questions conformably to the premises thus agreed on. The fact would hardly be worth mentioning, but for the circumstance, that the name I gave to the society I had planned was the Utilitarian Society. It was the first time that any one had taken the title of Utilitarian; and the term made its way into the language, from this humble source. I did not invent the word, but found it in one of Galt's novels, the 'Annals of the Parish,' in which the Scotch clergyman, of whom the book is a supposed autobiography, is represented as warning his parishioners not to leave the Gospel and become utilitarians. With a boy's fondness for a name and a banner I seized on the word, and for some years called myself and others by it as a sectarian appellation; and it came to be occasionally used by some others holding the opinions which it was intended to designate. As those opinions attracted more notice, the term was repeated by strangers and opponents, and got into rather common use just about the time when those who had originally assumed it, laid down that along with other sectarian characteristics. The Society so called consisted at first of no more than three members, one of whom, being Mr. Bentham's amanuensis, obtained for us permission to hold our meetings in his house. The number never, I think, reached ten, and the society was broken up in 1826. It had thus an existence of about three years and a half. The chief effect of it as regards myself, over and above the benefit of practice in oral discussion, was that of bringing me in contact with several young men at that time less advanced than myself, among whom, as they professed the same opinions, I was for some time a sort of leader, and had considerable influence on their mental progress. Any young man of education who fell in my way, and whose opinions were not incompatible with those of the Society, I endeavoured to press into its service ; and some others I probably should never have known, had they not joined it. Those of the members who became my intimate companions —no one of whom was in any sense of the word a disciple, but all of them independent thinkers on their own basis—were William Eyton Tooke, son of the eminent political economist, a young man of singular worth both moral and intellectual, lost to the world by an early death ; his friend William Ellis, an original thinker in the field of political economy, now honourably known by his apostolic exertions for the improvement of education ; George Graham, afterwards official assignee of the Bankruptcy Court, a thinker of originality and power on almost all abstract subjects ; and (from the time when he came first to England to study for the bar in 1824 or 1825) a man who has made considerably more noise in the world than any of these, John Arthur Roebuck.

In May, 1823, my professional occupation and status for the next thirty-five years of my life, were decided by my father's obtaining for me an appointment from the East India Company, in the office of the Examiner of India Correspondence, immediately under himself. I was appointed in the usual manner, at the bottom of the list of clerks, to rise, at least in the first instance, by seniority; but with the understanding that I should be employed from the beginning in preparing drafts of despatches, and be thus trained up as a successor to those who then filled the higher departments of the office. My drafts of course required, for some time, much revision from my immediate superiors, but I soon became well acquainted with the business, and by my father's instructions and the general growth of my own powers, I was in a few years qualified to be, and practically was, the chief conductor of the correspondence with India in one of the leading departments, that of the Native States. This continued to be my official duty until I was appointed Examiner, only two years before the time when the abolition of the East India Company as a political body determined my retirement. I do not know any one of the occupations by which a subsistence can now be gained, more suitable than such as this to any one who, not being in independent circumstances, desires to devote a part of the twenty-four hours to private intellectual pursuits. Writing for the press, cannot be recommended as a permanent resource to any one qualified to accomplish anything in the higher departments of literature or thought: not only on account of the uncertainty of this means of livelihood, especially if the writer has a conscience, and will not consent to serve any opinions except his own; but also because the writings by which one can live, are not the writings which themselves live, and are never those in which the writer does his best. Books destined to form future thinkers take too much time to write, and when written come, in general, too slowly into notice and repute, to be relied on for subsistence. Those who have to support themselves by their pen must depend on literary drudgery, or at best on writings addressed to the multitude; and can employ in the pursuits of their own choice, only such time as they can spare from those of necessity; which is generally less than the leisure allowed by office occupations, while the effect on the mind is far more enervating and fatiguing. For my own part I have, through life, found office duties an actual rest from the other mental occupations which I have carried on simultaneously with them. They were sufficiently intellectual not to be a distasteful drudgery, without being such as to cause any strain upon the mental powers of a person used to abstract thought, or to the labour of careful literary composition. The drawbacks, for every mode of life has its drawbacks, were not, however, unfelt by me. I cared little for the loss of the chances of riches and honours held out by some of the professions, particularly the bar, which had been, as I have already said, the profession thought of for me. But I was not indifferent to exclusion from Parliament, and public life: and I felt very sensibly the more immediate unpleasantness of confinement to London; the holiday allowed by India-House practice not exceeding a month in the year, while my taste was strong for a country life, and my sojourn in France had left behind it an ardent desire of travelling. But though these tastes could not be freely indulged, they were at no time entirely sacrificed. I passed most Sundays, throughout the year, in the country, taking long rural walks on that day even when residing in London. The month's holiday was, for a few years, passed at my father's house in the country: afterwards a part or the whole was spent in tours, chiefly pedestrian, with some one or more of the young men who were my chosen companions; and, at a later period, in longer journeys or excursions, alone or with other friends. France, Belgium, and Rhenish Germany were within easy reach of the annual holiday: and two longer absences, one of three, the other of six months, under medical advice, added Switzerland, the Tyrol, and Italy to my list. Fortunately, also, both these journeys occurred rather early, so as to give the benefit and charm of the remembrance to a large portion of life.

I am disposed to agree with what has been surmised by others, that the opportunity which my official position gave me of learning by personal observation the necessary conditions of the practical conduct of public affairs, has been of considerable value to me as a theoretical reformer of the opinions and institutions of my time. Not, indeed, that public business transacted on paper, to take effect on the other side of the globe, was of itself calculated to give much practical knowledge of life. But the occupation accustomed me to see and hear the difficulties of every course, and the means of obviating them, stated and discussed deliberately with a view to execution; it gave me opportunities of perceiving when public measures, and other political facts, did not produce the effects which had been expected of them, and from what causes; above all, it was valuable to me by making me, in this portion of my activity, merely one wheel in a machine, the whole of which had to work together. As a speculative writer, I should have had no one to consult but myself, and should have encountered in my speculations none of the obstacles which would have started up whenever they came to be applied to practice. But as a Secretary conducting political correspondence, I could not issue an order or express an opinion, without satisfying various persons very unlike myself, that the thing was fit to be done. I was thus in a good position for finding out by practice the mode of putting a thought which gives it easiest admittance into minds not prepared for it by habit; while I became practically conversant with the difficulties of moving bodies of men, the necessities of compromise, the art of sacrificing the non-essential to preserve the essential. I learnt how to obtain the best I could, when I could not obtain everything; instead of being indignant or dispirited because I could not have entirely my own way, to be pleased and encouraged when I could have the smallest part of it; and when even that could not be, to bear with complete equanimity the being overruled altogether. I have found, through life, these acquisitions to be of the greatest possible importance for personal happiness, and they are also a very necessary condition for enabling any one, either as theorist or as practical man, to effect the greatest amount of good compatible with his opportunities.

CHAPTER IV

YOUTHFUL PROPAGANDISM. THE WEST-
MINSTER REVIEW.

THE occupation of so much of my time by
office work did not relax my attention to my
own pursuits, which were never carried on more
vigorously. It was about this time that I began
to write in newspapers. The first writings
of mine which got into print were two letters
published towards the end of 1822, in the Traveller
evening newspaper. The Traveller (which afterwards grew into the 'Globe and Traveller,' by
the purchase and incorporation of the Globe)
was then the property of the well-known political
economist, Colonel Torrens, and under the editorship of an able man, Mr. Walter Coulson (who,
after being an amanuensis of Mr. Bentham,
became a reporter, then an editor, next a barrister
and conveyancer, and died Counsel to the Home
Office), it had become one of the most important
newspaper organs of Liberal politics. Colonel
Torrens himself wrote much of the political
economy of his paper; and had at this time made
an attack upon some opinion of Ricardo and
my father, to which, at my father's instigation,
I attempted an answer, and Coulson, out of
consideration for my father and goodwill to me,
inserted it. There was a reply by Torrens, to
which I again rejoined. I soon after attempted
something considerably more ambitious. The

prosecutions of Richard Carlile and his wife and sister for publications hostile to Christianity, were then exciting much attention, and nowhere more than among the people I frequented. Freedom of discussion even in politics, much more in religion, was at that time far from being, even in theory, the conceded point which it at least seems to be now; and the holders of obnoxious opinions had to be always ready to argue and re-argue for the liberty of expressing them. I wrote a series of five letters, under the signature of Wickliffe, going over the whole length and breadth of the question of free publication of all opinions on religion, and offered them to the Morning Chronicle. Three of them were published in January and February, 1823; the other two, containing things too outspoken for that journal, never appeared at all. But a paper which I wrote soon after on the same subject, *à propos* of a debate in the House of Commons, was inserted as a leading article; and during the whole of this year, 1823, a considerable number of my contributions were printed in the Chronicle and Traveller: sometimes notices of books but oftener letters, commenting on some nonsense talked in Parliament, or some defect of the law, or misdoings of the magistracy or the courts of justice. In this last department the Chronicle was now rendering signal service. After the death of Mr. Perry, the editorship and management of the paper had devolved on Mr. John Black, long a reporter on its establishment; a man of most extensive reading and information, great honesty and simplicity of mind; a particular friend of my father, imbued with many of his and Bentham's ideas, which he reproduced in his articles, among other valuable thoughts, with great facility and skill. From this time the Chronicle ceased to be the merely Whig organ it was before, and during the next ten years became to a considerable extent a vehicle of the opinions of the Utilitarian Radicals. This was mainly by what Black himself wrote, with some assistance from Fonblanque, who first showed his eminent qualities as a writer by articles and *jeux d'esprit* in the Chronicle. The defects of the law, and of the administration of justice, were the subject on which that paper rendered most service to improvement. Up to that time hardly a word had been said, except by Bentham and my father, against that most peccant part of English institutions and of their administration. It was the almost universal creed of Englishmen, that the law of England, the judicature of England, the unpaid magistracy of England, were models of excellence. I do not go beyond the mark in saying, that after Bentham, who supplied the principal materials, the greatest share of the merit of breaking down this wretched superstition belongs to Black, as editor of the Morning Chronicle. He kept up an incessant fire against it, exposing the absurdities and vices of the law and the courts of justice, paid and unpaid, until he forced some sense of them into people's minds. On many other questions he became the organ of opinions much in advance of any which had ever before found regular advocacy in the newspaper press. Black was a frequent visitor of my father, and Mr. Grote used to say that he always knew by the Monday morning's article, whether Black had been with my father on the Sunday. Black was one of the most influential of the many channels through which my father's conversation and personal influence made his opinions tell on the world; co-operating with the effect of his writings in making him a power in the country, such as it has rarely been the lot of an individual in a private station to be, through the mere force of intellect and character: and a power which was often acting the most efficiently where it was least seen and suspected. I have already noticed how much of what was done by Ricardo, Hume, and Grote, was the result, in part, of his prompting and persuasion. He was the good genius by the side of Brougham in most of what he did for the public, either on education, law reform, or any other subject. And his influence flowed in minor streams too numerous to be specified. This influence was now about to receive a great extension by the foundation of the Westminster Review.

Contrary to what may have been supposed, my father was in no degree a party to setting up the Westminster Review. The need of a Radical organ to make head against the Edinburgh and Quarterly (then in the period of their greatest reputation and influence), had been a topic of conversation between him and Mr. Bentham many years earlier, and it had been a part of their *Château en Espagne* that my father should be the editor; but the idea had never assumed any practical shape. In 1823, however, Mr. Bentham determined to establish the Review at his own cost, and offered the editorship to my father, who declined it as incompatible with his

India House appointment. It was then entrusted to Mr. (now Sir John) Bowring, at that time a merchant in the City. Mr. Bowring had been for two or three years previous an assiduous frequenter of Mr. Bentham, to whom he was recommended by many personal good qualities, by an ardent admiration for Bentham, a zealous adoption of many, though not all of his opinions, and, not least, by an extensive acquaintanceship and correspondence with Liberals of all countries, which seemed to qualify him for being a powerful agent in spreading Bentham's fame and doctrines through all quarters of the world. My father had seen little of Bowring, but knew enough of him to have formed a strong opinion, that he was a man of an entirely different type from what my father considered suitable for conducting a political and philosophical Review : and he augured so ill of the enterprise that he regretted it altogether, feeling persuaded not only that Mr. Bentham would lose his money, but that discredit would probably be brought upon Radical principles. He could not, however, desert Mr. Bentham, and he consented to write an article for the first number. As it had been a favourite portion of the scheme formerly talked of, that part of the work should be devoted to reviewing the other Reviews, this article of my father's was to be a general criticism of the Edinburgh Review from its commencement. Before writing it he made me read through all the volumes of the Review, or as much of each as seemed of any importance (which was not so arduous a task in 1823 as it would be now), and make notes for him of the articles which I thought he would wish

to examine, either on account of their good or
their bad qualities. This paper of my father's
was the chief cause of the sensation which the
Westminster Review produced at its first appearance, and is, both in conception and in execution,
one of the most striking of all his writings. He
began by an analysis of the tendencies of periodical
literature in general ; pointing out, that it cannot,
like books, wait for success, but must succeed
immediately, or not at all, and is hence almost
certain to profess and inculcate the opinions
already held by the public to which it addresses
itself, instead of attempting to rectify or improve
those opinions. He next, to characterize the
position of the Edinburgh Review as a political
organ, entered into a complete analysis, from
the Radical point of view, of the British Constitution. He held up to notice its thoroughly
aristocratic character : the nomination of a
majority of the House of Commons by a few
hundred families ; the entire identification of
the more independent portion, the county members,
with the great landholders ; the different classes
whom this narrow oligarchy was induced, for
convenience, to admit to a share of power ; and
finally, what he called its two props, the Church,
and the legal profession. He pointed out the
natural tendency of an aristocratic body of this
composition, to group itself into two parties, one
of them in possession of the executive, the other
endeavouring to supplant the former and become
the predominant section by the aid of public
opinion, without any essential sacrifice of the
aristocratical predominance. He described the
course likely to be pursued, and the political

ground occupied, by an aristocratic party in opposition, coquetting with popular principles for the sake of popular support. He showed how this idea was realized in the conduct of the Whig party, and of the Edinburgh Review as its chief literary organ. He described, as their main characteristic, what he termed 'seesaw;' writing alternately on both sides of every question which touched the power or interest of the governing classes; sometimes in different articles, sometimes in different parts of the same article: and illustrated his position by copious specimens. So formidable an attack on the Whig party and policy had never before been made; nor had so great a blow been ever struck, in this country, for Radicalism; nor was there, I believe, any living person capable of writing that article, except my father.[1]

In the meantime the nascent Review had formed a junction with another project, of a purely literary periodical, to be edited by Mr. Henry Southern, afterwards a diplomatist, then a literary man by profession. The two editors agreed to unite their corps, and divide the editorship, Bowring taking the political, Southern the literary department. Southern's Review was to have been published by Longman, and that firm, though part proprietors of the Edinburgh, were willing to be the publishers of the new journal. But when all the arrangements had been made,

---

[1] The continuation of this article in the second number of the Review was written by me under my father's eye, and (except as practice in composition, in which respect it was, to me, more useful than anything else I ever wrote) was of little or no value.

and the prospectuses sent out, the Longmans saw my father's attack on the Edinburgh, and drew back. My father was now appealed to for his interest with his own publisher, Baldwin, which was exerted with a successful result. And so, in April, 1824, amidst anything but hope on my father's part, and that of most of those who afterwards aided in carrying on the Review, the first number made its appearance.

That number was an agreeable surprise to most of us. The average of the articles was of much better quality than had been expected. The literary and artistic department had rested chiefly on Mr. Bingham, a barrister (subsequently a police magistrate), who had been for some years a frequenter of Bentham, was a friend of both the Austins, and had adopted with great ardour Mr. Bentham's philosophical opinions. Partly from accident, there were in the first number as many as five articles by Bingham; and we were extremely pleased with them. I well remember the mixed feeling I myself had about the Review; the joy at finding, what we did not at all expect, that it was sufficiently good to be capable of being made a creditable organ of those who held the opinions it professed; and extreme vexation, since it was so good on the whole, at what we thought the blemishes of it. When, however, in addition to our generally favourable opinion of it, we learned that it had an extraordinary large sale for a first number, and found that the appearance of a Radical Review, with pretensions equal to those of the established organs of parties, had excited much attention, there could be no room for hesitation, and we all became eager in doing everything we could to strengthen and improve it.

My father continued to write occasional articles. The Quarterly Review received its exposure, as a sequel to that of the Edinburgh. Of his other contributions, the most important were an attack on Southey's Book of the Church, in the fifth number, and a political article in the twelfth. Mr. Austin only contributed one paper, but one of great merit, an argument against primogeniture, in reply to an article then lately published in the Edinburgh Review by M'Culloch. Grote also was a contributor only once; all the time he could spare being already taken up with his History of Greece. The article he wrote was on his own subject, and was a very complete exposure and castigation of Mitford. Bingham and Charles Austin continued to write for some time; Fonblanque was a frequent contributor from the third number. Of my particular associates, Ellis was a regular writer up to the ninth number; and about the time when he left off, others of the set began; Eyton Tooke, Graham, and Roebuck. I was myself the most frequent writer of all, having contributed, from the second number to the eighteenth, thirteen articles; reviews of books on history and political economy, or discussions on special political topics, as corn laws, game laws, law of libel. Occasional articles of merit came in from other acquaintances of my father's and, in time, of mine; and some of Mr. Bowring's writers turned out well. On the whole, however, the conduct of the Review was never satisfactory to any of the persons strongly interested in its principles, with whom I came in contact. Hardly ever did a number come out without containing several things extremely offensive to us, either in point of opinion, of taste, or by mere want of ability. The unfavourable judgments passed by my father, Grote, the two Austins, and others, were re-echoed with exaggeration by us younger people; and as our youthful zeal rendered us by no means backward in making complaints, we led the two editors a sad life. From my knowledge of what I then was, I have no doubt that we were at least as often wrong as right; and I am very certain that if the Review had been carried on according to our notions (I mean those of the juniors), it would have been no better, perhaps not even so good as it was. But it is worth noting as a fact in the history of Benthamism, that the periodical organ, by which it was best known, was from the first extremely unsatisfactory to those whose opinions on all subjects it was supposed specially to represent.

Meanwhile, however, the Review made considerable noise in the world, and gave a recognised *status*, in the arena of opinion and discussion, to the Benthamic type of Radicalism, out of all proportion to the number of its adherents, and to the personal merits and abilities, at that time, of most of those who could be reckoned among them. It was a time, as is known, of rapidly rising Liberalism. When the fears and animosities accompanying the war with France had been brought to an end, and people had once more a place in their thoughts for home politics, the tide began to set towards reform. The renewed oppression of the Continent by the old reigning families, the countenance apparently given by the English Government to the conspiracy against liberty called the Holy Alliance, and the enormous weight of the national debt and taxation occasioned by so long and costly a war, rendered the government and parliament very unpopular. Radicalism, under the leadership of the Burdetts and Cobbetts, had assumed a character and importance which seriously alarmed the Administration : and their alarm had scarcely been temporarily assuaged by the celebrated Six Acts, when the trial of Queen Caroline roused a still wider and deeper feeling of hatred. Though the outward signs of this hatred passed away with its exciting cause, there arose on all sides a spirit which had never shown itself before, of opposition to abuses in detail. Mr. Hume's persevering scrutiny of the public expenditure, forcing the House of Commons to a division on every objectionable item in the estimates, had begun to tell with great force on public opinion, and had extorted many minor retrenchments from an unwilling administration. Political economy had asserted itself with great vigour in public affairs, by the petition of the merchants of London for free trade, drawn up in 1820 by Mr. Tooke and presented by Mr. Alexander Baring ; and by the noble exertions of Ricardo during the few years of his parliamentary life. His writings, following up the impulse given by the Bullion controversy, and followed up in their turn by the expositions and comments of my father and M'Culloch (whose writings in the Edinburgh Review during those years were most valuable), had drawn general attention to the subject, making at least partial converts in the Cabinet itself ; and Huskisson, supported by Canning, had commenced that gradual demolition of the protective system, which one of their colleagues virtually completed in 1846, though the last vestiges were only swept away by Mr. Gladstone in 1860. Mr. Peel, then Home Secretary, was entering cautiously into the untrodden and peculiarly Benthamic path of Law Reform. At this period, when Liberalism seemed to be becoming the tone of the time, when improvement of institutions was preached from the highest places, and a complete change of the constitution of Parliament was loudly demanded in the lowest, it is not strange that attention should have been roused by the regular appearance in controversy of what seemed a new school of writers, claiming to be the legislators and theorists of this new tendency. The air of strong conviction with which they wrote, when scarcely any one else seemed to have an equally strong faith in as definite a creed; the boldness with which they tilted against the very front of both the existing political parties; their uncompromising profession of opposition to many of the generally received opinions, and the suspicion they lay under of holding others still more heterodox than they professed; the talent and verve of at least my father's articles, and the appearance of a corps behind him sufficient to carry on a Review; and finally, the fact that the Review was bought and read, made the so-called Bentham school in philosophy and politics fill a greater place in the public mind than it had held before, or has ever again held since other equally earnest schools of thought have arisen in England. As I was in the headquarters of it, knew of what it was com-

posed, and as one of the most active of its very
small number, might say without undue assumtion, *quorum pars magna fui*, it belongs to me
more than to most others, to give some account
of it.

This supposed school, then, had no other
existence than what was constituted by the fact,
that my father's writings and conversation drew
round him a certain number of young men who
had already imbibed, or who imbibed from him,
a greater or smaller portion of his very decided
political and philosophical opinions. The notion
that Bentham was surrounded by a band of
disciples who received their opinions from his
lips, is a fable to which my father did justice in
his 'Fragment on Mackintosh,' and which, to
all who knew Mr. Bentham's habits of life and
manner of conversation, is simply ridiculous.
The influence which Bentham exercised was by
his writings. Through them he has produced,
and is producing, effects on the condition of mankind, wider and deeper, no doubt, than any which
can be attributed to my father. He is a much
greater name in history. But my father exercised
a far greater personal ascendancy. He *was*
sought for the vigour and instructiveness of his
conversation, and did use it largely as an instrument for the diffusion of his opinions. I have
never known any man who could do such ample
justice to his best thoughts in colloquial discussion.
His perfect command over his great mental
resources, the terseness and expressiveness of
his language and the moral earnestness as well
as intellectual force of his delivery, made him
one of the most striking of all argumentative

conversers : and he was full of anecdote, a hearty
laugher, and, when with people whom he liked,
a most lively and amusing companion. It was
not solely, or even chiefly, in diffusing his merely
intellectual convictions that his power showed
itself : it was still more through the influence
of a quality, of which I have only since learnt to
appreciate the extreme rarity : that exalted
public spirit, and regard above all things to the
good of the whole, which warmed into life and
activity every germ of similar virtue that existed
in the minds he came in contact with : the desire
he made them feel for his approbation, the shame
at his disapproval ; the moral support which
his conversation and his very existence gave to
those who were aiming at the same objects, and
the encouragement he afforded to the fainthearted
or desponding among them, by the firm confidence
which (though the reverse of sanguine as to the
results to be expected in any one particular case)
he always felt in the power of reason, the general
progress of improvement, and the good which
individuals could do by judicious effort.

It was my father's opinions which gave the
distinguishing character to the Benthamic or
utilitarian propagandism of that time. They fell
singly, scattered from him, in many directions,
but they flowed from him in a continued stream
principally in three channels. One was through me,
the only mind directly formed by his instructions, and through whom considerable influence
was exercised over various young men, who
became in their turn, propagandists. A second
was through some of the Cambridge contemporaries of Charles Austin, who, either initiated

by him or under the general mental impulse which he gave, had adopted many opinions allied to those of my father, and some of the more considerable of whom afterwards sought my father's acquaintance and frequented his house. Among these may be mentioned Strutt, afterwards Lord Belper, and the present Lord Romilly, with whose eminent father, Sir Samuel, my father had of old been on terms of friendship. The third channel was that of a younger generation of Cambridge undergraduates, contemporary, not with Austin, but with Eyton Tooke, who were drawn to that estimable person by affinity of opinions, and introduced by him to my father: the most notable of these was Charles Buller. Various other persons individually received and transmitted a considerable amount of my father's influence: for example, Black (as before mentioned) and Fonblanque: most of these, however, we accounted only partial allies; Fonblanque, for instance, was always divergent from us on many important points. But indeed there was by no means complete unanimity among any portion of us, nor had any of us adopted implicitly all my father's opinions. For example, although his Essay on Government was regarded probably by all of us as a masterpiece of political wisdom, our adhesion by no means extended to the paragraph of it, in which he maintains that women may consistently with good government, be excluded from the suffrage, because their interest is the same with that of men. From this doctrine, I, and all those who formed my chosen associates, most positively dissented. It is due to my father to say that he denied having intended to affirm

that women *should* be excluded, any more than
men under the age of forty, concerning whom he
maintained, in the very next paragraph, an
exactly similar thesis. He was, as he truly said,
not discussing whether the suffrage had better
be restricted, but only (assuming that it is to be
restricted) what is the utmost limit of restriction, which does not necessarily involve a sacrifice of the securities for good government. But
I thought then, as I have always thought since,
that the opinion which he acknowledged, no less
than that which he disclaimed, is as great an
error as any of those against which the Essay
was directed; that the interest of women is
included in that of men exactly as much and
no more, as the interest of subjects is included
in that of kings; and that every reason which
exists for giving the suffrage to anybody, demands
that it should not be withheld from women.
This was also the general opinion of the younger
proselytes; and it is pleasant to be able to say
that Mr. Bentham, on this important point, was
wholly on our side.

But though none of us, probably, agreed in
every respect with my father, his opinions, as
I said before, were the principal element which
gave its colour and character to the little group
of young men who were the first propagators of
what was afterwards called ' Philosophic Radicalism.' Their mode of thinking was not characterized
by Benthamism in any sense which has relation
to Bentham as a chief or guide, but rather by
a combination of Bentham's point of view with
that of the modern political economy, and with
the Hartleian metaphysics. Malthus's population

principle was quite as much a banner, and point of union among us, as any opinion specially belonging to Bentham. This great doctrine, originally brought forward as an argument against the indefinite improvability of human affairs, we took up with ardent zeal in the contrary sense, as indicating the sole means of realizing that improvability by securing full employment at high wages to the whole labouring population through a voluntary restriction of the increase of their numbers. The other leading characteristics of the creed, which we held in common with my father, may be stated as follows :

In politics, an almost unbounded confidence in the efficacy of two things : representative government, and complete freedom of discussion. So complete was my father's reliance on the influence of reason over the minds of mankind, whenever it is allowed to reach them, that he felt as if all would be gained if the whole population were taught to read, if all sorts of opinions were allowed to be addressed to them by word and in writing, and if by means of the suffrage they could nominate a legislature to give effect to the opinions they adopted. He thought that when the legislature no longer represented a class interest, it would aim at the general interest, honestly and with adequate wisdom ; since the people would be sufficiently under the guidance of educated intelligence, to make in general a good choice of persons to represent them, and having done so, to leave to those whom they had chosen a liberal discretion. Accordingly aristocratic rule, the government of the Few in any of its shapes, being in his eyes the only thing which stood between mankind and an administration of their affairs by the best wisdom to be found among them, was the object of his sternest disapprobation, and a democratic suffrage the principal article of his political creed, not on the ground of liberty, Rights of Man, or any of the phrases, more or less significant, by which, up to that time, democracy had usually been defended, but as the most essential of 'securities for good government.' In this, too, he held fast only to what he deemed essentials; he was comparatively indifferent to monarchical or republican forms —far more so than Bentham, to whom a king, in the character of 'corrupter-general,' appeared necessarily very noxious. Next to aristocracy, an established church, or corporation of priests, as being by position the great depravers of religion, and interested in opposing the progress of the human mind, was the object of his greatest detestation; though he disliked no clergyman personally who did not deserve it, and was on terms of sincere friendship with several. In ethics, his moral feelings were energetic and rigid on all points which he deemed important to human well being, while he was supremely indifferent in opinion (though his indifference did not show itself in personal conduct) to all those doctrines of the common morality, which he thought had no foundation but in asceticism and priestcraft. He looked forward, for example, to a considerable increase of freedom in the relations between the sexes, though without pretending to define exactly what would be, or ought to be, the precise conditions of that freedom. This opinion was connected in him with no sensuality either of a theoretical or of a practical kind. He anticipated, on the contrary, as one of the beneficial effects of increased freedom, that the imagination would no longer dwell upon the physical relation and its adjuncts, and swell this into one of the principal objects of life; a perversion of the imagination and feelings, which he regarded as one of the deepest seated and most pervading evils in the human mind. In psychology, his fundamental doctrine was the formation of all human character by circumstances, through the universal Principle of Association, and the consequent unlimited possibility of improving the moral and intellectual condition of mankind by education. Of all his doctrines none was more important than this, or needs more to be insisted on: unfortunately there is none which is more contradictory to the prevailing tendencies of speculation, both in his time and since.

These various opinions were seized on with youthful fanaticism by the little knot of young men of whom I was one: and we put into them a sectarian spirit, from which, in intention at least, my father was wholly free. What we (or rather a phantom substituted in the place of us) were sometimes, by a ridiculous exaggeration, called by others, namely a 'school,' some of us for a time really hoped and aspired to be. The French *philosophes* of the eighteenth century were the example we sought to imitate, and we hoped to accomplish no less results. No one of the set went to so great excesses in this boyish ambition as I did; which might be shown by many particulars, were it not an useless waste of space and time.

All this, however, is properly only the outside of our existence; or, at least, the intellectual part alone, and no more than one side of that. In attempting to penetrate inward, and give any indication of what we were as human beings, I must be understood as speaking only of myself, of whom alone I can speak from sufficient knowledge; and I do not believe that the picture would suit any of my companions without many and great modifications.

I conceive that the description so often given of a Benthamite, as a mere reasoning machine, though extremely inapplicable to most of those who have been designated by that title, was during two or three years of my life not altogether untrue of me. It was perhaps as applicable to me as it can well be to any one just entering into life, to whom the common objects of desire must in general have at least the attraction of novelty. There is nothing very extraordinary in this fact: no youth of the age I then was, can be expected to be more than one thing, and this was the thing I happened to be. Ambition and desire of distinction, I had in abundance; and zeal for what I thought the good of mankind was my strongest sentiment, mixing with and colouring all others. But my zeal was as yet little else, at that period of my life, than zeal for speculative opinions. It had not its root in genuine benevolence, or sympathy with mankind; though these qualities held their due place in my ethical standard. Nor was it connected with any high enthusiasm for ideal nobleness. Yet of this feeling I was imaginatively very susceptible; but there was at that time an intermission of its natural aliment, poetical culture, while there was a superabundance of the discipline antagonistic to it, that of mere logic and analysis. Add to this that, as already mentioned, my father's teachings tended to the undervaluing of feeling. It was not that he was himself cold-hearted or insensible; I believe it was rather from the contrary quality; he thought that feeling could take care of itself; that there was sure to be enough of it if actions were properly cared about. Offended by the frequency with which, in ethical and philosophical controversy, feeling is made the ultimate reason and justification of conduct, instead of being itself called on for a justification, while, in practice, actions the effect of which on human happiness is mischievous, are defended as being required by feeling, and the character of a person of feeling obtains a credit for desert, which he thought only due to actions, he had a real impatience of attributing praise to feeling, or of any but the most sparing reference to it, either in the estimation of persons or in the discussion of things. In addition to the influence which this characteristic in him, had on me and others, we found all the opinions to which we attached most importance, constantly attacked on the ground of feeling. Utility was denounced as cold calculation; political economy as hard-hearted; anti-population doctrines as repulsive to the natural feelings of mankind. We retorted by the word 'sentimentality,' which, along with 'declamation' and 'vague generalities,' served us as common terms of opprobrium. Although we were generally in the right, as against those who were opposed to us, the effect was that the cultivation of feeling (except the feelings of public and private duty), was not in much esteem among us, and had very little place in the thoughts of most of us, myself in particular. What we principally thought of, was to alter people's opinions; to make them believe according to evidence, and know what was their real interest, which when they once knew, they would, we thought, by the instrument of opinion, enforce a regard to it upon one another. While fully recognising the superior excellence of unselfish benevolence and love of justice, we did not expect the regeneration of mankind from any direct action on those sentiments, but from the effect of educated intellect, enlightening the selfish feelings. Although this last is prodigiously important as a means of improvement in the hands of those who are themselves impelled by nobler principles of action, I do not believe that any one of the survivors of the Benthamites or Utilitarians of that day, now relies mainly upon it for the general amendment of human conduct.

From this neglect both in theory and in practice of the cultivation of feeling, naturally resulted, among other things, an undervaluing of poetry, and of Imagination generally, as an element of human nature. It is, or was, part of the popular notion of Benthamites, that they are enemies of poetry: this was partly true of Bentham himself; he used to say that 'all poetry is misrepresentation:' but in the sense in which he said it, the same might have been said of all impressive speech; of all representation or inculcation more oratorical in its character than a sum in arithmetic. An article of Bingham's in the first number of the Westminster Review, in which he offered as an explanation of something which he disliked in Moore, that ' Mr. Moore *is* a poet, and therefore is *not* a reasoner,' did a good deal to attach the notion of hating poetry to the writers in the Review. But the truth was that many of us were great readers of poetry ; Bingham himself had been a writer of it, while as regards me (and the same thing might be said of my father), the correct statement would be, not that I disliked poetry, but that I was theoretically indifferent to it. I disliked any sentiments in poetry which I should have disliked in prose ; and that included a great deal. And I was wholly blind to its place in human culture, as a means of educating the feelings. But I was always personally very susceptible to some kinds of it. In the most sectarian period of my Benthamism, I happened to look into Pope's Essay on Man, and though every opinion in it was contrary to mine, I well remember how powerfully it acted on my imagination. Perhaps at that time poetical composition of any higher type than eloquent discussion in verse, might not have produced a similar effect on me : at all events I seldom gave it an opportunity. This, however, was a mere passive state. Long before I had enlarged in any considerable degree, the basis of my intellectual creed, I had obtained in the natural course of my mental progress, poetic culture of the most valuable kind, by means of reverential admiration for the lives and characters of heroic persons ; especially the heroes of philosophy. The same inspiring effect which so many of the benefactors of mankind have left on record that they had experienced from Plutarch's Lives, was produced

on me by Plato's pictures of Socrates, and by
some modern biographies, above all by Condorcet's
Life of Turgot; a book well calculated to rouse
the best sort of enthusiasm, since it contains one
of the wisest and noblest of lives, delineated by
one of the wisest and noblest of men. The heroic
virtue of these glorious representatives of the
opinions with which I sympathized, deeply
affected me, and I perpetually recurred to them
as others do to a favourite poet, when needing
to be carried up into the more elevated regions
of feeling and thought. I may observe by the
way that this book cured me of my sectarian
follies. The two or three pages beginning ' Il
regardait toute secte comme nuisible,' and explaining why Turgot always kept himself perfectly
distinct from the Encyclopedists, sank deeply
into my mind. I left off designating myself and
others as Utilitarians, and by the pronoun ' we '
or any other collective designation, I ceased to
afficher sectarianism. My real inward sectarianism
I did not get rid of till later, and much more
gradually.

About the end of 1824, or beginning of 1825,
Mr. Bentham, having lately got back his papers
on Evidence from M. Dumont (whose Traité
des Preuves Judiciaires, grounded on them, was
then first completed and published) resolved to
have them printed in the original, and bethought
himself of me as capable of preparing them for
the press; in the same manner as his Book of
Fallacies had been recently edited by Bingham.
I gladly undertook this task, and it occupied
nearly all my leisure for about a year, exclusive
of the time afterwards spent in seeing the five

large volumes through the press. Mr. Bentham
had begun this treatise three times, at considerable intervals, each time in a different manner,
and each time without reference to the preceding :
two of the three times he had gone over nearly
the whole subject. These three masses of manuscript it was my business to condense into a
single treatise ; adopting the one last written
as the groundwork, and incorporating with it
as much of the two others as it had not completely
superseded. I had also to unroll such of Bentham's
involved and parenthetical sentences, as seemed
to overpass by their complexity the measure of
what readers were likely to take the pains to
understand. It was further Mr. Bentham's particular desire that I should, from myself, endeavour
to supply any *lacunæ* which he had left ; and at
his instance I read, for this purpose, the most
authoritative treatises on the English Law of
Evidence, and commented on a few of the objectionable points of the English rules, which had
escaped Bentham's notice. I also replied to the
objections which had been made to some of his
doctrines by reviewers of Dumont's book, and
added a few supplementary remarks on some
of the more abstract parts of the subject, such
as the theory of improbability and impossibility.
The controversial part of these editorial additions
was written in a more assuming tone than became
one so young and inexperienced as I was : but
indeed I had never contemplated coming forward
in my own person ; and as an anonymous editor
of Bentham, I fell into the tone of my author, not
thinking it unsuitable to him or to the subject,
however it might be so to me. My name as editor

was put to the book after it was printed, at
Mr. Bentham's positive desire, which I in vain
attempted to persuade him to forego.

The time occupied in this editorial work was
extremely well employed in respect to my own
improvement. The 'Rationale of Judicial Evidence' is one of the richest in matter of all Bentham's productions. The theory of evidence
being in itself one of the most important of his
subjects, and ramifying into most of the others,
the book contains, very fully developed, a great
proportion of all his best thoughts : while, among
more special things, it comprises the most elaborate
exposure of the vices and defects of English law,
as it then was, which is to be found in his works :
not confined to the law of evidence, but including,
by way of illustrative episode, the entire procedure
or practice of Westminster Hall. The direct
knowledge, therefore, which I obtained from
the book, and which was imprinted upon me much
more thoroughly than it could have been by mere
reading, was itself no small acquisition. But this
occupation did for me what might seem less to
be expected ; it gave a great start to my powers of
composition. Everything which I wrote subsequently to this editorial employment, was markedly
superior to anything that I had written before
it. Bentham's later style, as the world knows,
was heavy and cumbersome, from the excess
of a good quality, the love of precision, which
made him introduce clause within clause into
the heart of every sentence, that the reader might
receive into his mind all the modifications and
qualifications simultaneously with the main proposition : and the habit grew on him until his

sentences became, to those not accustomed to them, most laborious reading. But his earlier style, that of the Fragment on Government, Plan of a Judicial Establishment, &c., is a model of liveliness and ease combined with fulness of matter, scarcely ever surpassed : and of this earlier style there were many striking specimens in the manuscripts on Evidence, all of which I endeavoured to preserve. So long a course of this admirable writing had a considerable effect upon my own ; and I added to it by the assiduous reading of other writers, both French and English, who combined, in a remarkable degree, ease with force, such as Goldsmith, Fielding, Pascal, Voltaire, and Courier. Through these influences my writing lost the jejuneness of my early compositions ; the bones and cartilages began to clothe themselves with flesh, and the style became, at times, lively and almost light.

This improvement was first exhibited in a new field. Mr. Marshall, of Leeds, father of the present generation of Marshalls, the same who was brought into Parliament for Yorkshire, when the representation forfeited by Grampound was transferred to it, an earnest Parliamentary reformer, and a man of large fortune, of which he made a liberal use, had been much struck with Bentham's Book of Fallacies : and the thought had occurred to him that it would be useful to publish annually the Parliamentary Debates, not in the chronological order of Hansard, but classified according to subjects, and accompanied by a commentary pointing out the fallacies of the speakers. With this intention, he very naturally addressed himself to the editor of the Book of Fallacies ; and

Bingham, with the assistance of Charles Austin, undertook the editorship. The work was called 'Parliamentary History and Review.' Its sale was not sufficient to keep it in existence, and it only lasted three years. It excited, however, some attention among parliamentary and political people. The best strength of the party was put forth in it; and its execution did them much more credit than that of the Westminster Review had ever done. Bingham and Charles Austin wrote much in it; as did Strutt, Romilly, and several other Liberal lawyers. My father wrote one article in his best style; the elder Austin another. Coulson wrote one of great merit. It fell to my lot to lead off the first number by an article on the principal topic of the session (that of 1825), the Catholic Association and the Catholic Disabilities. In the second number I wrote an elaborate Essay on the Commercial Crisis of 1825 and the Currency Debates. In the third I had two articles, one on a minor subject, the other on the Reciprocity principle in commerce, à propos of a celebrated diplomatic correspondence between Canning and Gallatin. These writings were no longer mere reproductions and applications of the doctrines I had been taught; they were original thinking, as far as that name can be applied to old ideas in new forms and connexions: and I do not exceed the truth in saying that there was a maturity, and a well-digested character about them, which there had not been in any of my previous performances. In execution, therefore, they were not at all juvenile; but their subjects have either gone by, or have been so much better treated since that they are entirely superseded, and should remain buried in the same oblivion with my contributions to the first dynasty of the Westminster Review.

While thus engaged in writing for the public, I did not neglect other modes of self-cultivation. It was at this time that I learnt German; beginning it on the Hamiltonian method, for which purpose I and several of my companions formed a class. For several years from this period, our social studies assumed a shape which contributed very much to my mental progress. The idea occurred to us of carrying on, by reading and conversation, a joint study of several of the branches of science which we wished to be masters of. We assembled to the number of a dozen or more. Mr. Grote lent a room of his house in Threadneedle Street for the purpose, and his partner, Prescott, one of the three original members of the Utilitarian Society, made one among us. We met two mornings in every week, from half-past eight till ten, at which hour most of us were called off to our daily occupations. Our first subject was Political Economy. We chose some systematic treatise as our text-book; my father's 'Elements' being our first choice. One of us read aloud a chapter, or some smaller portion of the book. The discussion was then opened, and any one who had an objection, or other remark to make, made it. Our rule was to discuss thoroughly every point raised, whether great or small, prolonging the discussion until all who took part were satisfied with the conclusion they had individually arrived at; and to follow up every topic of collateral speculation which the chapter or the conversation suggested, never leaving it

until we had untied every knot which we found.
We repeatedly kept up the discussion of some
one point for several weeks, thinking intently
on it during the intervals of our meetings, and
contriving solutions of the new difficulties which
had risen up in the last morning's discussion.
When we had finished in this way my father's
Elements, we went in the same manner through
Ricardo's Principles of Political Economy, and
Bailey's Dissertation on Value. These close
and vigorous discussions were not only improving
in a high degree to those who took part in them,
but brought out new views of some topics of
abstract Political Economy. The theory of
International Values which I afterwards published,
emanated from these conversations, as did also
the modified form of Ricardo's theory of Profits,
laid down in my Essay on Profits and Interest.
Those among us with whom new speculations
chiefly originated, were Ellis, Graham, and I;
though others gave valuable aid to the discussions,
especially Prescott and Roebuck, the one by his
knowledge, the other by his dialectical acuteness.
The theories of International Values and of
Profits were excogitated and worked out in about
equal proportions by myself and Graham: and
if our original project had been executed, my
' Essays on Some Unsettled Questions of Political
Economy ' would have been brought out along
with some papers of his, under our joint names.
But when my exposition came to be written,
I found that I had so much over-estimated my
agreement with him, and he dissented so much
from the most original of the two Essays, that
on International Values, that I was obliged to

consider the theory as now exclusively mine, and it came out as such when published many years later. I may mention that among the alterations which my father made in revising his Elements for the third edition, several were founded on criticisms elicited by these conversations; and in particular he modified his opinions (though not to the extent of our new speculations) on both the points to which I have adverted.

When we had enough of political economy, we took up the syllogistic logic in the same manner, Grote now joining us. Our first text-book was Aldrich, but being disgusted with its superficiality, we reprinted one of the most finished among the many manuals of the school logic, which my father, a great collector of such books, possessed, the Manuductio ad Logicam of the Jesuit Du Trieu. After finishing this, we took up Whately's Logic, then first republished from the Encyclopædia Metropolitana, and finally the 'Computatio sive Logica' of Hobbes. These books, dealt with in our manner, afforded a wide range for original metaphysical speculation: and most of what has been done in the First Book of my System of Logic, to rationalize and correct the principles and distinctions of the school logicians, and to improve the theory of the Import of Propositions, had its origin in these discussions; Graham and I originating most of the novelties, while Grote and others furnished an excellent tribunal or test. From this time I formed the project of writing a book on Logic, though on a much humbler scale than the one I ultimately executed.

Having done with Logic, we launched into Analytic Psychology, and having chosen Hartley for our textbook, we raised Priestley's edition to an extravagant price by searching through London to furnish each of us with a copy. When we had finished Hartley, we suspended our meetings; but my father's Analysis of the Mind being published soon after, we reassembled for the purpose of reading it. With this our exercises ended. I have always dated from these conversations my own real inauguration as an original and independent thinker. It was also through them that I acquired, or very much strengthened, a mental habit to which I attribute all that I have ever done, or ever shall do, in speculation; that of never accepting half-solutions of difficulties as complete; never abandoning a puzzle, but again and again returning to it until it was cleared up; never allowing obscure corners of a subject to remain unexplored, because they did not appear important; never thinking that I perfectly understood any part of a subject until I understood the whole.

Our doings from 1825 to 1830 in the way of public speaking, filled a considerable place in my life during those years, and as they had important effects on my development, something ought to be said of them.

There was for some time in existence a society of Owenites, called the Co-operation Society, which met for weekly public discussions in Chancery Lane. In the early part of 1825, accident brought Roebuck in contact with several of its members, and led to his attending one or two of the meetings and taking part in the debate in opposition to Owenism. Some one of us started the notion of going there in a body and having a general battle : and Charles Austin and some of his friends who did not usually take part in our joint exercises, entered into the project. It was carried out by concert with the principal members of the Society, themselves nothing loth, as they naturally preferred a controversy with opponents to a tame discussion among their own body. The question of population was proposed as the subject of debate : Charles Austin led the case on our side with a brilliant speech, and the fight was kept up by adjournment through five or six weekly meetings before crowded auditories, including along with the members of the Society and their friends, many hearers and some speakers from the Inns of Court. When this debate was ended, another was commenced on the general merits of Owen's system : and the contest altogether lasted about three months. It was a *lutte corps à corps* between Owenites and political economists, whom the Owenites regarded as their most inveterate opponents : but it was a perfectly friendly dispute. We who represented political economy, had the same objects in view as they had, and took pains to show it ; and the principal champion on their side was a very estimable man, with whom I was well acquainted, Mr. William Thompson, of Cork, author of a book on the Distribution of Wealth, and of an 'Appeal' in behalf of women against the passage relating to them in my father's Essay on Government. Ellis, Roebuck, and I took an active part in the debate, and among those from the Inns of Court who joined in it, I remember Charles Villiers. The other side obtained also, on the population question, very

efficient support from without. The well-known
Gale Jones, then an elderly man, made one of
his florid speeches; but the speaker with whom
I was most struck, though I dissented from
nearly every word he said, was Thirlwall, the
historian, since Bishop of St. David's, then a
Chancery barrister, unknown except by a high
reputation for eloquence acquired at the Cambridge
Union before the era of Austin and Macaulay.
His speech was in answer to one of mine. Before
he had uttered ten sentences, I set him down as
the best speaker I had ever heard, and I have
never since heard any one whom I placed above
him.

The great interest of these debates predisposed
some of those who took part in them, to catch
at a suggestion thrown out by M'Culloch, the
political economist, that a Society was wanted
in London similar to the Speculative Society at
Edinburgh, in which Brougham, Horner, and
others first cultivated public speaking.   Our
experience at the Co-operative Society seemed
to give cause for being sanguine as to the sort of
men who might be brought together in London
for such a purpose.   M'Culloch mentioned the
matter to several young men of influence, to
whom he was then giving private lessons in
political economy.   Some of these entered warmly
into the project, particularly George Villiers,
afterwards Earl of Clarendon.   He and his brothers,
Hyde and Charles, Romilly, Charles Austin and
I, with some others, met and agreed on a plan.
We determined to meet once a fortnight from
November to June, at the Freemasons' Tavern,
and we had soon a fine list of members, containing,

along with several members of Parliament,
nearly all the most noted speakers of the Cambridge
Union and of the Oxford United Debating Society.
It is curiously illustrative of the tendencies of
the time, that our principal difficulty in recruiting
for the Society was to find a sufficient number
of Tory speakers. Almost all whom we could
press into the service were Liberals, of different
orders and degrees. Besides those already named,
we had Macaulay, Thirlwall, Praed, Lord Howick,
Samuel Wilberforce (afterwards Bishop of Oxford),
Charles Poulett Thomson (afterwards Lord Syden-
ham), Edward and Henry Lytton Bulwer,
Fonblanque, and many others whom I cannot
now recollect, but who made themselves afterwards more or less conspicuous in public or
literary life. Nothing could seem more promising.
But when the time for action drew near, and
it was necessary to fix on a President, and find
somebody to open the first debate, none of our
celebrities would consent to perform either office.
Of the many who were pressed on the subject,
the only one who could be prevailed on was a
man of whom I knew very little, but who had
taken high honours at Oxford and was said to
have acquired a great oratorical reputation
there; who some time afterwards became a
Tory member of Parliament. He accordingly
was fixed on, both for filling the President's chair
and for making the first speech. The important
day arrived; the benches were crowded; all our
great speakers were present, to judge of, but not
to help our efforts. The Oxford orator's speech
was a complete failure. This threw a damp on
the whole concern: the speakers who followed

were few, and none of them did their best : the
affair was a complete *fiasco* ; and the oratorical
celebrities we had counted on went away never
to return, giving to me at least a lesson in knowledge of the world. This unexpected breakdown
altered my whole relation to the project. I had
not anticipated taking a prominent part, or
speaking much or often, particularly at first,
but I now saw that the success of the scheme
depended on the new men, and I put my shoulder
to the wheel. I opened the second question,
and from that time spoke in nearly every debate.
It was very uphill work for some time. The three
Villiers and Romilly stuck to us for some time
longer, but the patience of all the founders of
the Society was at last exhausted, except me
and Roebuck. In the season following, 1826–7,
things began to mend. We had acquired two
excellent Tory speakers, Hayward and Shee
(afterwards Sergeant Shee) : the Radical side
was reinforced by Charles Buller, Cockburn, and
others of the second generation of Cambridge
Benthamites ; and with their and other occasional
aid, and the two Tories as well as Roebuck and
me for regular speakers, almost every debate
was a *bataille rangée* between the ' philosophic
Radicals ' and the Tory lawyers ; until our conflicts were talked about, and several persons of
note and consideration came to hear us. This
happened still more in the subsequent seasons,
1828 and 1829, when the Coleridgians, in the
persons of Maurice and Sterling, made their
appearance in the Society as a second Liberal
and even Radical party, on totally different
grounds from Benthamism and vehemently

opposed to it; bringing into these discussions the general doctrines and modes of thought of the European reaction against the philosophy of the eighteenth century; and adding a third and very important belligerent party to our contests, which were now no bad exponents of the movement of opinion among the most cultivated part of the new generation. Our debates were very different from those of common debating societies, for they habitually consisted of the strongest arguments and most philosophic principles which either side was able to produce, thrown often into close and *serré* confutations of one another. The practice was necessarily very useful to us, and eminently so to me. I never, indeed, acquired real fluency, and had always a bad and ungraceful delivery; but I could make myself listened to: and as I always wrote my speeches when, from the feelings involved or the nature of the ideas to be developed, expression seemed important, I greatly increased my power of effective writing; acquiring not only an ear for smoothness and rhythm, but a practical sense for *telling* sentences, and an immediate criterion of their telling property, by their effect on a mixed audience.

The Society, and the preparation for it, together with the preparation for the morning conversations which were going on simultaneously, occupied the greater part of my leisure; and made me feel it a relief when, in the spring of 1828, I ceased to write for the Westminster. The Review had fallen into difficulties. Though the sale of the first number had been very encouraging, the permanent sale had never, I believe, been sufficient to pay the expenses, on the scale on which the Review was carried on. Those expenses had been considerably, but not sufficiently, reduced. One of the editors, Southern, had resigned; and several of the writers, including my father and me, who had been paid like other contributors for our earlier articles, had latterly written without payment. Nevertheless, the original funds were nearly or quite exhausted, and if the Review was to be continued some new arrangement of its affairs had become indispensable. My father and I had several conferences with Bowring on the subject. We were willing to do our utmost for maintaining the Review as an organ of our opinions, but not under Bowring's editorship: while the impossibility of its any longer supporting a paid editor, afforded a ground on which, without affront to him, we could propose to dispense with his services. We and some of our friends were prepared to carry on the Review as unpaid writers, either finding among ourselves an unpaid editor, or sharing the editorship among us. But while this negotiation was proceeding with Bowring's apparent acquiescence, he was carrying on another in a different quarter (with Colonel Perronet Thompson), of which we received the first intimation in a letter from Bowring as editor, informing us merely that an arrangement had been made, and proposing to us to write for the next number, with promise of payment. We did not dispute Bowring's right to bring about, if he could, an arrangement more favourable to himself than the one we had proposed; but we thought the concealment which he had practised towards us, while seemingly entering into our own project, an affront : and even had we not thought so, we were indisposed to expend any more of our time and trouble in attempting to write up the Review under his management. Accordingly my father excused himself from writing ; though two or three years later, on great pressure, he did write one more political article. As for me, I positively refused. And thus ended my connexion with the original Westminster. The last article which I wrote in it had cost me more labour than any previous ; but it was a labour of love, being a defence of the early French Revolutionists against the Tory misrepresentations of Sir Walter Scott, in the introduction to his Life of Napoleon. The number of books which I read for this purpose, making notes and extracts—even the number I had to buy (for in those days there was no public or subscription library from which books of reference could be taken home), far exceeded the worth of the immediate object ; but I had at that time a half-formed intention of writing a History of the French Revolution ; and though I never executed it, my collections afterwards were very useful to Carlyle for a similar purpose.

CHAPTER V

A CRISIS IN MY MENTAL HISTORY. ONE STAGE ONWARD.

FOR some years after this time I wrote very little, and nothing regularly, for publication : and great were the advantages which I derived from the intermission. It was of no common importance to me, at this period, to be able to digest and mature my thoughts for my own mind only, without any immediate call for giving them out in print. Had I gone on writing, it would have much disturbed the important transformation in my opinions and character, which took place during those years. The origin of this transformation, or at least the process by which I was prepared for it, can only be explained by turning some distance back.

From the winter of 1821, when I first read Bentham, and especially from the commencement of the Westminster Review, I had what might truly be called an object in life ; to be a reformer of the world. My conception of my own happiness was entirely identified with this object. The personal sympathies I wished for were those of fellow labourers in this enterprise. I endeavoured to pick up as many flowers as I could by the way ; but as a serious and permanent personal satisfaction to rest upon, my whole reliance was placed on this ; and I was accustomed to felicitate myself on the certainty of a happy life which I enjoyed, through placing my happiness in something durable and distant, in which some progress might be always making, while it could never be exhausted by complete attainment. This did very well for several years, during which the general improvement going on in the world and the idea of myself as engaged with others in struggling to promote it, seemed enough to fill up an interesting and animated existence. But the time came when I awakened from this as from a dream. It was in the autumn of 1826. I was in a dull state of nerves, such as everybody is occasionally liable to; unsusceptible to enjoyment or pleasurable excitement; one of those moods when what is pleasure at other times, becomes insipid or indifferent; the state, I should think, in which converts to Methodism usually are, when smitten by their first 'conviction of sin.' In this frame of mind it occurred to me to put the question directly to myself: 'Suppose that all your objects in life were realized; that all the changes in institutions and opinions which you are looking forward to, could be completely effected at this very instant: would this be a great joy and happiness to you?' And an irrepressible self-consciousness distinctly answered, 'No!' At this my heart sank within me: the whole foundation on which my life was constructed fell down. All my happiness was to have been found in the continual pursuit of this end. The end had ceased to charm, and how could there ever again be any interest in the means? I seemed to have nothing left to live for.

At first I hoped that the cloud would pass away of itself; but it did not. A night's sleep, the sovereign remedy for the smaller vexations of life, had no effect on it. I awoke to a renewed consciousness of the woful fact. I carried it with me into all companies, into all occupations. Hardly anything had power to cause me even a few minutes' oblivion of it. For some months the cloud seemed to grow thicker and thicker. The lines in Coleridge's ' Dejection '—I was not then acquainted with them—exactly describe my case :

> A grief without a pang, void, dark and drear,
> A drowsy, stifled, unimpassioned grief,
> Which finds no natural outlet or relief
> In word, or sigh, or tear.

In vain I sought relief from my favourite books ; those memorials of past nobleness and greatness from which I had always hitherto drawn strength and animation. I read them now without feeling, or with the accustomed feeling *minus* all its charm ; and I became persuaded, that my love of mankind, and of excellence for its own sake, had worn itself out. I sought no comfort by speaking to others of what I felt. If I had loved any one sufficiently to make confiding my griefs a necessity, I should not have been in the condition I was. I felt, too, that mine was not an interesting, or in any way respectable distress. There was nothing in it to attract sympathy. Advice, if I had known where to seek it, would have been most precious. The words of Macbeth to the physician often occurred to my thoughts. But there was no one on whom I could build the faintest hope of such assistance. My father, to whom it would have been natural to me to have recourse in any practical difficulties, was the last person to whom, in such a case as this, I looked for help. Everything convinced me that he had no knowledge of any such mental state as I was suffering from, and that even if he could be made to understand it, he was not the physician who could heal it. My education, which was wholly his work, had been conducted without any regard to the possibility of its ending in this result; and I saw no use in giving him the pain of thinking that his plans had failed, when the failure was probably irremediable, and, at all events, beyond the power of *his* remedies. Of other friends, I had at that time none to whom I had any hope of making my condition intelligible. It was however abundantly intelligible to myself; and the more I dwelt upon it, the more hopeless it appeared.

My course of study had led me to believe, that all mental and moral feelings and qualities, whether of a good or of a bad kind, were the results of association; that we love one thing, and hate another, take pleasure in one sort of action or contemplation, and pain in another sort, through the clinging of pleasurable or painful ideas to those things, from the effect of education or of experience. As a corollary from this, I had always heard it maintained by my father, and was myself convinced, that the object of education should be to form the strongest possible associations of the salutary class; associations of pleasure with all things beneficial to the great whole, and of pain with all things hurtful to it. This doctrine appeared inexpugnable; but it now seemed to me, on retrospect, that my teachers had occupied themselves but superficially with the means of forming and keeping up these salutary associations.

They seemed to have trusted altogether to the old familiar instruments, praise and blame, reward and punishment. Now, I did not doubt that by these means, begun early, and applied unremittingly, intense associations of pain and pleasure, especially of pain, might be created, and might produce desires and aversions capable of lasting undiminished to the end of life. But there must always be something artificial and casual in associations thus produced. The pains and pleasures thus forcibly associated with things, are not connected with them by any natural tie; and it is therefore, I thought, essential to the durability of these associations, that they should have become so intense and inveterate as to be practically indissoluble, before the habitual exercise of the power of analysis had commenced. For I now saw, or thought I saw, what I had always before received with incredulity—that the habit of analysis has a tendency to wear away the feelings: as indeed it has, when no other mental habit is cultivated, and the analysing spirit remains without its natural complements and correctives. The very excellence of analysis (I argued) is that it tends to weaken and undermine whatever is the result of prejudice; that it enables us mentally to separate ideas which have only casually clung together: and no associations whatever could ultimately resist this dissolving force, were it not that we owe to analysis our clearest knowledge of the permanent sequences in nature; the real connexions between Things, not dependent on our will and feelings; natural laws, by virtue of which, in many cases, one thing is inseparable from another in fact; which laws, in proportion as they are clearly perceived and imaginatively realized, cause our ideas of things which are always joined together in Nature, to cohere more and more closely in our thoughts. Analytic habits may thus even strengthen the associations between causes and effects, means and ends, but tend altogether to weaken those which are, to speak familiarly, a *mere* matter of feeling. They are therefore (I thought) favourable to prudence and clear-sightedness, but a perpetual worm at the root both of the passions and of the virtues; and, above all, fearfully undermine all desires, and all pleasures, which are the effects of association, that is, according to the theory I held, all except the purely physical and organic; of the entire insufficiency of which to make life desirable, no one had a stronger conviction than I had. These were the laws of human nature, by which, as it seemed to me, I had been brought to my present state. All those to whom I looked up, were of opinion that the pleasure of sympathy with human beings, and the feelings which made the good of others, and especially of mankind on a large scale, the object of existence, were the greatest and surest sources of happiness. Of the truth of this I was convinced, but to know that a feeling would make me happy if I had it, did not give me the feeling. My education, I thought, had failed to create these feelings in sufficient strength to resist the dissolving influence of analysis, while the whole course of my intellectual cultivation had made precocious and premature analysis the inveterate habit of my mind. I was thus, as I said to myself, left stranded at the commencement of my voyage, with a well-equipped ship and a rudder, but no sail; without any real desire for the ends which I had been so carefully fitted out to work for: no delight in virtue, or the general good, but also just as little in anything else. The fountains of vanity and ambition seemed to have dried up within me, as completely as those of benevolence. I had had (as I reflected) some gratification of vanity at too early an age: I had obtained some distinction, and felt myself of some importance, before the desire of distinction and of importance had grown into a passion: and little as it was which I had attained, yet having been attained too early, like all pleasures enjoyed too soon, it had made me *blasé* and indifferent to the pursuit. Thus neither selfish nor unselfish pleasures were pleasures to me. And there seemed no power in nature sufficient to begin the formation of my character anew, and create in a mind now irretrievably analytic, fresh associations of pleasure with any of the objects of human desire.

These were the thoughts which mingled with the dry heavy dejection of the melancholy winter of 1826–7. During this time I was not incapable of my usual occupations. I went on with them mechanically, by the mere force of habit. I had been so drilled in a certain sort of mental exercise, that I could still carry it on when all the spirit had gone out of it. I even composed and spoke several speeches at the debating society, how, or with what degree of success, I know not. Of four years continual speaking at that society, this is the only year of which I remember next to nothing. Two lines of Coleridge, in whom alone of all writers I have found a true description of what I felt, were often in my thoughts, not at this time (for I had never read them), but in a later period of the same mental malady :

> Work without hope draws nectar in a sieve,
> And hope without an object cannot live.

In all probability my case was by no means so peculiar as I fancied it, and I doubt not that many others have passed through a similar state ; but the idiosyncrasies of my education had given to the general phenomenon a special character, which made it seem the natural effect of causes that it was hardly possible for time to remove. I frequently asked myself, if I could, or if I was bound to go on living, when life must be passed in this manner. I generally answered to myself, that I did not think I could possibly bear it beyond a year. When, however, not more than half that duration of time had elapsed, a small ray of light broke in upon my gloom. I was reading, accidentally, Marmontel's 'Memoires,' and came to the passage which relates his father's death, the distressed position of the family, and the sudden inspiration by which he, then a mere boy, felt and made them feel that he would be everything to them—would supply the place of all that they had lost. A vivid conception of the scene and its feelings came over me, and I was moved to tears. From this moment my burden grew lighter. The oppression of the thought that all feeling was dead within me, was gone. I was no longer hopeless : I was not a stock or a stone. I had still, it seemed, some of the material out of which all worth of character, and all capacity for happiness, are made. Relieved from my ever present sense of irremediable wretchedness, I gradually found that the ordinary incidents of life could again give me some pleasure ; that I could again find enjoyment, not intense, but sufficient for cheerfulness, in sunshine and sky, in books, in conversation, in public affairs ; and that there was, once more, excitement, though of a moderate kind, in exerting myself for my opinions, and for the public good. Thus the cloud gradually drew off, and I again enjoyed life : and though I had several relapses, some of which lasted many months, I never again was as miserable as I had been.

The experiences of this period had two very marked effects on my opinions and character. In the first place, they led me to adopt a theory of life, very unlike that on which I had before acted, and having much in common with what at that time I certainly had never heard of, the anti-self-consciousness theory of Carlyle. I never, indeed, wavered in the conviction that happiness is the test of all rules of conduct, and the end of life. But I now thought that this end was only to be attained by not making it the direct end. Those only are happy (I thought) who have their minds fixed on some object other than their own happiness ; on the happiness of others, on the improvement of mankind, even on some art or pursuit, followed not as a means, but as itself an ideal end. Aiming thus at something else, they find happiness by the way. The enjoyments of life (such was now my theory) are sufficient to make it a pleasant thing, when they are taken *en passant*, without being made a principal object. Once make them so, and they are immediately felt to be insufficient. They will not bear a scrutinizing examination. Ask yourself whether you are happy, and you cease to be so. The only chance is to treat, not happiness, but some end external to it, as the purpose of life. Let your self-consciousness, your scrutiny, your self-interrogation, exhaust themselves on that; and if otherwise fortunately circumstanced you will inhale happiness with the air you breathe, without dwelling on it or thinking about it, without either forestalling it in imagination, or putting it to flight by fatal questioning. This theory now became the basis of my philosophy of life. And I still hold to it as the best theory for all those who have but a moderate degree of sensibility and of capacity for enjoyment, that is, for the great majority of mankind.

The other important change which my opinions at this time underwent, was that I, for the first time, gave its proper place, among the prime necessities of human well-being, to the internal culture of the individual. I ceased to attach almost exclusive importance to the ordering of outward circumstances, and the training of the human being for speculation and for action.

I had now learnt by experience that the passive susceptibilities needed to be cultivated as well as the active capacities, and required to be nourished and enriched as well as guided. I did not, for an instant, lose sight of, or undervalue, that part of the truth which I had seen before; I never turned recreant to intellectual culture, or ceased to consider the power and practice of analysis as an essential condition both of individual and of social improvement. But I thought that it had consequences which required to be corrected, by joining other kinds of cultivation with it. The maintenance of a due balance among the faculties, now seemed to me of primary importance. The cultivation of the feelings became one of the cardinal points in my ethical and philosophical creed. And my thoughts and inclinations turned in an increasing degree towards whatever seemed capable of being instrumental to that object.

I now began to find meaning in the things which I had read or heard about the importance of poetry and art as instruments of human culture. But it was some time longer before I began to know this by personal experience. The only one of the imaginative arts in which I had from childhood taken great pleasure, was music; the best effect of which (and in this it surpasses perhaps every other art) consists in exciting enthusiasm; in winding up to a high pitch those feelings of an elevated kind which are already in the character, but to which this excitement gives a glow and a fervour, which, though transitory at its utmost height, is precious for sustaining them at other times. This effect of music I had often experienced; but like all my pleasurable susceptibilities it was suspended during the gloomy period. I had sought relief again and again from this quarter, but found none. After the tide had turned, and I was in process of recovery, I had been helped forward by music, but in a much less elevated manner. I at this time first became acquainted with Weber's Oberon, and the extreme pleasure which I drew from its delicious melodies did me good, by showing me a source of pleasure to which I was as susceptible as ever. The good, however, was much impaired by the thought, that the pleasure of music (as is quite true of such pleasure as this was, that of mere tune) fades with familiarity, and requires either to be revived by intermittence, or fed by continual novelty. And it is very characteristic both of my then state, and of the general tone of my mind at this period of my life, that I was seriously tormented by the thought of the exhaustibility of musical combinations. The octave consists only of five tones and two semitones, which can be put together in only a limited number of ways, of which but a small proportion are beautiful: most of these, it seemed to me, must have been already discovered, and there could not be room for a long succession of Mozarts and Webers, to strike out, as these had done, entirely new and surpassingly rich veins of musical beauty. This source of anxiety may, perhaps, be thought to resemble that of the philosophers of Laputa, who feared lest the sun should be burnt out. It was, however, connected with the best feature in my character, and the only good point to be found in my very unromantic and in no way honourable distress. For though my dejection, honestly looked at, could not be called other than egotistical, produced by the ruin, as I thought, of my fabric of happiness, yet the destiny of mankind in general was ever in my thoughts, and could not be separated from my own. I felt that the flaw in my life, must be a flaw in life itself; that the question was, whether, if the reformers of society and government could succeed in their objects, and every person in the community were free and in a state of physical comfort, the pleasures of life, being no longer kept up by struggle and privation, would cease to be pleasures. And I felt that unless I could see my way to some better hope than this for human happiness in general, my dejection must continue ; but that if I could see such an outlet, I should then look on the world with pleasure ; content as far as I was myself concerned, with any fair share of the general lot.

This state of my thoughts and feelings made the fact of my reading Wordsworth for the first time (in the autumn of 1828), an important event in my life. I took up the collection of his poems from curiosity, with no expectation of mental relief from it, though I had before resorted to poetry with that hope. In the worst period of my depression, I had read through the whole of Byron (then new to me), to try whether a poet, whose peculiar department was supposed to be that of the intenser feelings, could rouse any feeling in me. As might be expected, I got no good from this reading, but the reverse. The poet's state of mind was too like my own. His was the lament of a man who had worn out all pleasures, and who seemed to think that life, to all who possess the good things of it, must necessarily be the vapid, uninteresting thing which I found it. His Harold and Manfred had the same burden on them which I had ; and I was not in a frame of mind to desire any comfort from the vehement sensual passion of his Giaours, or the sullenness of his Laras. But while Byron was exactly what did not suit my condition, Wordsworth was exactly what did. I had looked into the Excursion two or three years before, and found little in it ; and I should probably have found as little, had I read it at this time. But the miscellaneous poems, in the two-volume edition of 1815 (to which little of value was added in the latter part of the author's life), proved to be

the precise thing for my mental wants at that
particular juncture.

In the first place, these poems addressed themselves powerfully to one of the strongest of my
pleasurable susceptibilities, the love of rural
objects and natural scenery ; to which I had been
indebted not only for much of the pleasure of my
life, but quite recently for relief from one of my
longest relapses into depression. In this power
of rural beauty over me, there was a foundation
laid for taking pleasure in Wordsworth's poetry ;
the more so, as his scenery lies mostly among
mountains, which, owing to my early Pyrenean
excursion, were my ideal of natural beauty. But
Wordsworth would never have had any great
effect on me, if he had merely placed before me
beautiful pictures of natural scenery. Scott does
this still better than Wordsworth, and a very
second-rate landscape does it more effectually
than any poet. What made Wordsworth's poems
a medicine for my state of mind, was that they
expressed, not mere outward beauty, but states
of feeling, and of thought coloured by feeling, under
the excitement of beauty. They seemed to be the
very culture of the feelings, which I was in quest
of. In them I seemed to draw from a source of
inward joy, of sympathetic and imaginative
pleasure, which could be shared in by all human
beings ; which had no connexion with struggle or
imperfection, but would be made richer by every
improvement in the physical or social condition of
mankind. From them I seemed to learn what
would be the perennial sources of happiness, when
all the greater evils of life shall have been removed.
And I felt myself at once better and happier as

I came under their influence. There have certainly
been, even in our own age, greater poets than
Wordsworth; but poetry of deeper and loftier
feeling could not have done for me at that time
what his did. I needed to be made to feel that
there was real, permanent happiness in tranquil
contemplation. Wordsworth taught me this, not
only without turning away from, but with a greatly
increased interest in the common feelings and
common destiny of human beings. And the
delight which these poems gave me, proved that
with culture of this sort, there was nothing to
dread from the most confirmed habit of analysis.
At the conclusion of the Poems came the famous
Ode, falsely called Platonic, 'Intimations of
Immortality:' in which, along with more than his
usual sweetness of melody and rhythm, and along
with the two passages of grand imagery but bad
philosophy so often quoted, I found that he too had
had similar experience to mine; that he also had
felt that the first freshness of youthful enjoyment
of life was not lasting; but that he had sought for
compensation, and found it, in the way in which
he was now teaching me to find it. The result was
that I gradually, but completely, emerged from my
habitual depression, and was never again subject
to it. I long continued to value Wordsworth less
according to his intrinsic merits, than by the measure
of what he had done for me. Compared with the
greatest poets, he may be said to be the poet of
unpoetical natures, possessed of quiet and contemplative tastes. But unpoetical natures are precisely
those which require poetic cultivation. This cultivation Wordsworth is much more fitted to give, than
poets who are intrinsically far more poets than he.

It so fell out that the merits of Wordsworth were the occasion of my first public declaration of my new way of thinking, and separation from those of my habitual companions who had not undergone a similar change. The person with whom at that time I was most in the habit of comparing notes on such subjects was Roebuck, and I induced him to read Wordsworth, in whom he also at first seemed to find much to admire : but I, like most Wordsworthians, threw myself into strong antagonism to Byron, both as a poet and as to his influence on the character. Roebuck, all whose instincts were those of action and struggle, had, on the contrary, a strong relish and great admiration of Byron, whose writings he regarded as the poetry of human life, while Wordsworth's, according to him, was that of flowers and butterflies. We agreed to have the fight out at our Debating Society, where we accordingly discussed for two evenings the comparative merits of Byron and Wordsworth, propounding and illustrating by long recitations our respective theories of poetry : Sterling also, in a brilliant speech, putting forward his particular theory. This was the first debate on any weighty subject in which Roebuck and I had been on opposite sides. The schism between us widened from this time more and more, though we continued for some years longer to be companions. In the beginning, our chief divergence related to the cultivation of the feelings. Roebuck was in many respects very different from the vulgar notion of a Benthamite or Utilitarian. He was a lover of poetry and of most of the fine arts. He took great pleasure in music, in dramatic performances, especially in painting, and himself drew and designed landscapes with great facility and beauty. But he never could be made to see that these things have any value as aids in the formation of character. Personally, instead of being, as Benthamites are supposed to be, void of feeling, he had very quick and strong sensibilities. But, like most Englishmen who have feelings, he found his feelings stand very much in his way. He was much more susceptible to the painful sympathies than to the pleasurable, and looking for his happiness elsewhere, he wished that his feelings should be deadened rather than quickened. And, in truth, the English character, and English social circumstances, make it so seldom possible to derive happiness from the exercise of the sympathies, that it is not wonderful if they count for little in an Englishman's scheme of life. In most other countries the paramount importance of the sympathies as a constituent of individual happiness is an axiom, taken for granted rather than needing any formal statement; but most English thinkers almost seem to regard them as necessary evils, required for keeping men's actions benevolent and compassionate. Roebuck was, or appeared to be, this kind of Englishman. He saw little good in any cultivation of the feelings, and none at all in cultivating them through the imagination, which he thought was only cultivating illusions. It was in vain I urged on him that the imaginative emotion which an idea, when vividly conceived, excites in us, is not an illusion but a fact, as real as any of the other qualities of objects; and far from implying anything erroneous and delusive in our mental apprehension of the object, is quite consistent with the most accurate knowledge and most perfect practical recognition of all its physical and intellectual laws and relations. The intensest feeling of the beauty of a cloud lighted by the setting sun, is no hindrance to my knowing that the cloud is vapour of water, subject to all the laws of vapours in a state of suspension ; and I am just as likely to allow for, and act on, these physical laws whenever there is occasion to do so, as if I had been incapable of perceiving any distinction between beauty and ugliness.

While my intimacy with Roebuck diminished, I fell more and more into friendly intercourse with our Coleridgian adversaries in the Society, Frederick Maurice and John Sterling, both subsequently so well known, the former by his writings, the latter through the biographies by Hare and Carlyle. Of these two friends, Maurice was the thinker, Sterling the orator, and impassioned expositor of thoughts which, at this period, were almost entirely formed for him by Maurice.

With Maurice I had for some time been acquainted through Eyton Tooke, who had known him at Cambridge, and although my discussions with him were almost always disputes, I had carried away from them much that helped to build up my new fabric of thought, in the same way as I was deriving much from Coleridge, and from the writings of Goethe and other German authors which I read during these years. I have so deep a respect for Maurice's character and purposes, as well as for his great mental gifts, that it is with some unwillingness I say anything which may seem to place him on a less high eminence than I would gladly be able to accord to him. But I have always thought that there was more intellectual

power wasted in Maurice than in any other of
my contemporaries. Few of them certainly have
had so much to waste. Great powers of generalization, rare ingenuity and subtlety, and a wide
perception of important and unobvious truths,
served him not for putting something better into
the place of the worthless heap of received opinions
on the great subjects of thought, but for proving
to his own mind that the Church of England had
known everything from the first, and that all the
truths on the ground of which the Church and
orthodoxy have been attacked (many of which he
saw as clearly as any one) are not only consistent
with the Thirty-nine Articles, but are better understood and expressed in those Articles than by any
one who rejects them. I have never been able to
find any other explanation of this, than by attributing it to that timidity of conscience, combined
with original sensitiveness of temperament, which
has so often driven highly gifted men into Roman-
ism from the need of a firmer support than they
can find in the independent conclusions of their
own judgment. Any more vulgar kind of timidity
no one who knew Maurice would ever think of
imputing to him, even if he had not given public
proof of his freedom from it, by his ultimate
collision with some of the opinions commonly
regarded as orthodox, and by his noble origination
of the Christian Socialist movement. The nearest
parallel to him, in a moral point of view, is
Coleridge, to whom, in merely intellectual power,
apart from poetical genius, I think him decidedly
superior. At this time, however, he might be
described as a disciple of Coleridge, and Sterling
as a disciple of Coleridge and of him. The modifica-

tions which were taking place in my old opinions
gave me some points of contact with them ; and
both Maurice and Sterling were of considerable
use to my development. With Sterling I soon
became very intimate, and was more attached to
him than I have ever been to any other man. He
was indeed one of the most loveable of men. His
frank, cordial, affectionate, and expansive character ; a love of truth alike conspicuous in the
highest things and the humblest ; a generous and
ardent nature which threw itself with impetuosity
into the opinions it adopted, but was as eager to
do justice to the doctrines and the men it was
opposed to, as to make war on what it thought
their errors ; and an equal devotion to the two
cardinal points of Liberty and Duty, formed a
combination of qualities as attractive to me, as to
all others who knew him as well as I did. With
his open mind and heart, he found no difficulty in
joining hands with me across the gulf which as yet
divided our opinions. He told me how he and
others had looked upon me (from hearsay information), as a ' made ' or manufactured man, having
had a certain impress of opinion stamped on me
which I could only reproduce ; and what a change
took place in his feelings when he found, in the
discussion on Wordsworth and Byron, that
Wordsworth, and all which that name implies,
' belonged ' to me as much as to him and his
friends. The failure of his health soon scattered
all his plans of life, and compelled him to live at a
distance from London, so that after the first year
or two of our acquaintance, we only saw each
other at distant intervals. But (as he said himself
in one of his letters to Carlyle) when we did meet

it was like brothers. Though he was never, in the full sense of the word, a profound thinker, his openness of mind, and the moral courage in which he greatly surpassed Maurice, made him outgrow the dominion which Maurice and Coleridge had once exercised over his intellect; though he retained to the last a great but discriminating admiration of both, and towards Maurice a warm affection. Except in that short and transitory phasis of his life, during which he made the mistake of becoming a clergyman, his mind was ever progressive: and the advance he always seemed to have made when I saw him after an interval, made me apply to him what Goethe said of Schiller, ' er hatte eine furchtliche Fortschreitung.' He and I started from intellectual points almost as wide apart as the poles, but the distance between us was always diminishing: if I made steps towards some of his opinions, he, during his short life, was constantly approximating more and more to several of mine : and if he had lived, and had health and vigour to prosecute his ever assiduous self-culture, there is no knowing how much further this spontaneous assimilation might have proceeded.

After 1829 I withdrew from attendance on the Debating Society. I had had enough of speech-making, and was glad to carry on my private studies and meditations without any immediate call for outward assertion of their results. I found the fabric of my old and taught opinions giving way in many fresh places, and I never allowed it to fall to pieces, but was incessantly occupied in weaving it anew. I never, in the course of my transition, was content to remain. for ever so short a time, confused and unsettled. When I had taken in any new idea, I could not rest till I had adjusted its relation to my old opinions, and ascertained exactly how far its effect ought to extend in modifying or superseding them.

The conflicts which I had so often had to sustain in defending the theory of government laid down in Bentham's and my father's writings, and the acquaintance I had obtained with other schools of political thinking, made me aware of many things which that doctrine, professing to be a theory of government in general, ought to have made room for, and did not. But these things, as yet, remained with me rather as corrections to be made in applying the theory to practice, than as defects in the theory. I felt that politics could not be a science of specific experience; and that the accusations against the Benthamic theory of *being* a theory, of proceeding *à priori* by way of general reasoning, instead of Baconian experiment, showed complete ignorance of Bacon's principles, and of the necessary conditions of experimental investigation. At this juncture appeared in the Edinburgh Review, Macaulay's famous attack on my father's Essay on Government. This gave me much to think about. I saw that Macaulay's conception of the logic of politics was erroneous; that he stood up for the empirical mode of treating political phenomena, against the philosophical; that even in physical science his notions of philosophizing might have recognised Kepler, but would have excluded Newton and Laplace. But I could not help feeling, that though the tone was unbecoming (an error for which the writer, at a later period, made the most ample and honourable amends),

there was truth in several of his strictures on my
father's treatment of the subject ; that my father's
premises were really too narrow, and included but
a small number of the general truths, on which,
in politics, the important consequences depend.
Identity of interest between the governing body
and the community at large, is not, in any practical
sense which can be attached to it, the only thing
on which good government depends ; neither can
this identity of interest be secured by the mere
conditions of election. I was not at all satisfied
with the mode in which my father met the criticisms
of Macaulay. He did not, as I thought he ought
to have done, justify himself by saying, ' I was
not writing a scientific treatise on politics, I was
writing an argument for parliamentary reform.'
He treated Macaulay's argument as simply irrational ; an attack upon the reasoning faculty ;
an example of the saying of Hobbes, that when
reason is against a man, a man will be against
reason. This made me think that there was really
something more fundamentally erroneous in my
father's conception of philosophical method, as
applicable to politics, than I had hitherto supposed
there was. But I did not at first see clearly what
the error might be. At last it flashed upon me all
at once in the course of other studies. In the early
part of 1830 I had begun to put on paper the ideas
on Logic (chiefly on the distinctions among Terms,
and the import of Propositions) which had
been suggested and in part worked out in the
morning conversations already spoken of. Having
secured these thoughts from being lost, I pushed
on into the other parts of the subject, to try
whether I could do anything further towards

clearing up the theory of logic generally. I grappled at once with the problem of Induction, postponing that of Reasoning, on the ground that it is necessary to obtain premises before we can reason from them. Now, Induction is mainly a process for finding the causes of effects : and in attempting to fathom the mode of tracing causes and effects in physical science, I soon saw that in the more perfect of the sciences, we ascend, by generalization from particulars, to the tendencies of causes considered singly, and then reason downward from those separate tendencies, to the effect of the same causes when combined. I then asked myself, what is the ultimate analysis of this deductive process ; the common theory of the syllogism evidently throwing no light upon it. My practice (learnt from Hobbes and my father) being to study abstract principles by means of the best concrete instances I could find, the Composition of Forces, in dynamics, occurred to me as the most complete example of the logical process I was investigating. On examining, accordingly, what the mind does when it applies the principle of the Composition of Forces, I found that it performs a simple act of addition. It adds the separate effect of the one force to the separate effect of the other, and puts down the sum of these separate effects as the joint effect. But is this a legitimate process ? In dynamics, and in all the mathematical branches of physics, it is ; but in some other cases, as in chemistry, it is not ; and I then recollected that something not unlike this was pointed out as one of the distinctions between chemical and mechanical phenomena, in the introduction to that favourite of my boyhood, Thomson's System of Chemistry.

This distinction at once made my mind clear as to what was perplexing me in respect to the philosophy of politics. I now saw, that a science is either deductive or experimental, according as, in the province it deals with, the effects of causes when conjoined, are or are not the sums of the effects which the same causes produce when separate. It followed that politics must be a deductive science. It thus appeared, that both Macaulay and my father were wrong; the one in assimilating the method of philosophizing in politics to the purely experimental method of chemistry; while the other, though right in adopting a deductive method, had made a wrong selection of one, having taken as the type of deduction, not the appropriate process, that of the deductive branches of natural philosophy, but the inappropriate one of pure geometry, which, not being a science of causation at all, does not require or admit of any summing-up of effects. A foundation was thus laid in my thoughts for the principal chapters of what I afterwards published on the Logic of the Moral Sciences; and my new position in respect to my old political creed, now became perfectly definite.

If I am asked, what system of political philosophy I substituted for that which, as a philosophy, I had abandoned, I answer, No system: only a conviction that the true system was something much more complex and many-sided than I had previously had any idea of, and that its office was to supply, not a set of model institutions, but principles from which the institutions suitable to any given circumstances might be deduced. The influences of European, that is to say, Continental,

thought, and especially those of the reaction of
the nineteenth century against the eighteenth,
were now streaming in upon me. They came from
various quarters : from the writings of Coleridge,
which I had begun to read with interest even
before the change in my opinions ; from the
Coleridgians with whom I was in personal intercourse ; from what I had read of Goethe ; from
Carlyle's early articles in the Edinburgh and
Foreign Reviews, though for a long time I saw
nothing in these (as my father saw nothing in
them to the last) but insane rhapsody. From these
sources, and from the acquaintance I kept up with
the French literature of the time, I derived, among
other ideas which the general turning upside down
of the opinions of European thinkers had brought
uppermost, these in particular : That the human
mind has a certain order of possible progress, in
which some things must precede others, an order
which governments and public instructors can
modify to some, but not to an unlimited extent :
that all questions of political institutions are
relative, not absolute, and that different stages of
human progress not only *will* have, but *ought* to
have, different institutions : that government is
always either in the hands, or passing into the
hands, of whatever is the strongest power in
society, and that what this power is, does not
depend on institutions, but institutions on it :
that any general theory or philosophy of politics
supposes a previous theory of human progress, and
that this is the same thing with a philosophy of
history. These opinions, true in the main, were
held in exaggerated and violent manner by the
thinkers with whom I was now most accustomed

to compare notes, and who, as usual with a reaction, ignored that half of the truth which the thinkers of the eighteenth century saw. But though, at one period of my progress, I for some time under-valued that great century, I never joined in the reaction against it, but kept as firm hold of one side of the truth as I took of the other. The fight between the nineteenth century and the eighteenth always reminded me of the battle about the shield, one side of which was white and the other black. I marvelled at the blind rage with which the combatants rushed against one another. I applied to them, and to Coleridge himself, many of Coleridge's sayings about half truths; and Goethe's device, 'many-sidedness,' was one which I would most willingly, at this period, have taken for mine.

The writers by whom, more than by any others, a new mode of political thinking was brought home to me, were those of the St. Simonian school in France. In 1829 and 1830 I became acquainted with some of their writings. They were then only in the earlier stages of their speculations. They had not yet dressed out their philosophy as a religion, nor had they organized their scheme of Socialism. They were just beginning to question the principle of hereditary property. I was by no means prepared to go with them even this length; but I was greatly struck with the connected view which they for the first time presented to me, of the natural order of human progress; and especi-ally with their division of all history into organic periods and critical periods. During the organic periods (they said) mankind accept with firm conviction some positive creed, claiming juris-

diction over all their actions, and containing more
or less of truth and adaptation to the needs of
humanity. Under its influence they make all the
progress compatible with the creed, and finally
outgrow it; when a period follows of criticism
and negation, in which mankind lose their old
convictions without acquiring any new ones, of
a general or authoritative character, except the
conviction that the old are false. The period of
Greek and Roman polytheism, so long as really
believed in by instructed Greeks and Romans, was
an organic period, succeeded by the critical or
sceptical period of the Greek philosophers.
Another organic period came in with Christianity.
The corresponding critical period began with the
Reformation, has lasted ever since, still lasts, and
cannot altogether cease until a new organic period
has been inaugurated by the triumph of a yet more
advanced creed. These ideas, I knew, were not
peculiar to the St. Simonians; on the contrary,
they were the general property of Europe, or at
least of Germany and France, but they had never,
to my knowledge, been so completely systematized
as by these writers, nor the distinguishing characteristics of a critical period so powerfully set forth;
for I was not then acquainted with Fichte's
Lectures on 'The Characteristics of the Present
Age.' In Carlyle, indeed, I found bitter denunciations of an 'age of unbelief,' and of the present
age as such, which I, like most people at that time,
supposed to be passionate protests in favour of
the old modes of belief. But all that was true in
these denunciations, I thought that I found more
calmly and philosophically stated by the St.
Simonians. Among their publications, too, there

was one which seemed to me far superior to the
rest; in which the general idea was matured into
something much more definite and instructive.
This was an early work of Auguste Comte, who then
called himself, and even announced himself in the
title-page as, a pupil of Saint Simon. In this tract
M. Comte first put forth the doctrine, which he
afterwards so copiously illustrated, of the natural
succession of three stages in every department of
human knowledge: first, the theological, next the
metaphysical, and lastly, the positive stage; and
contended, that social science must be subject
to the same law; that the feudal and Catholic
system was the concluding phasis of the theological
state of the social science, Protestantism the
commencement, and the doctrines of the French
Revolution the consummation, of the metaphysical; and that its positive state was yet to
come. This doctrine harmonized well with my
existing notions, to which it seemed to give a
scientific shape. I already regarded the methods
of physical science as the proper models for
political. But the chief benefit which I derived
at this time from the trains of thought suggested
by the St. Simonians and by Comte, was, that
I obtained a clearer conception than ever before
of the peculiarities of an era of transition in
opinion, and ceased to mistake the moral and
intellectual characteristics of such an era, for the
normal attributes of humanity. I looked forward,
through the present age of loud disputes but
generally weak convictions, to a future which
shall unite the best qualities of the critical with
the best qualities of the organic periods; un-
checked liberty of thought, unbounded freedom

of individual action in all modes not hurtful to others ; but also, convictions as to what is right and wrong, useful and pernicious, deeply engraven on the feelings by early education and general unanimity of sentiment, and so firmly grounded in reason and in the true exigencies of life, that they shall not, like all former and present creeds, religious, ethical, and political, require to be periodically thrown off and replaced by others.

M. Comte soon left the St. Simonians, and I lost sight of him and his writings for a number of years. But the St. Simonians I continued to cultivate. I was kept *au courant* of their progress by one of their most enthusiastic disciples, M. Gustave d'Eichthal, who about that time passed a considerable interval in England. I was introduced to their chiefs, Bazard and Enfantin, in 1830 ; and as long as their public teachings and proselytism continued, I read nearly everything they wrote. Their criticisms on the common doctrines of Liberalism seemed to me full of important truth ; and it was partly by their writings that my eyes were opened to the very limited and temporary value of the old political economy, which assumes private property and inheritance as indefeasible facts, and freedom of production and exchange as the *dernier mot* of social improvement. The scheme gradually unfolded by the St. Simonians, under which the labour and capital of society would be managed for the general account of the community, every individual being required to take a share of labour, either as thinker, teacher, artist, or producer, all being classed according to their capacity, and remunerated according to their work, appeared to me a far superior description of Socialism to Owen's. Their aim seemed to me desirable and rational, however their means might be inefficacious; and though I neither believed in the practicability, nor in the beneficial operation of their social machinery, I felt that the proclamation of such an ideal of human society could not but tend to give a beneficial direction to the efforts of others to bring society, as at present constituted, nearer to some ideal standard. I honoured them most of all for what they have been most cried down for—the boldness and freedom from prejudice with which they treated the subject of family, the most important of any, and needing more fundamental alterations than remain to be made in any other great social institution, but on which scarcely any reformer has the courage to touch. In proclaiming the perfect equality of men and women, and an entirely new order of things in regard to their relations with one another, the St. Simonians, in common with Owen and Fourier, have entitled themselves to the grateful remembrance of future generations.

In giving an account of this period of my life, I have only specified such of my new impressions as appeared to me, both at the time and since, to be a kind of turning points, marking a definite progress in my mode of thought. But these few selected points give a very insufficient idea of the quantity of thinking which I carried on respecting a host of subjects during these years of transition. Much of this, it is true, consisted in rediscovering things known to all the world, which I had previously disbelieved, or disregarded. But the rediscovery was to me a discovery, giving me plenary possession of the truths, not as traditional

platitudes, but fresh from their source : and it
seldom failed to place them in some new light, by
which they were reconciled with, and seemed to
confirm while they modified, the truths less
generally known which lay in my early opinions,
and in no essential part of which I at any time
wavered. All my new thinking only laid the
foundation of these more deeply and strongly,
while it often removed misapprehension and confusion of ideas which had perverted their effect.
For example, during the later returns of my
dejection, the doctrine of what is called Philosophical Necessity weighed on my existence like
an incubus. I felt as if I was scientifically proved
to be the helpless slave of antecedent circumstances ; as if my character and that of all others
had been formed for us by agencies beyond our
control, and was wholly out of our own power.
I often said to myself, what a relief it would be if
I could disbelieve the doctrine of the formation
of character by circumstances ; and remembering
the wish of Fox respecting the doctrine of resistance
to governments, that it might never be forgotten
by kings, nor remembered by subjects, I said that
it would be a blessing if the doctrine of necessity
could be believed by all *quoad* the characters of
others, and disbelieved in regard to their own.
I pondered painfully on the subject, till gradually
I saw light through it. I perceived, that the word
Necessity, as a name for the doctrine of Cause and
Effect applied to human action, carried with it
a misleading association ; and that this association
was the operative force in the depressing and
paralysing influence which I had experienced :
I saw that though our character is formed by

circumstances, our own desires can do much to shape those circumstances; and that what is really inspiriting and ennobling in the doctrine of freewill, is the conviction that we have real power over the formation of our own character; that our will, by influencing some of our circumstances, can modify our future habits or capabilities of willing. All this was entirely consistent with the doctrine of circumstances, or rather, was that doctrine itself, properly understood. From that time I drew in my own mind, a clear distinction between the doctrine of circumstances, and Fatalism; discarding altogether the misleading word Necessity. The theory, which I now for the first time rightly apprehended, ceased altogether to be discouraging, and besides the relief to my spirits, I no longer suffered under the burden, so heavy to one who aims at being a reformer in opinions, of thinking one doctrine true, and the contrary doctrine morally beneficial. The train of thought which had extricated me from this dilemma, seemed to me, in after years, fitted to render a similar service to others; and it now forms the chapter on Liberty and Necessity in the concluding Book of my system of Logic.

Again, in politics, though I no longer accepted the doctrine of the Essay on Government as a scientific theory; though I ceased to consider representative democracy as an absolute principle, and regarded it as a question of time, place, and circumstance; though I now looked upon the choice of political institutions as a moral and educational question more than one of material interests, thinking that it ought to be decided mainly by the consideration, what great improve-

ment in life and culture stands next in order for
the people concerned, as the condition of their
further progress, and what institutions are most
likely to promote that; nevertheless, this change
in the premises of my political philosophy did not
alter my practical political creed as to the requirements of my own time and country. I was as
much as ever a Radical and Democrat for Europe,
and especially for England. I thought the predominance of the aristocratic classes, the noble
and the rich, in the English constitution, an evil
worth any struggle to get rid of; not on account
of taxes, or any such comparatively small incon-
venience, but as the great demoralizing agency in
the country. Demoralizing, first, because it made
the conduct of the Government an example of
gross public immorality, through the predominance
of private over public interests in the State, and
the abuse of the powers of legislation for the
advantage of classes. Secondly, and in a still
greater degree, because the respect of the multitude always attaching itself principally to that
which, in the existing state of society, is the chief
passport to power; and under English institutions, riches, hereditary or acquired, being the
almost exclusive source of political importance;
riches, and the signs of riches, were almost the
only things really respected, and the life of the
people was mainly devoted to the pursuit of them.
I thought, that while the higher and richer classes
held the power of government, the instruction
and improvement of the mass of the people were
contrary to the self-interest of those classes,
because tending to render the people more powerful
for throwing off the yoke: but if the democracy

obtained a large, and perhaps the principal share, in the governing power, it would become the interest of the opulent classes to promote their education, in order to ward off really mischievous errors, and especially those which would lead to unjust violations of property. On these grounds I was not only as ardent as ever for democratic institutions, but earnestly hoped that Owenite, St. Simonian, and all other anti-property doctrines might spread widely among the poorer classes; not that I thought those doctrines true, or desired that they should be acted on, but in order that the higher classes might be made to see that they had more to fear from the poor when uneducated, than when educated.

In this frame of mind the French Revolution of July found me. It roused my utmost enthusiasm, and gave me, as it were, a new existence. I went at once to Paris, was introduced to Lafayette, and laid the groundwork of the intercourse I afterwards kept up with several of the active chiefs of the extreme popular party. After my return I entered warmly, as a writer, into the political discussions of the time; which soon became still more exciting, by the coming in of Lord Grey's Ministry, and the proposing of the Reform Bill. For the next few years I wrote copiously in newspapers. It was about this time that Fonblanque, who had for some time written the political articles in the Examiner, became the proprietor and editor of the paper. It is not forgotten with what verve and talent, as well as fine wit, he carried it on, during the whole period of Lord Grey's Ministry, and what importance it assumed as the principal representative, in the newspaper press, of Radical opinions. The distinguishing character of the paper was given to it entirely by his own articles, which formed at least three-fourths of all the original writing contained in it: but of the remaining fourth I contributed during those years a much larger share than any one else. I wrote nearly all the articles on French subjects, including a weekly summary of French politics, often extending to considerable length; together with many leading articles on general politics, commercial and financial legislation, and any miscellaneous subjects in which I felt interested, and which were suitable to the paper, including occasional reviews of books. Mere newspaper articles on the occurrences or questions of the moment, gave no opportunity for the development of any general mode of thought; but I attempted, in the beginning of 1831, to embody in a series of articles, headed 'The Spirit of the Age,' some of my new opinions, and especially to point out in the character of the present age, the anomalies and evils characteristic of the transition from a system of opinions which had worn out, to another only in process of being formed. These articles were, I fancy, lumbering in style, and not lively or striking enough to be, at any time, acceptable to newspaper readers; but had they been far more attractive, still, at that particular moment, when great political changes were impending, and engrossing all minds, these discussions were ill-timed, and missed fire altogether. The only effect which I know to have been produced by them, was that Carlyle, then living in a secluded part of Scotland, read them in his solitude, and saying to himself (as he afterwards told me) 'Here is a new Mystic,' inquired on coming to London that autumn respecting their authorship; an inquiry which was the immediate cause of our becoming personally acquainted.

I have already mentioned Carlyle's earlier writings as one of the channels through which I received the influences which enlarged my early narrow creed; but I do not think that those writings, by themselves, would ever have had any effect on my opinions. What truths they contained, though of the very kind which I was already receiving from other quarters, were presented in a form and vesture less suited than any other to give them access to a mind trained as mine had been. They seemed a haze of poetry and German metaphysics, in which almost the only clear thing was a strong animosity to most of the opinions which were the basis of my mode of thought; religious scepticism, utilitarianism, the doctrine of circumstances, and the attaching any importance to democracy, logic, or political economy. Instead of my having been taught anything, in the first instance, by Carlyle, it was only in proportion as I came to see the same truths through media more suited to my mental constitution, that I recognised them in his writings. Then, indeed, the wonderful power with which he put them forth made a deep impression upon me, and I was during a long period one of his most fervent admirers; but the good his writings did me, was not as philosophy to instruct, but as poetry to animate. Even at the time when our acquaintance commenced, I was not sufficiently advanced in my new modes of thought, to appreciate him fully; a proof of which is, that on his showing me the manuscript of Sartor

Resartus, his best and greatest work, which he had just then finished, I made little of it; though when it came out about two years afterwards in Fraser's Magazine I read it with enthusiastic admiration and the keenest delight. I did not seek and cultivate Carlyle less on account of the fundamental differences in our philosophy. He soon found out that I was not ' another mystic,' and when for the sake of my own integrity I wrote to him a distinct profession of all those of my opinions which I knew he most disliked, he replied that the chief difference between us was that I ' was as yet consciously nothing of a mystic.' I do not know at what period he gave up the expectation that I was destined to become one; but though both his and my opinions underwent in subsequent years considerable changes, we never approached much nearer to each other's modes of thought than we were in the first years of our acquaintance. I did not, however, deem myself a competent judge of Carlyle. I felt that he was a poet, and that I was not; that he was a man of intuition, which I was not; and that as such, he not only saw many things long before me, which I could only when they were pointed out to me, hobble after and prove, but that it was highly probable he could see many things which were not visible to me even after they were pointed out. I knew that I could not see round him, and could never be certain that I saw over him; and I never presumed to judge him with any definiteness, until he was interpreted to me by one greatly the superior of us both—who was more a poet than he, and more a thinker than I—whose own mind and nature included his, and infinitely more.

Among the persons of intellect whom I had known of old, the one with whom I had now most points of agreement was the elder Austin. I have mentioned that he always set himself in opposition to our early sectarianism ; and latterly he had, like myself, come under new influences. Having been appointed Professor of Jurisprudence in the London University (now University College), he had lived for some time at Bonn to study for his Lectures ; and the influences of German literature and of the German character and state of society had made a very perceptible change in his views of life. His personal disposition was much softened ; he was less militant and polemic ; his tastes had begun to turn themselves towards the poetic and contemplative. He attached much less importance than formerly to outward changes ; unless accompanied by a better cultivation of the inward nature. He had a strong distaste for the general meanness of English life, the absence of enlarged thoughts and unselfish desires, the low objects on which the faculties of all classes of the English are intent. Even the kind of public interests which Englishmen care for, he held in very little esteem. He thought that there was more practical good government, and (which is true enough) infinitely more care for the education and mental improvement of all ranks of the people, under the Prussian monarchy, than under the English representative government : and he held, with the French *Economistes*, that the real security for good government is ' un peuple éclairé,' which is not always the fruit of popular institutions, and which if it could be had without them, would do their work better than they. Though he approved of the Reform

Bill, he predicted, what in fact occurred, that it would not produce the great immediate improvements in government, which many expected from it. The men, he said, who could do these great things, did not exist in the country. There were many points of sympathy between him and me, both in the new opinions he had adopted and in the old ones which he retained. Like me, he never ceased to be an utilitarian, and with all his love of the Germans, and enjoyment of their literature, never became in the smallest degree reconciled to the innate-principle metaphysics. He cultivated more and more a kind of German religion, a religion of poetry and feeling with little, if anything, of positive dogma ; while, in politics (and here it was that I most differed with him) he acquired an indifference, bordering on contempt, for the progress of popular institutions : though he rejoiced in that of Socialism, as the most effectual means of compelling the powerful classes to educate the people, and to impress on them the only real means of permanently improving their material condition, a limitation of their numbers. Neither was he, at this time, fundamentally opposed to Socialism in itself as an ultimate result of improvement. He professed great disrespect for what he called ' the universal principles of human nature of the political economists,' and insisted on the evidence which history and daily experience afford of the ' extraordinary pliability of human nature ' (a phrase which I have somewhere borrowed from him) ; nor did he think it possible to set any positive bounds to the moral capabilities which might unfold themselves in mankind, under an enlightened direction of social and educational influences. Whether he retained all these opinions to the end of life I know not. Certainly the modes of thinking of his later years, and especially of his last publication, were much more Tory in their general character than those which he held at this time.

My father's tone of thought and feeling, I now felt myself at a great distance from: greater, indeed, than a full and calm explanation and reconsideration on both sides, might have shown to exist in reality. But my father was not one with whom calm and full explanations on fundamental points of doctrine could be expected, at least with one whom he might consider as, in some sort, a deserter from his standard. Fortunately we were almost always in strong agreement on the political questions of the day, which engrossed a large part of his interest and of his conversation. On those matters of opinion on which we differed, we talked little. He knew that the habit of thinking for myself, which his mode of education had fostered, sometimes led me to opinions different from his, and he perceived from time to time that I did not always tell him *how* different. I expected no good, but only pain to both of us, from discussing our differences: and I never expressed them but when he gave utterance to some opinion or feeling repugnant to mine, in a manner which would have made it disingenuousness on my part to remain silent.

It remains to speak of what I wrote during these years, which, independently of my contributions to newspapers, was considerable. In 1830 and 1831 I wrote the five Essays since published under the title of 'Essays on some Unsettled Questions of Political Economy,' almost as they now stand, except that in 1833 I partially rewrote the fifth Essay. They were written with no immediate purpose of publication; and when, some years later, I offered them to a publisher, he declined them. They were only printed in 1844, after the success of the ' System of Logic.' I also resumed my speculations on this last subject, and puzzled myself, like others before me, with the great paradox of the discovery of new truths by general reasoning. As to the fact, there could be no doubt. As little could it be doubted, that all reasoning is resolvable into syllogisms, and that in every syllogism the conclusion is actually contained and implied in the premises. How, being so contained and implied, it could be new truth, and how the theorems of geometry, so different in appearance from the definitions and axioms, could be all contained in these, was a difficulty which no one, I thought, had sufficiently felt, and which, at all events, no one had succeeded in clearing up. The explanations offered by Whately and others, though they might give a temporary satisfaction, always, in my mind, left a mist still hanging over the subject. At last, when reading a second or third time the chapters on Reasoning in the second volume of Dugald Stewart, interrogating myself on every point, and following out, as far as I knew how, every topic of thought which the book suggested, I came upon an idea of his respecting the use of axioms in ratiocination, which I did not remember to have before noticed, but which now, in meditating on it, seemed to me not only true of axioms, but of all general propositions whatever, and to be the key of the whole perplexity. From

this germ grew the theory of the Syllogism propounded in the Second Book of the Logic ; which
I immediately fixed by writing it out. And now,
with greatly increased hope of being able to produce
a work on Logic, of some originality and value,
I proceeded to write the First Book, from the rough
and imperfect draft I had already made. What
I now wrote became the basis of that part of the
subsequent Treatise ; except that it did not
contain the Theory of Kinds, which was a later
addition, suggested by otherwise inextricable
difficulties which met me in my first attempt to
work out the subject of some of the concluding
chapters of the Third Book. At the point which
I had now reached I made a halt, which lasted five
years. I had come to the end of my tether ;
I could make nothing satisfactory of Induction,
at this time. I continued to read any book which
seemed to promise light on the subject, and
appropriated, as well as I could, the results ; but
for a long time I found nothing which seemed to
open to me any very important vein of meditation.

In 1832 I wrote several papers for the first series
of Tait's Magazine, and one for a quarterly periodical called the Jurist, which had been founded, and
for a short time carried on, by a set of friends, all
lawyers and law reformers, with several of whom
I was acquainted. The paper in question is the
one on the rights and duties of the State respecting
Corporation and Church Property, now standing
first among the collected ' Dissertations and
Discussions ; ' where one of my articles in ' Tait,'
' The Currency Juggle,' also appears. In the whole
mass of what I wrote previous to these, there is
nothing of sufficient permanent value to justify

reprinting. The paper in the Jurist, which I still think a very complete discussion of the rights of the State over Foundations, showed both sides of my opinions, asserting as firmly as I should have done at any time, the doctrine that all endowments are national property, which the government may and ought to control; but not, as I should once have done, condemning endowments in themselves, and proposing that they should be taken to pay off the national debt. On the contrary, I urged strenuously the importance of having a provision for education, not dependent on the mere demand of the market, that is, on the knowledge and discernment of average parents, but calculated to establish and keep up a higher standard of instruction than is likely to be spontaneously demanded by the buyers of the article. All these opinions have been confirmed and strengthened by the whole course of my subsequent reflections.

CHAPTER VI

COMMENCEMENT OF THE MOST VALUABLE
FRIENDSHIP OF MY LIFE. MY FATHER'S
DEATH. WRITINGS AND OTHER PRO-
CEEDINGS UP TO 1840.

It was at the period of my mental progress which
I have now reached that I formed the friendship
which has been the honour and chief blessing of my
existence, as well as the source of a great part of all
that I have attempted to do, or hope to effect here-
after, for human improvement. My first introduction to the lady who, after a friendship of
twenty years, consented to become my wife, was
in 1830, when I was in my twenty-fifth and she
in her twenty-third year. With her husband's
family it was the renewal of an old acquaintanceship. His grandfather lived in the next house to
my father's in Newington Green, and I had, sometimes when a boy, been invited to play in the old
gentleman's garden. He was a fine specimen of
the old Scotch Puritan ; stern, severe, and powerful, but very kind to children, on whom such men
make a lasting impression. Although it was years
after my introduction to Mrs. Taylor before my
acquaintance with her became at all intimate or
confidential, I very soon felt her to be the most
admirable person I had ever known. It is not to
be supposed that she was, or that any one, at the
age at which I first saw her, could be, all that she
afterwards became. Least of all could this be true

of her, with whom self-improvement, progress in the highest and in all senses, was a law of her nature ; a necessity equally from the ardour with which she sought it, and from the spontaneous tendency of faculties which could not receive an impression or an experience without making it the source or the occasion of an accession of wisdom. Up to the time when I first saw her, her rich and powerful nature had chiefly unfolded itself according to the received type of feminine genius. To her outer circle she was a beauty and a wit, with an air of natural distinction, felt by all who approached her : to the inner, a woman of deep and strong feeling, of penetrating and intuitive intelligence, and of an eminently meditative and poetic nature. Married at an early age, to a most upright, brave, and honourable man, of liberal opinions and good education, but without the intellectual or artistic tastes which would have made him a companion for her, though a steady and affectionate friend, for whom she had true esteem and the strongest affection through life, and whom she most deeply lamented when dead ; shut out by the social disabilities of women from any adequate exercise of her highest faculties in action on the world without ; her life was one of inward meditation, varied by familiar intercourse with a small circle of friends, of whom one only (long since deceased) was a person of genius, or of capacities of feeling or intellect kindred with her own, but all had more or less of alliance with her in sentiments and opinions. Into this circle I had the good fortune to be admitted, and I soon perceived that she possessed in combination, the qualities which in all other persons whom I had known I had been only too happy to find singly. In her, complete emancipation from every kind of superstition (including that which attributes a pretended perfection to the order of nature and the universe), and an earnest protest against many things which are still part of the established constitution of society, resulted not from the hard intellect, but from strength of noble and elevated feeling, and co-existed with a highly reverential nature. In general spiritual characteristics, as well as in temperament and organization, I have often compared her, as she was at this time, to Shelley : but in thought and intellect, Shelley, so far as his powers were developed in his short life, was but a child compared with what she ultimately became. Alike in the highest regions of speculation and in the smaller practical concerns of daily life, her mind was the same perfect instrument, piercing to the very heart and marrow of the matter ; always seizing the essential idea or principle. The same exactness and rapidity of operation, pervading as it did her sensitive as well as her mental faculties, would, with her gifts of feeling and imagination, have fitted her to be a consummate artist, as her fiery and tender soul and her vigorous eloquence would certainly have made her a great orator, and her profound knowledge of human nature and discernment and sagacity in practical life, would, in the times when such a *carrière* was open to women, have made her eminent among the rulers of mankind. Her intellectual gifts did but minister to a moral character at once the noblest and the best balanced which I have ever met with in life. Her unselfishness was not that of a taught system of duties, but of a heart which thoroughly identified itself with the feelings of others, and often went to excess in consideration for them by imaginatively investing their feelings with the intensity of its own. The passion of justice might have been thought to be her strongest feeling, but for her boundless generosity, and a lovingness ever ready to pour itself forth upon any or all human beings who were capable of giving the smallest feeling in return. The rest of her moral characteristics were such as naturally accompany these qualities of mind and heart : the most genuine modesty combined with the loftiest pride ; a simplicity and sincerity which were absolute, towards all who were fit to receive them ; the utmost scorn of whatever was mean and cowardly, and a burning indignation at everything brutal or tyrannical, faithless or dishonourable in conduct and character, while making the broadest distinction between *mala in se* and mere *mala prohibita*— between acts giving evidence of intrinsic badness in feeling and character, and those which are only violations of conventions either good or bad, violations which whether in themselves right or wrong, are capable of being committed by persons in every other respect loveable or admirable.

To be admitted into any degree of mental intercourse with a being of these qualities, could not but have a most beneficial influence on my development ; though the effect was only gradual, and many years elapsed before her mental progress and mine went forward in the complete companionship they at last attained. The benefit I received was far greater than any which I could hope to give ; though to her, who had at first reached her opinions by the moral intuition of a character of strong feeling, there was doubtless help as well as encouragement to be derived from one who had arrived at many of the same results by study and reasoning : and in the rapidity of her intellectual growth, her mental activity, which converted everything into knowledge, doubtless drew from me, as it did from other sources, many of its materials. What I owe, even intellectually, to her, is in its detail, almost infinite ; of its general character a few words will give some, though a very imperfect, idea.

With those who, like all the best and wisest of mankind, are dissatisfied with human life as it is, and whose feelings are wholly identified with its radical amendment, there are two main regions of thought. One is the region of ultimate aims ; the constituent elements of the highest realizable ideal of human life. The other is that of the immediately useful and practically attainable. In both these departments, I have acquired more from her teaching, than from all other sources taken together. And, to say truth, it is in these two extremes principally, that real certainty lies. My own strength lay wholly in the uncertain and slippery intermediate region, that of theory, or moral and political science : respecting the conclusions of which, in any of the forms in which I have received or originated them, whether as political economy, analytic psychology, logic, philosophy of history, or anything else, it is not the least of my intellectual obligations to her that I have derived from her a wise scepticism, which, while it has not hindered me from following out the honest exercise of my thinking faculties to whatever conclusions might result from it, has put me on my guard against holding or announcing these conclusions with a degree of confidence which the nature of such speculations does not warrant, and has kept my mind not only open to admit, but prompt to welcome and eager to seek, even on the questions on which I have most meditated, any prospect of clearer perceptions and better evidence. I have often received praise, which in my own right I only partially deserve, for the greater practicality which is supposed to be found in my writings compared with those of most thinkers who have been equally addicted to large generalizations. The writings in which this quality has been observed, were not the work of one mind, but of the fusion of two, one of them as pre-eminently practical in its judgments and perceptions of things present, as it was high and bold in its anticipations for a remote futurity.

At the present period, however, this influence was only one among many which were helping to shape the character of my future development and even after it became, I may truly say, the presiding principle of my mental progress, it did not alter the path, but only made me move forward more boldly, and, at the same time, more cautiously, in the same course. The only actual revolution which has ever taken place in my modes of thinking was already complete. My new tendencies had to be confirmed in some respects, moderated in others : but the only substantial changes of opinion that were yet to come, related to politics, and consisted, on one hand, in a greater approximation, so far as regards the ultimate prospects of humanity, to a qualified Socialism, and on the other, a shifting of my political ideal from pure democracy, as

commonly understood by its partizans, to the
modified form of it, which is set forth in my
' Considerations on Representative Government.'

This last change, which took place very gradually,
dates its commencement from my reading, or
rather study, of M. de Tocqueville's ' Democracy in
America,' which fell into my hands immediately
after its first appearance. In that remarkable
work, the excellences of democracy were pointed
out in a more conclusive, because a more specific
manner than I had ever known them to be, even
by the most enthusiastic democrats ; while the
specific dangers which beset democracy, considered as the government of the numerical
majority, were brought into equally strong light,
and subjected to a masterly analysis, not as
reasons for resisting what the author considered
as an inevitable result of human progress, but as
indications of the weak points of popular government, the defences by which it needs to be
guarded, and the correctives which must be added
to it in order that while full play is given to its
beneficial tendencies, those which are of a different
nature may be neutralized or mitigated. I was now
well prepared for speculations of this character,
and from this time onward my own thoughts moved
more and more in the same channel, though the consequent modifications in my practical political creed
were spread over many years, as would be shown
by comparing my first review of ' Democracy in
America,' written and published in 1835, with the
one in 1840 (reprinted in the ' Dissertations '), and
this last, with the ' Considerations on Representative Government.'

A collateral subject on which also I derived great

benefit from the study of Tocqueville, was the fundamental question of centralization. The powerful philosophic analysis which he applied to American and to French experience, led him to attach the utmost importance to the performance of as much of the collective business of society, as can safely be so performed, by the people themselves, without any intervention of the executive government, either to supersede their agency, or to dictate the manner of its exercise. He viewed this practical political activity of the individual citizen, not only as one of the most effectual means of training the social feelings and practical intelligence of the people, so important in themselves and so indispensable to good government, but also as the specific counteractive to some of the characteristic infirmities of democracy, and a necessary protection against its degenerating into the only despotism of which, in the modern world, there is real danger—the absolute rule of the head of the executive over a congregation of isolated individuals, all equals but all slaves. There was, indeed, no immediate peril from this source on the British side of the channel, where nine-tenths of the internal business which elsewhere devolves on the government, was transacted by agencies independent of it; where centralization was, and is, the subject not only of rational disapprobation, but of unreasoning prejudice; where jealousy of government interference was a blind feeling preventing or resisting even the most beneficial exertion of legislative authority to correct the abuses of what pretends to be local self-government, but is, too often, selfish mismanagement of local interests, by a jobbing and *borné* local oligarchy. But the more certain the public were to go wrong on the side opposed to centralization, the greater danger was there lest philosophic reformers should fall into the contrary error, and overlook the mischiefs of which they had been spared the painful experience. I was myself, at this very time, actively engaged in defending important measures, such as the great Poor Law Reform of 1834, against an irrational clamour grounded on the anti-centralization prejudice: and had it not been for the lessons of Tocqueville, I do not know that I might not, like many reformers before me, have been hurried into the excess opposite to that, which, being the one prevalent in my own country, it was generally my business to combat. As it is, I have steered carefully between the two errors, and whether I have or have not drawn the line between them exactly in the right place, I have at least insisted with equal emphasis upon the evils on both sides, and have made the means of reconciling the advantages of both, a subject of serious study.

In the meanwhile had taken place the election of the first Reformed Parliament, which included several of the most notable of my Radical friends and acquaintances—Grote, Roebuck, Buller, Sir William Molesworth, John and Edward Romilly, and several more; besides Warburton, Strutt, and others, who were in Parliament already. These who thought themselves, and were called by their friends, the philosophic Radicals, had now, it seemed, a fair opportunity, in a more advantageous position than they had ever before occupied, for showing what was in them; and I, as well as my father, founded great hopes on them.

These hopes were destined to be disappointed. The men were honest, and faithful to their opinions, as far as votes were concerned ; often in spite of much discouragement. When measures were proposed, flagrantly at variance with their principles, such as the Irish Coercion Bill, or the Canada Coercion in 1837, they came forward manfully, and braved any amount of hostility and prejudice rather than desert the right. But on the whole they did very little to promote any opinions ; they had little enterprise, little activity : they left the lead of the Radical portion of the House to the old hands, to Hume and O'Connell. A partial exception must be made in favour of one or two of the younger men ; and in the case of Roebuck, it is his title to permanent remembrance, that in the very first year during which he sat in Parliament, he originated (or re-originated after the unsuccessful attempt of Mr. Brougham) the parliamentary movement for National Education ; and that he was the first to commence, and for years carried on almost alone, the contest for the self-government of the Colonies. Nothing, on the whole equal to these two things, was done by any other individual, even of those from whom most was expected. And now, on a calm retrospect, I can perceive that the men were less in fault than we supposed, and that we had expected too much from them. They were in unfavourable circumstances. Their lot was cast in the ten years of inevitable reaction, when, the Reform excitement being over, and the few legislative improvements which the public really called for having been rapidly effected, power gravitated back in its natural direction, to those who were for keeping things as they were; when the public mind desired rest, and was less disposed than at any other period since the peace, to let itself be moved by attempts to work up the Reform feeling into fresh activity in favour of new things. It would have required a great political leader, which no one is to be blamed for not being, to have effected really great things by parliamentary discussion when the nation was in this mood. My father and I had hoped that some competent leader might arise; some man of philosophic attainments and popular talents, who could have put heart into the many younger or less distinguished men that would have been ready to join him—could have made them available, to the extent of their talents, in bringing advanced ideas before the public—could have used the House of Commons as a rostra or a teacher's chair for instructing and impelling the public mind; and would either have forced the Whigs to receive their measures from him, or have taken the lead of the Reform party out of their hands. Such a leader there would have been, if my father had been in Parliament. For want of such a man, the instructed Radicals sank into a mere *Côté Gauche* of the Whig party. With a keen, and as I now think, an exaggerated sense of the possibilities which were open to the Radicals if they made even ordinary exertion for their opinions, I laboured from this time till 1839, both by personal influence with some of them, and by writings, to put ideas into their heads, and purpose into their hearts. I did some good with Charles Buller, and some with Sir William Molesworth; both of whom did valuable service, but were unhappily cut off almost in the beginning of their usefulness. On the whole, however, my attempt was vain. To have had a chance of succeeding in it, required a different position from mine. It was a task only for one who, being himself in Parliament, could have mixed with the Radical members in daily consultation, could himself have taken the initiative, and instead of urging others to lead, could have summoned them to follow.

What I could do by writing, I did. During the year 1833 I continued working in the Examiner with Fonblanque, who at that time was zealous in keeping up the fight for Radicalism against the Whig ministry. During the session of 1834 I wrote comments on passing events, of the nature of newspaper articles (under the title of ' Notes on the Newspapers '), in the Monthly Repository, a magazine conducted by Mr. Fox, well known as a preacher and political orator, and subsequently as member of Parliament for Oldham ; with whom I had lately become acquainted, and for whose sake chiefly I wrote in his magazine. I contributed several other articles to this periodical, the most considerable of which (on the theory of Poetry), is reprinted in the ' Dissertations.' Altogether, the writings (independently of those in newspapers) which I published from 1832 to 1834, amount to a large volume. This, however, includes abstracts of several of Plato's Dialogues, with introductory remarks, which, though not published until 1834, had been written several years earlier ; and which I afterwards, on various occasions, found to have been read, and their authorship known, by more people than were aware of anything else which I had written, up to that time. To complete the tale of my writings at this period, I may add that in 1833, at the request of Bulwer, who was just then completing his 'England and the English' (a work, at that time, greatly in advance of the public mind), I wrote for him a critical account of Bentham's philosophy, a small part of which he incorporated in his text, and printed the rest (with an honourable acknowledgment), as an appendix.   In this, along with the favourable, a part also of the unfavourable side of my estimation of Bentham's doctrines, considered as a complete philosophy, was for the first time put into print.

But an opportunity soon offered, by which, as it seemed, I might have it in my power to give more effectual aid, and, at the same time, stimulus, to the 'philosophic Radical' party, than I had done hitherto.   One of the projects occasionally talked of between my father and me, and some of the parliamentary and other Radicals who frequented his house, was the foundation of a periodical organ of philosophic radicalism, to take the place which the Westminster Review had been intended to fill : and the scheme had gone so far as to bring under discussion the pecuniary contributions which could be looked for, and the choice of an editor. Nothing, however, came of it for some time : but in the summer of 1834 Sir William Molesworth, himself a laborious student, and a precise and metaphysical thinker, capable of aiding the cause by his pen as well as by his purse, spontaneously proposed to establish a Review, provided I would consent to be the real, if I could not be the ostensible, editor.   Such a proposal was not to be refused ; and the Review was founded, at first under the title of the London Review, and afterwards under that of the London and Westminster, Molesworth having bought the Westminster from its proprietor, General Thompson, and merged the two into one. In the years between 1834 and 1840 the conduct of this Review occupied the greater part of my spare time. In the beginning, it did not, as a whole, by any means represent my opinions. I was under the necessity of conceding much to my inevitable associates. The Review was established to be the representative of the 'philosophic Radicals,' with most of whom I was now at issue on many essential points, and among whom I could not even claim to be the most important individual. My father's co-operation as a writer we all deemed indispensable, and he wrote largely in it until prevented by his last illness. The subjects of his articles, and the strength and decision with which his opinions were expressed in them, made the Review at first derive its tone and colouring from him much more than from any of the other writers. I could not exercise editorial control over his articles, and I was sometimes obliged to sacrifice to him portions of my own. The old Westminster Review doctrines, but little modified, thus formed the staple of the Review ; but I hoped, by the side of these, to introduce other ideas and another tone, and to obtain for my own shade of opinion a fair representation, along with those of other members of the party. With this end chiefly in view, I made it one of the peculiarities of the work that every article should bear an initial, or some other signature, and be held to express the opinions solely of the individual writer ; the editor being only responsible for its being worth publishing, and not in conflict with

the objects for which the Review was set on foot.
I had an opportunity of putting in practice my
scheme of conciliation between the old and the
new 'philosophic radicalism,' by the choice of
a subject for my own first contribution. Professor
Sedgwick, a man of eminence in a particular walk
of natural science, but who should not have
trespassed into philosophy, had lately published
his Discourse on the Studies of Cambridge, which
had as its most prominent feature an intemperate
assault on analytic psychology and utilitarian
ethics, in the form of an attack on Locke and Paley.
This had excited great indignation in my father
and others, which I thought it fully deserved.
And here, I imagined, was an opportunity of at the
same time repelling an unjust attack, and inserting
into my defence of Hartleianism and Utilitarianism
a number of the opinions which constituted my
view of those subjects, as distinguished from that
of my old associates. In this I partially succeeded,
though my relation to my father would have made
it painful to me in any case, and impossible in
a Review for which he wrote, to speak out my
whole mind on the subject at this time.

I am, however, inclined to think that my father
was not so much opposed as he seemed, to the
modes of thought in which I believed myself to
differ from him; that he did injustice to his own
opinions by the unconscious exaggerations of an
intellect emphatically polemical; and that when
thinking without an adversary in view, he was
willing to make room for a great portion of the
truths he seemed to deny. I have frequently
observed that he made large allowance in practice
for considerations which seemed to have no place

in his theory. His 'Fragment on Mackintosh,' which he wrote and published about this time, although I greatly admired some parts of it, I read as a whole with more pain than pleasure; yet on reading it again, long after, I found little in the opinions it contains, but what I think in the main just; and I can even sympathize in his disgust at the *verbiage* of Mackintosh, though his asperity towards it went not only beyond what was judicious, but beyond what was even fair. One thing, which I thought, at the time, of good augury, was the very favourable reception he gave to Tocqueville's 'Democracy in America.' It is true, he said and thought much more about what Tocqueville said in favour of democracy, than about what he said of its disadvantages. Still, his high appreciation of a book which was at any rate an example of a mode of treating the question of government almost the reverse of his—wholly inductive and analytical, instead of purely ratiocinative—gave me great encouragement. He also approved of an article which I published in the first number following the junction of the two reviews, the essay reprinted in the 'Dissertations,' under the title 'Civilization;' into which I threw many of my new opinions, and criticised rather emphatically the mental and moral tendencies of the time, on grounds and in a manner which I certainly had not learnt from him.

All speculation, however, on the possible future developments of my father's opinions, and on the probabilities of permanent co-operation between him and me in the promulgation of our thoughts, was doomed to be cut short. During the whole of 1835 his health had been declining: his symptoms became unequivocally those of pulmonary consumption, and after lingering to the last stage of debility, he died on the 23rd of June, 1836. Until the last few days of his life there was no apparent abatement of intellectual vigour; his interest in all things and persons that had interested him through life was undiminished, nor did the approach of death cause the smallest wavering (as in so strong and firm a mind it was impossible that it should) in his convictions on the subject of religion. His principal satisfaction, after he knew that his end was near, seemed to be the thought of what he had done to make the world better than he found it; and his chief regret in not living longer, that he had not had time to do more.

His place is an eminent one in the literary, and even in the political history of his country; and it is far from honourable to the generation which has benefited by his worth, that he is so seldom mentioned, and, compared with men far his inferiors, so little remembered. This is probably to be ascribed mainly to two causes. In the first place, the thought of him merges too much in the deservedly superior fame of Bentham. Yet he was anything but Bentham's mere follower or disciple. Precisely because he was himself one of the most original thinkers of his time, he was one of the earliest to appreciate and adopt the most important mass of original thought which had been produced by the generation preceding him. His mind and Bentham's were essentially of different construction. He had not all Bentham's high qualities, but neither had Bentham all his. It would, indeed, be ridiculous to claim for him the praise of having accomplished for mankind such splendid services as Bentham's. He did not revolutionize, or rather create, one of the great departments of human thought. But, leaving out of the reckoning all that portion of his labours in which he benefited by what Bentham had done, and counting only what he achieved in a province in which Bentham had done nothing, that of analytic psychology, he will be known to posterity as one of the greatest names in that most important branch of specula-tion, on which all the moral and political sciences ultimately rest, and will mark one of the essential stages in its progress. The other reason which has made his fame less than he deserved, is that notwithstanding the great number of his opinions which, partly through his own efforts, have now been generally adopted, there was, on the whole, a marked opposition between his spirit and that of the present time. As Brutus was called the last of the Romans, so was he the last of the eighteenth century : he continued its tone of thought and sentiment into the nineteenth (though not unmodified nor unimproved), par-taking neither in the good nor in the bad influences of the reaction against the eighteenth century, which was the great characteristic of the first half of the nineteenth. The eighteenth century was a great age, an age of strong and brave men, and he was a fit companion for its strongest and bravest. By his writings and his personal in-fluence he was a great centre of light to his generation. During his later years he was quite as much the head and leader of the intellectual radicals in England, as Voltaire was of the *philo-sophes* of France. It is only one of his minor merits, that he was the originator of all sound statesmanship in regard to the subject of his largest work, India. He wrote on no subject which he did not enrich with valuable thought, and excepting the 'Elements of Political Economy,' a very useful book when first written, but which has now for some time finished its work, it will be long before any of his books will be wholly superseded, or will cease to be instructive reading to students of their subjects. In the power of influencing by mere force of mind and character, the convictions and purposes of others, and in the strenuous exertion of that power to promote freedom and progress, he left, as my knowledge extends, no equal among men, and but one among women.

Though acutely sensible of my own inferiority in the qualities by which he acquired his personal ascendancy, I had now to try what it might be possible for me to accomplish without him: and the Review was the instrument on which I built my chief hopes of establishing a useful influence over the liberal and democratic section of the public mind. Deprived of my father's aid, I was also exempted from the restraints and reticences [1] by which that aid had been purchased. I did not feel that there was any other radical writer or politician to whom I was bound to defer, further than consisted with my own opinions: and having the complete confidence of Molesworth, I resolved henceforth to give full scope to my own opinions and modes of thought, and to open the Review widely to all writers who were in sympathy with Progress as I understood it, even though I should lose by it the support of my former associates. Carlyle, consequently, became from this time

[1] retinences *1873*: qy. misprint. Cf. *O. E. D.*

a frequent writer in the Review; Sterling, soon after, an occasional one; and though each individual article continued to be the expression of the private sentiments of its writer, the general tone conformed in some tolerable degree to my opinions. For the conduct of the Review, under, and in conjunction with me, I associated with myself a young Scotchman of the name of Robertson, who had some ability and information, much industry, and an active scheming head, full of devices for making the Review more saleable, and on whose capacities in that direction I founded a good deal of hope: insomuch, that when Molesworth, in the beginning of 1837, became tired of carrying on the Review at a loss, and desirous of getting rid of it (he had done his part honourably, and at no small pecuniary cost), I, very imprudently for my own pecuniary interest, and very much from reliance on Robertson's devices, determined to continue it at my own risk, until his plans should have had a fair trial. The devices were good, and I never had any reason to change my opinion of them. But I do not believe that any devices would have made a radical and democratic review defray its expenses, including a paid editor or sub-editor, and a liberal payment to writers. I myself and several frequent contributors gave our labour gratuitously, as we had done for Molesworth; but the paid contributors continued to be remunerated on the usual scale of the Edinburgh and Quarterly Reviews; and this could not be done from the proceeds of the sale.

In the same year, 1837, and in the midst of these occupations, I resumed the Logic. I had not touched my pen on the subject for five years, having been stopped and brought to a halt on the threshold of Induction. I had gradually discovered that what was mainly wanting, to overcome the difficulties of that branch of the subject, was a comprehensive, and, at the same time, accurate view of the whole circle of physical science, which I feared it would take me a long course of study to acquire; since I knew not of any book, or other guide, that would spread out before me the generalities and processes of the sciences, and I apprehended that I should have no choice but to extract them for myself, as I best could, from the details. Happily for me, Dr. Whewell, early in this year, published his History of the Inductive Sciences. I read it with eagerness, and found in it a considerable approximation to what I wanted. Much, if not most, of the philosophy of the work appeared open to objection; but the materials were there, for my own thoughts to work upon: and the author had given to those materials that first degree of elaboration, which so greatly facilitates and abridges the subsequent labour. I had now obtained what I had been waiting for. Under the impulse given me by the thoughts excited by Dr. Whewell, I read again Sir J. Herschel's discourse on the Study of Natural Philosophy: and I was able to measure the progress my mind had made, by the great help I now found in this work—though I had read and even reviewed it several years before with little profit. I now set myself vigorously to work out the subject in thought and in writing. The time I bestowed on this had to be stolen from occupations more urgent. I had just two months to spare, at this period, in the intervals of writing for the Review. In these two months

I completed the first draft of about a third, the most difficult third, of the book. What I had before written, I estimate at another third, so that only one-third remained. What I wrote at this time consisted of the remainder of the doctrine of Reasoning (the theory of Trains of Reasoning, and Demonstrative Science), and the greater part of the Book on Induction. When this was done, I had, as it seemed to me, untied all the really hard knots, and the completion of the book had become only a question of time. Having got thus far, I had to leave off in order to write two articles for the next number of the Review. When these were written, I returned to the subject, and now for the first time fell in with Comte's Cour de Philosophie Positive, or rather with the two volumes of it which were all that had at that time been published.

My theory of Induction was substantially completed before I knew of Comte's book; and it is perhaps well that I came to it by a different road from his, since the consequence has been that my treatise contains, what his certainly does not, a reduction of the inductive process to strict rules and to a scientific test, such as the syllogism is for ratiocination. Comte is always precise and profound on the method of investigation, but he does not even attempt any exact definition of the conditions of proof: and his writings show that he never attained a just conception of them. This, however, was specifically the problem which, in treating of Induction, I had proposed to myself. Nevertheless, I gained much from Comte, with which to enrich my chapters in the subsequent rewriting: and his book was of essential service

to me in some of the parts which still remained
to be thought out. As his subsequent volumes
successively made their appearance, I read them
with avidity, but, when he reached the subject of
Social Science, with varying feelings. The fourth
volume disappointed me: it contained those of
his opinions on social subjects with which I most
disagree. But the fifth, containing the connected
view of history, rekindled all my enthusiasm;
which the sixth (or concluding) volume did not
materially abate. In a merely logical point of
view, the only leading conception for which I am
indebted to him is that of the Inverse Deductive
Method, as the one chiefly applicable to the complicated subjects of History and Statistics: a
process differing from the more common form of
the deductive method in this—that instead of
arriving at its conclusions by general reasoning,
and verifying them by specific experience (as is the
natural order in the deductive branches of physical
science), it obtains its generalizations by a collation
of specific experience, and verifies them by ascertaining whether they are such as would follow
from known general principles. This was an idea
entirely new to me when I found it in Comte: and
but for him I might not soon (if ever) have arrived
at it.

I had been long an ardent admirer of Comte's
writings before I had any communication with himself; nor did I ever, to the last, see him in the body.
But for some years we were frequent correspondents,
until our correspondence became controversial,
and our zeal cooled. I was the first to slacken
correspondence; he was the first to drop it.
I found, and he probably found likewise, that I

could do no good to his mind, and that all the good he could do to mine, he did by his books. This would never have led to discontinuance of intercourse, if the differences between us had been on matters of simple doctrine. But they were chiefly on those points of opinion which blended in both of us with our strongest feelings, and determined the entire direction of our aspirations. I had fully agreed with him when he maintained that the mass of mankind, including even their rulers in all the practical departments of life, must, from the necessity of the case, accept most of their opinions on political and social matters, as they do on physical, from the authority of those who have bestowed more study on those subjects than they generally have it in their power to do. This lesson had been strongly impressed on me by the early work of Comte, to which I have adverted. And there was nothing in his great Treatise which I admired more than his remarkable exposition of the benefits which the nations of modern Europe have historically derived from the separation, during the Middle Ages, of temporal and spiritual power, and the distinct organization of the latter. I agreed with him that the moral and intellectual ascendancy, once exercised by priests, must in time pass into the hands of philosophers, and will naturally do so when they become sufficiently unanimous, and in other respects worthy to possess it. But when he exaggerated this line of thought into a practical system, in which philosophers were to be organized into a kind of corporate hierarchy, invested with almost the same spiritual supremacy (though without any secular power) once possessed by the Catholic Church ; when I found him relying on this spiritual authority as the only security for good government, the sole bulwark against practical oppression, and expecting that by it a system of despotism in the state and despotism in the family would be rendered innocuous and beneficial; it is not surprising, that while as logicians we were nearly at one, as sociologists we could travel together no further. M. Comte lived to carry out these doctrines to their extremest consequences, by planning, in his last work, the 'Système de Politique Positive,' the completest system of spiritual and temporal despotism which ever yet emanated from a human brain, unless possibly that of Ignatius Loyola: a system by which the yoke of general opinion, wielded by an organized body of spiritual teachers and rulers, would be made supreme over every action, and as far as is in human possibility, every thought, of every member of the community, as well in the things which regard only himself, as in those which concern the interests of others. It is but just to say that this work is a considerable improvement, in many points of feeling, over Comte's previous writings on the same subjects: but as an accession to social philosophy, the only value it seems to me to possess, consists in putting an end to the notion that no effectual moral authority can be maintained over society without the aid of religious belief; for Comte's work recognises no religion except that of Humanity, yet it leaves an irresistible conviction that any moral beliefs concurred in by the community generally, may be brought to bear upon the whole conduct and lives of its individual members, with an energy and potency truly alarming to think of. The book stands a monumental warning to thinkers on society and politics, of what happens when once men lose sight in their speculations, of the value of Liberty and of Individuality.

To return to myself. The Review engrossed, for some time longer, nearly all the time I could devote to authorship, or to thinking with authorship in view. The articles from the London and Westminster Review which are reprinted in the ' Dissertations,' are scarcely a fourth part of those I wrote. In the conduct of the Review I had two principal objects. One was to free philosophic radicalism from the reproach of sectarian Benthamism. I desired, while retaining the precision of expression, the definiteness of meaning, the contempt of declamatory phrases and vague generalities, which were so honourably characteristic both of Bentham and of my father, to give a wider basis and a more free and genial character to Radical speculations; to show that there was a Radical philosophy, better and more complete than Bentham's, while recognizing and incorporating all of Bentham's which is permanently valuable. In this first object I, to a certain extent, succeeded. The other thing I attempted, was to stir up the educated Radicals, in and out of Parliament, to exertion, and induce them to make themselves, what I thought by using the proper means they might become—a powerful party capable of taking the government of the country, or at least of dictating the terms on which they should share it with the Whigs. This attempt was from the first chimerical: partly because the time was unpropitious, the Reform fervour being in its period of ebb, and the Tory influences powerfully rallying; but still more, because, as Austin so truly said, ' the country did not contain the men.' Among the Radicals in Parliament there were several qualified to be useful members of an enlightened Radical party, but none capable of forming and leading such a party. The exhortations I addressed to them found no response. One occasion did present itself when there seemed to be room for a bold and successful stroke for Radicalism. Lord Durham had left the Ministry, by reason, as was thought, of their not being sufficiently Liberal; he afterwards accepted from them the task of ascertaining and removing the causes of the Canadian rebellion; he had shown a disposition to surround himself at the outset with Radical advisers; one of his earliest measures, a good measure both in intention and in effect, having been disapproved and reversed by the Government at home, he had resigned his post, and placed himself openly in a position of quarrel with the Ministers. Here was a possible chief for a Radical party in the person of a man of importance, who was hated by the Tories and had just been injured by the Whigs. Any one who had the most elementary notions of party tactics, must have attempted to make something of such an opportunity. Lord Durham was bitterly attacked from all sides, inveighed against by enemies, given up by timid friends; while those who would willingly have defended him did not know what to say. He appeared to be returning a defeated and discredited man. I had followed the Canadian events from the beginning; I had been one of the prompters of his prompters; his policy was almost exactly what mine would have been, and I was in a position to defend it. I wrote and published a manifesto in the Review, in which I took the very highest ground in his behalf, claiming for him not mere acquittal, but praise and honour. Instantly a number of other writers took up the tone: I believe there was a portion of truth in what Lord Durham, soon after, with polite exaggeration, said to me—that to this article might be ascribed the almost triumphal reception which he met with on his arrival in England. I believe it to have been the word in season, which, at a critical moment, does much to decide the result; the touch which determines whether a stone, set in motion at the top of an eminence, shall roll down on one side or on the other. All hopes connected with Lord Durham as a politician soon vanished; but with regard to Canadian, and generally to colonial policy, the cause was gained: Lord Durham's report, written by Charles Buller, partly under the inspiration of Wakefield, began a new era; its recommendations, extending to complete internal self-government, were in full operation in Canada within two or three years, and have been since extended to nearly all the other colonies, of European race, which have any claim to the character of important communities. And I may say that in successfully upholding the reputation of Lord Durham and his advisers at the most important moment, I contributed materially to this result.

One other case occurred during my conduct of the Review, which similarly illustrated the effect of taking a prompt initiative. I believe that the early success and reputation of Carlyle's French Revolution, were considerably accelerated by what I wrote about it in the Review. Immediately on its publication, and before the commonplace critics, all whose rules and modes of judgment it set at defiance, had time to pre-occupy the public with their disapproval of it, I wrote and published a review of the book, hailing it as one of those productions of genius which are above all rules, and are a law to themselves. Neither in this case nor in that of Lord Durham do I ascribe the impression, which I think was produced by what I wrote, to any particular merit of execution: indeed, in at least one of the cases (the article on Carlyle) I do not think the execution was good. And in both instances, I am persuaded that anybody, in a position to be read, who had expressed the same opinion at the same precise time, and had made any tolerable statement of the just grounds for it, would have produced the same effect. But, after the complete failure of my hopes of putting a new life into Radical politics by means of the Review, I am glad to look back on these two instances of an honest attempt to do immediate service to things and persons that deserved it.

After the last hope of the formation of a Radical party had disappeared, it was time for me to stop the heavy expenditure of time and money which the Review cost me. It had to some extent answered my personal purpose as a vehicle for my opinions. It had enabled me to express in print much of my altered mode of thought, and to separate myself in a marked manner from the narrower Benthamism of my early writings. This was done by the general tone of all I wrote, including various purely literary articles, but especially by the two papers (reprinted in the Dissertations) which attempted a philosophical estimate of Bentham and of Coleridge. In the first of these, while doing full justice to the merits of Bentham, I pointed out what I thought the errors and deficiencies of his philosophy. The substance of this criticism I still think perfectly just; but I have sometimes doubted whether it was right to publish it at that time. I have often felt that Bentham's philosophy, as an instrument of progress, has been to some extent discredited before it had done its work, and that to lend a hand towards lowering its reputation was doing more harm than service to improvement. Now, however, when a counter-reaction appears to be setting in towards what is good in Benthamism, I can look with more satisfaction on this criticism of its defects, especially as I have myself balanced it by vindications of the fundamental principles of Bentham's philosophy, which are reprinted along with it in the same collection. In the essay on Coleridge I attempted to characterize the European reaction against the negative philosophy of the eighteenth century: and here, if the effect only of this one paper were to be considered, I might be thought to have erred by giving undue prominence to the favourable side, as I had done in the case of Bentham to the unfavourable. In both cases, the impetus with which I had detached myself from what was untenable in the doctrines of Bentham and of the eighteenth century, may have carried me, though in appearance rather than in reality, too far on the contrary side. But as far as relates to the article on Coleridge, my defence is, that I was writing for Radicals and Liberals, and it was my business to dwell most on that, in writers of a different school, from the knowledge of which, they might derive most improvement.

The number of the Review which contained the paper on Coleridge, was the last which was published during my proprietorship. In the spring of 1840 I made over the Review to Mr. Hickson, who had been a frequent and very useful unpaid contributor under my management : only stipulating that the change should be marked by a resumption of the old name, that of Westminster Review. Under that name Mr. Hickson conducted it for ten years, on the plan of dividing among contributors only the net proceeds of the Review, giving his own labour as writer and editor gratuitously. Under the difficulty in obtaining writers, which arose from this low scale of payment, it is highly creditable to him that he was able to maintain, in some tolerable degree, the character of the Review as an organ of radicalism and progress. I did not cease altogether to write for the Review, but continued to send it occasional contributions, not, however, exclusively ; for the greater circulation of the Edinburgh Review induced me from this time to offer articles to it also when I had anything to say for which it appeared to be a suitable vehicle. And the concluding volumes of ' Democracy in America,' having just then come out, I inaugurated myself as a contributor to the Edinburgh, by the article on that work, which heads the second volume of the ' Dissertations.'

CHAPTER VII

GENERAL VIEW OF THE REMAINDER OF MY LIFE.

FROM this time, what is worth relating of my life will come into a very small compass; for I have no further mental changes to tell of, but only, as I hope, a continued mental progress; which does not admit of a consecutive history, and the results of which, if real, will be best found in my writings. I shall, therefore, greatly abridge the chronicle of my subsequent years.

The first use I made of the leisure which I gained by disconnecting myself from the Review, was to finish the Logic. In July and August 1838, I had found an interval in which to execute what was still undone of the original draft of the Third Book. In working out the logical theory of those laws of nature which are not laws of Causation, nor corollaries from such laws, I was led to recognise kinds as realities in nature and not mere distinctions for convenience; a light which I had not obtained when the First Book was written, and which made it necessary for me to modify and enlarge several chapters of that Book. The Book on Language and Classification, and the chapter on the Classification of Fallacies, were drafted in the autumn of the same year; the remainder of the work, in the summer and autumn of 1840. From April following, to the end of 1841, my spare time was devoted to a complete re-writing of the book from its commencement. It is in this way that all my books have been composed. They were always written at least twice over; a first draft of the entire work was completed to the very end of the subject, then the whole begun again *de novo*; but incorporating, in the second writing, all sentences and parts of sentences of the old draft, which appeared as suitable to my purpose as anything which I could write in lieu of them. I have found great advantages in this system of double redaction. It combines, better than any other mode of composition, the freshness and vigour of the first conception, with the superior precision and completeness resulting from prolonged thought. In my own case, moreover, I have found that the patience necessary for a careful elaboration of the details of composition and expression, costs much less effort after the entire subject has been once gone through, and the substance of all that I find to say has in some manner, however imperfect, been got upon paper. The only thing which I am careful, in the first draft, to make as perfect as I am able, is the arrangement. If that is bad, the whole thread on which the ideas string themselves becomes twisted; thoughts placed in a wrong connexion are not expounded in a manner that suits the right, and a first draft with this original vice is next to useless as a foundation for the final treatment.

During the re-writing of the Logic, Dr. Whewell's Philosophy of the Inductive Sciences made its appearance; a circumstance fortunate for me, as it gave me what I greatly desired, a full treat-

ment of the subject by an antagonist, and enabled
me to present my ideas with greater clearness
and emphasis as well as fuller and more varied
development, in defending them against definite
objections, or confronting them distinctly with
an opposite theory. The controversies with
Dr. Whewell, as well as much matter derived
from Comte, were first introduced into the book
in the course of the re-writing.

At the end of 1841, the book being ready for
the press, I offered it to Murray, who kept it
until too late for publication that season, and
then refused it, for reasons which could just as
well have been given at first. But I have had no
cause to regret a rejection which led to my offering
it to Mr. Parker, by whom it was published in the
spring of 1843. My original expectations of success
were extremely limited. Archbishop Whately had,
indeed, rehabilitated the name of Logic, and the
study of the forms, rules, and fallacies of Ratiocination; and Dr. Whewell's writings had begun to excite
an interest in the other part of my subject, the
theory of Induction. A treatise, however, on
a matter so abstract, could not be expected to
be popular; it could only be a book for students,
and students on such subjects were not only (at
least in England) few, but addicted chiefly to
the opposite school of metaphysics, the ontological
and 'innate principles' school. I therefore did
not expect that the book would have many
readers, or approvers; and looked for little
practical effect from it, save that of keeping the
tradition unbroken of what I thought a better
philosophy. What hopes I had of exciting any
immediate attention, were mainly grounded on

the polemical propensities of Dr. Whewell; who,
I thought, from observation of his conduct in
other cases, would probably do something to
bring the book into notice, by replying, and that
promptly, to the attack on his opinions.   He
did reply, but not till 1850, just in time for me
to answer him in the third edition. How the book
came to have, for a work of the kind, so much
success, and what sort of persons compose the
bulk of those who have bought, I will not venture
to say read, it, I have never thoroughly understood. But taken in conjunction with the many
proofs which have since been given of a revival
of speculation, speculation too of a free kind, in
many quarters, and above all (where at one time
I should have least expected it) in the Universities,
the fact becomes partially intelligible. I have
never indulged the illusion that the book had
made any considerable impression on philosophical
opinion. The German, or *à priori* view of human
knowledge, and of the knowing faculties, is likely
for some time longer (though it may be hoped
in a diminishing degree) to predominate among
those who occupy themselves with such inquiries,
both here and on the Continent. But the ' System
of Logic ' supplies what was much wanted, a
text-book of the opposite doctrine—that which
derives all knowledge from experience, and all
moral and intellectual qualities principally from
the direction given to the associations. I make
as humble an estimate as anybody of what either
an analysis of logical processes, or any possible
canons of evidence, can do by themselves, towards
guiding or rectifying the operations of the understanding. Combined with other requisites, I

certainly do think them of great use; but whatever may be the practical value of a true philosophy
of these matters, it is hardly possible to exaggerate
the mischiefs of a false one. The notion that
truths external to the mind may be known by
intuition or consciousness, independently of
observation and experience, is, I am persuaded,
in these times, the great intellectual support of
false doctrines and bad institutions. By the aid
of this theory, every inveterate belief and every
intense feeling, of which the origin is not remembered, is enabled to dispense with the obligation
of justifying itself by reason, and is erected into
its own all-sufficient voucher and justification.
There never was such an instrument devised
for consecrating all deep-seated prejudices. And
the chief strength of this false philosophy in
morals, politics, and religion, lies in the appeal
which it is accustomed to make to the evidence
of mathematics and of the cognate branches
of physical science. To expel it from these, is
to drive it from its stronghold: and because
this had never been effectually done, the intuitive
school, even after what my father had written
in his Analysis of the Mind, had in appearance,
and as far as published writings were concerned,
on the whole the best of the argument. In
attempting to clear up the real nature of the
evidence of mathematical and physical truths,
the 'System of Logic' met the intuitive philosophers on ground on which they had previously
been deemed unassailable; and gave its own
explanation, from experience and association,
of that peculiar character of what are called
necessary truths, which is adduced as proof that

their evidence must come from a deeper source than experience. Whether this has been done effectually, is still *sub judice;* and even then, to deprive a mode of thought so strongly rooted in human prejudices and partialities, of its mere speculative support, goes but a very little way towards overcoming it; but though only a step, it is a quite indispensable one; for since, after all, prejudice can only be successfully combated by philosophy, no way can really be made against it permanently until it has been shown not to have philosophy on its side.

Being now released from any active concern in temporary politics, and from any literary occupation involving personal communication with contributors and others, I was enabled to indulge the inclination, natural to thinking persons when the age of boyish vanity is once past, for limiting my own society to a very few persons. General society, as now carried on in England, is so insipid an affair, even to the persons who make it what it is, that it is kept up for any reason rather than the pleasure it affords. All serious discussion on matters on which opinions differ, being considered ill-bred, and the national deficiency in liveliness and sociability having prevented the cultivation of the art of talking agreeably on trifles, in which the French of the last century so much excelled, the sole attraction of what is called society to those who are not at the top of the tree, is the hope of being aided to climb a little higher in it; while to those who are already at the top, it is chiefly a compliance with custom, and with the supposed requirements of their station. To a person of any but a very common order in thought or feeling, such society, unless he has personal objects to serve by it, must be supremely unattractive : and most people, in the present day, of any really high class of intellect, make their contact with it so slight, and at such long intervals, as to be almost considered as retiring from it altogether. Those persons of any mental superiority who do otherwise, are, almost without exception, greatly deteriorated by it. Not to mention loss of time, the tone of their feelings is lowered : they become less in earnest about those of their opinions respecting which they must remain silent in the society they frequent : they come to look upon their most elevated objects as unpractical, or, at least, too remote from realization to be more than a vision, or a theory ; and if, more fortunate than most, they retain their higher principles unimpaired, yet with respect to the persons and affairs of their own day they insensibly adopt the modes of feeling and judgment in which they can hope for sympathy from the company they keep. A person of high intellect should never go into unintellectual society unless he can enter it as an apostle ; yet he is the only person with high objects who can safely enter it at all. Persons even of intellectual aspirations had much better, if they can, make their habitual associates of at least their equals, and, as far as possible, their superiors, in knowledge, intellect, and elevation of sentiment. Moreover, if the character is formed, and the mind made up, on the few cardinal points of human opinion, agreement of conviction and feeling on these, has been felt in all times to be an essential requisite of anything worthy the name of friendship, in a really earnest mind. All these circumstances united, made the number very small of those whose society, and still more whose intimacy, I now voluntarily sought.

Among these, the principal was the incomparable friend of whom I have already spoken. At this period she lived mostly with one young daughter, in a quiet part of the country, and only occasionally in town, with her first husband, Mr. Taylor. I visited her equally in both places: and was greatly indebted to the strength of character which enabled her to disregard the false interpretations liable to be put on the frequency of my visits to her while living generally apart from Mr. Taylor, and on our occasionally travelling together, though in all other respects our conduct during those years gave not the slightest ground for any other supposition than the true one, that our relation to each other at that time was one of strong affection and confidential intimacy only. For though we did not consider the ordinances of society binding on a subject so entirely personal, we did feel bound that our conduct should be such as in no degree to bring discredit on her husband, nor therefore on herself.

In this third period (as it may be termed) of my mental progress, which now went hand in hand with hers, my opinions gained equally in breadth and depth, I understood more things, and those which I had understood before, I now understood more thoroughly. I had now completely turned back from what there had been of excess in my reaction against Benthamism. I had, at the height of that reaction, certainly become much more indulgent to the common opinions of society and the world, and more willing to be content with seconding the superficial improvement which had begun to take place in those common opinions, than became one whose convictions, on so many points, differed fundamentally from them. I was much more inclined, than I can now approve, to put in abeyance the more decidedly heretical part of my opinions, which I now look upon as almost the only ones, the assertion of which tends in any way to regenerate society. But in addition to this, our opinions were far *more* heretical than mine had been in the days of my most extreme Benthamism. In those days I had seen little further than the old school of political economists into the possibilities of fundamental improvement in social arrangements. Private property, as now understood, and inheritance, appeared to me, as to them, the *dernier mot* of legislation : and I looked no further than to mitigating the inequalities consequent on these institutions, by getting rid of primogeniture and entails. The notion that it was possible to go further than this in removing the injustice—for injustice it is, whether admitting of a complete remedy or not—involved in the fact that some are born to riches and the vast majority to poverty, I then reckoned chimerical, and only hoped that by universal education, leading to voluntary restraint on population, the portion of the poor might be made more tolerable. In short, I was a democrat, but not the least of a Socialist. We were now much less democrats than I had been, because so long as education continues to be so

wretchedly imperfect, we dreaded the ignorance
and especially the selfishness and brutality of
the mass: but our ideal of ultimate improvement
went far beyond Democracy, and would class
us decidedly under the general designation of
Socialists. While we repudiated with the greatest
energy that tyranny of society over the individual
which most Socialistic systems are supposed to
involve, we yet looked forward to a time when
society will no longer be divided into the idle
and the industrious; when the rule that they
who do not work shall not eat, will be applied
not to paupers only, but impartially to all;
when the division of the produce of labour,
instead of depending, as in so great a degree it
now does, on the accident of birth, will be made
by concert on an acknowledged principle of
justice; and when it will no longer either be,
or be thought to be, impossible for human beings
to exert themselves strenuously in procuring
benefits which are not to be exclusively their
own, but to be shared with the society they belong
to. The social problem of the future we considered to be, how to unite the greatest individual
liberty of action, with a common ownership in
the raw material of the globe, and an equal
participation of all in the benefits of combined
labour. We had not the presumption to suppose
that we could already foresee, by what precise
form of institutions these objects could most
effectually be attained, or at how near or how
distant a period they would become practicable.
We saw clearly that to render any such social
transformation either possible or desirable, an
equivalent change of character must take place

both in the uncultivated herd who now compose the labouring masses, and in the immense majority of their employers. Both these classes must learn by practice to labour and combine for generous, or at all events for public and social purposes, and not, as hitherto, solely for narrowly interested ones. But the capacity to do this has always existed in mankind, and is not, nor is ever likely to be, extinct. Education, habit, and the cultivation of the sentiments, will make a common man dig or weave for his country, as readily as fight for his country. True enough, it is only by slow degrees, and a system of culture prolonged through successive generations, that men in general can be brought up to this point. But the hindrance is not in the essential constitution of human nature. Interest in the common good is at present so weak a motive in the generality, not because it can never be otherwise, but because the mind is not accustomed to dwell on it as it dwells from morning till night on things which tend only to personal advantage. When called into activity, as only self-interest now is, by the daily course of life, and spurred from behind by the love of distinction and the fear of shame, it is capable of producing, even in common men, the most strenuous exertions as well as the most heroic sacrifices. The deep-rooted selfishness which forms the general character of the existing state of society, is *so* deeply rooted, only because the whole course of existing institutions tends to foster it ; and modern institutions in some respects more than ancient, since the occasion on which the individual is called on to do anything for the public without receiving its pay, are far less frequent in modern life, than in the smaller commonwealths of antiquity. These considerations did not make us overlook the folly of premature attempts to dispense with the inducements of private interest in social affairs, while no substitute for them has been or can be provided : but we regarded all existing institutions and social arrangements as being (in a phrase I once heard from Austin) ' merely provisional,' and we welcomed with the greatest pleasure and interest all socialistic experiments by select individuals (such as the Co-operative Societies), which, whether they succeeded or failed, could not but operate as a most useful education of those who took part in them, by cultivating their capacity of acting upon motives pointing directly to the general good, or making them aware of the defects which render them and others incapable of doing so.

In the ' Principles of Political Economy,' these opinions were promulgated, less clearly and fully in the first edition, rather more so in the second, and quite unequivocally in the third The difference arose partly from the change o. times, the first edition having been written and sent to press before the French Revolution o 1848, after which the public mind became more open to the reception of novelties in opinion, and doctrines appeared moderate which would have been thought very startling a short time before In the first edition the difficulties of socialism were stated so strongly, that the tone was on the whole that of opposition to it. In the yea or two which followed, much time was given to the study of the best Socialistic writers on th

Continent, and to meditation and discussion on the whole range of topics involved in the controversy : and the result was that most of what had been written on the subject in the first edition was cancelled, and replaced by arguments and reflections which represent a more advanced opinion.

The Political Economy was far more rapidly executed than the Logic, or indeed than anything of importance which I had previously written. It was commenced in the autumn of 1845, and was ready for the press before the end of 1847. In this period of little more than two years there was an interval of six months during which the work was laid aside, while I was writing articles in the Morning Chronicle (which unexpectedly entered warmly into my purpose) urging the formation of peasant properties on the waste lands of Ireland. This was during the period of the Famine, the winter of 1846–47, when the stern necessities of the time seemed to afford a chance of gaining attention for what appeared to me the only mode of combining relief to immediate destitution with permanent improvement of the social and economical condition of the Irish people. But the idea was new and strange ; there was no English precedent for such a proceeding : and the profound ignorance of English politicians and the English public concerning all social phenomena not generally met with in England (however common elsewhere), made my endeavours an entire failure. Instead of a great operation on the waste lands, and the conversion of cottiers into proprietors, Parliament passed a Poor Law for maintaining them as paupers: and if the nation has not since found itself in inextricable difficulties from the joint operation of the old evils and the quack remedy, it is indebted for its deliverance to that most unexpected and surprising fact, the depopulation of Ireland, commenced by famine, and continued by emigration.

The rapid success of the Political Economy showed that the public wanted, and were prepared for such a book. Published early in 1848, an edition of a thousand copies was sold in less than a year. Another similar edition was published in the spring of 1849; and a third, of 1250 copies, early in 1852. It was, from the first, continually cited and referred to as an authority, because it was not a book merely of abstract science, but also of application, and treated Political Economy not as a thing by itself, but as a fragment of a greater whole; a branch of Social Philosophy, so interlinked with all the other branches, that its conclusions, even in its own peculiar province, are only true conditionally, subject to interference and counteraction from causes not directly within its scope: while to the character of a practical guide it has no pretension, apart from other classes of considerations. Political Economy, in truth, has never pretended to give advice to mankind with no lights but its own; though people who knew nothing but political economy (and therefore knew that ill) have taken upon themselves to advise, and could only do so by such lights as they had. But the numerous sentimental enemies of political economy, and its still more numerous interested enemies in sentimental guise, have been very successful in gaining belief for this among other unmerited imputations against it, and the ' Principles ' having, in spite of the freedom of many of its opinions, become for the present the most popular treatise on the subject, has helped to disarm the enemies of so important a study. The amount of its worth as an exposition of the science, and the value of the different applications which it suggests, others of course must judge.

For a considerable time after this, I published no work of magnitude ; though I still occasionally wrote in periodicals, and my correspondence (much of it with persons quite unknown to me), on subjects of public interest, swelled to a considerable bulk. During these years I wrote or commenced various Essays, for eventual publication, on some of the fundamental questions of human and social life, with regard to several of which I have already much exceeded the severity of the Horatian precept. I continued to watch with keen interest the progress of public events. But it was not, on the whole, very encouraging to me. The European reaction after 1848, and the success of an unprincipled usurper in December, 1851, put an end, as it seemed, to all present hope of freedom or social improvement in France and the Continent. In England, I had seen and continued to see many of the opinions of my youth obtain general recognition, and many of the reforms in institutions, for which I had through life contended, either effected or in course of being so. But these changes had been attended with much less benefit to human well-being than I should formerly have anticipated, because they had produced very little improvement in that which all real amelioration in the lot of mankind depends on, their intellectual and moral state : and it might even be questioned if the various causes of deterioration which had been at work in the meanwhile, had not more than counterbalanced the tendencies to improvement. I had learnt from experience that many false opinions may be exchanged for true ones, without in the least altering the habits of mind of which false opinions are the result. The English public, for example, are quite as raw and undiscerning on subjects of political economy since the nation has been converted to free-trade, as they were before ; and are still further from having acquired better habits of thought or feeling, or being in any way better fortified against error, on subjects of a more elevated character. For, though they have thrown off certain errors, the general discipline of their minds, intellectually and morally, is not altered. I am now convinced, that no great improvements in the lot of mankind are possible, until a great change takes place in the fundamental constitution of their modes of thought. The old opinions in religion, morals, and politics, are so much discredited in the more intellectual minds as to have lost the greater part of their efficacy for good, while they have still life enough in them to be a powerful obstacle to the growing up of any better opinions on those subjects. When the philosophic minds of the world can no longer believe its religion, or can only believe it with modifications amounting to an essential change of its character, a transitional period commences, of weak convictions, paralysed intellects, and growing laxity of principle which cannot terminate until a renovation has been effected in the basis of their belief, leading to the evolution of some faith, whether religious or merely human, which they can really believe : and when things are in this state, all thinking or writing which does not tend to promote such a renovation, is of very little value beyond the moment. Since there was little in the apparent condition of the public mind, indicative of any tendency in this direction, my view of the immediate prospects of human improvement was not sanguine. More recently a spirit of free speculation has sprung up, giving a more encouraging prospect of the gradual mental emancipation of England ; and concurring with the renewal under better auspices, of the movement for political freedom in the rest of Europe, has given to the present condition of human affairs a more hopeful aspect.[1]

Between the time of which I have now spoken, and the present, took place the most important events of my private life. The first of these was my marriage, in April, 1851, to the lady whose incomparable worth had made her friendship the greatest source to me both of happiness and of improvement, during many years in which we never expected to be in any closer relation to one another. Ardently as I should have aspired to this complete union of our lives at any time in the course of my existence at which it had been practicable, I, as much as my wife, would far rather have foregone that privilege for ever, than have owed it to the premature death of one for whom I had the sincerest respect,

[1] Written about 1861.

and she the strongest affection. That event, however, having taken place in July, 1849, it was granted to me to derive from that evil my own greatest good, by adding to the partnership of thought, feeling, and writing which had long existed, a partnership of our entire existence. For seven and a-half years that blessing was mine; for seven and a-half only! I can say nothing which could describe, even in the faintest manner, what that loss was and is. But because I know that she would have wished it, I endeavour to make the best of what life I have left, and to work on for her purposes with such diminished strength as can be derived from thoughts of her, and communion with her memory.

When two persons have their thoughts and speculations completely in common; when all subjects of intellectual or moral interest are discussed between them in daily life, and probed to much greater depths than are usually or conveniently sounded in writings intended for general readers; when they set out from the same principles, and arrive at their conclusions by processes pursued jointly, it is of little consequence in respect to the question of originality, which of them holds the pen; the one who contributes least to the composition may contribute most to the thought; the writings which result are the joint product of both, and it must often be impossible to disentangle their respective parts, and affirm that this belongs to one and that to the other. In this wide sense, not only during the years of our married life, but during many of the years of confidential friendship which preceded, all my published writings were as much her work

as mine ; her share in them constantly increasing
as years advanced. But in certain cases, what
belongs to her can be distinguished, and specially
identified. Over and above the general influence
which her mind had over mine, the most valuable
ideas and features in these joint productions—
those which have been most fruitful of important
results, and have contributed most to the success
and reputation of the works themselves—originated with her, were emanations from her mind,
my part in them being no greater than in any of
the thoughts which I found in previous writers,
and made my own only by incorporating them
with my own system of thought. During the
greater part of my literary life I have performed
the office in relation to her, which from a rather
early period I had considered as the most useful
part that I was qualified to take in the domain
of thought, that of an interpreter of original
thinkers, and mediator between them and the
public ; for I had always a humble opinion of
my own powers as an original thinker, except
in abstract science (logic, metaphysics, and the
theoretic principles of political economy and
politics), but thought myself much superior to
most of my contemporaries in willingness and
ability to learn from everybody ; as I found
hardly any one who made such a point of examining
what was said in defence of all opinions, however
new or however old, in the conviction that even
if they were errors there might be a substratum
of truth underneath them, and that in any case
the discovery of what it was that made them
plausible, would be a benefit to truth. I had,
in consequence, marked this out as a sphere of

usefulness in which I was under a special obligation to make myself active : the more so, as the
acquaintance I had formed with the ideas of the
Coleridgians, of the German thinkers, and of
Carlyle, all of them fiercely opposed to the mode
of thought in which I had been brought up, had
convinced me that along with much error they
possessed much truth, which was veiled from
minds otherwise capable of receiving it by the
transcendental and mystical phraseology in which
they were accustomed to shut it up, and from
which they neither cared, nor knew how, to
disengage it ; and I did not despair of separating
the truth from the error, and exposing it in terms
which would be intelligible and not repulsive
to those on my own side in philosophy. Thus
prepared, it will easily be believed that when I
came into close intellectual communion with
a person of the most eminent faculties, whose
genius, as it grew and unfolded itself in thought,
continually struck out truths far in advance of
me, but in which I could not, as I had done in
those others, detect any mixture of error, the
greatest part of my mental growth consisted in
the assimilation of those truths, and the most
valuable part of my intellectual work was in
building the bridges and clearing the paths which
connected them with my general system of
thought.[1]

[1] The steps in my mental growth for which I was
indebted to her were far from being those which a person
wholly uninformed on the subject would probably suspect.
It might be supposed, for instance, that my strong convictions on the complete equality in all legal, political,
social and domestic relations, which ought to exist between
men and women, may have been adopted or learnt from

The first of my books in which her share was conspicuous was the 'Principles of Political Economy.' The 'System of Logic' owed little to her except in the minuter matters of composition, in which respect my writings, both great and small, have largely benefited by her accurate and clear-sighted criticism.[1] The chapter of

her. This was so far from being the fact, that those convictions were among the earliest results of the application of my mind to political subjects, and the strength with which I held them was, as I believe, more than anything else, the originating cause of the interest she felt in me. What is true is, that until I knew her, the opinion was in my mind, little more than an abstract principle. I saw no more reason why women should be held in legal subjection to other people, than why men should. I was certain that their interests required fully as much protection as those of men, and were quite as little likely to obtain it without an equal voice in making the laws by which they were to be bound. But that perception of the vast practical bearings of women's disabilities which found expression in the book on the 'Subjection of Women' was acquired mainly through her teaching. But for her rare knowledge of human nature and comprehension of moral and social influences, though I should doubtless have held my present opinions, I should have had a very insufficient perception of the mode in which the consequences of the inferior position of women intertwine themselves with all the evils of existing society and with all the difficulties of human improvement. I am indeed painfully conscious of how much of her best thoughts on the subject I have failed to reproduce, and how greatly that little treatise falls short of what would have been if she had put on paper her entire mind on this question, or had lived to revise and improve, as she certainly would have done, my imperfect statement of the case.

[1] The only person from whom I received any direct assistance in the preparation of the System of Logic was Mr. Bain, since so justly celebrated for his philosophical writings. He went carefully through the manuscript

the Political Economy which has had a greater
influence on opinion than all the rest, that on
'the Probable Future of the Labouring Classes,'
is entirely due to her : in the first draft of the
book, that chapter did not exist. She pointed
out the need of such a chapter, and the extreme
imperfection of the book without it : she was
the cause of my writing it ; and the more general
part of the chapter, the statement and discussion
of the two opposite theories respecting the proper
condition of the labouring classes, was wholly
an exposition of her thoughts, often in words
taken from her own lips. The purely scientific
part of the Political Economy I did not learn
from her ; but it was chiefly her influence that
gave to the book that general tone by which it
is distinguished from all previous expositions
of Political Economy that had any pretension

before it was sent to press, and enriched it with a great
number of additional examples and illustrations from
science ; many of which, as well as some detached remarks
of his own in confirmation of my logical views, I inserted
nearly in his own words.

My obligations to Comte were only to his writings—
to the part which had then been published of his ' Système
de Philosophie Positive :' and, as has been seen from
what I have already said in this narrative, the amount
of these obligations is far less than has sometimes been
asserted. The first volume, which contains all the fundamental doctrines of the book, was substantially complete
before I had seen Comte's treatise. I derived from him
many valuable thoughts, conspicuously in the chapter
on Hypotheses and in the view taken of the logic of
Algebra : but it is only in the concluding Book, on the
Logic of the Moral Sciences, that I owe to him any radical
improvement in my conception of the application of
logical method. This improvement I have stated and
characterized in a former part of the present Memoir.

to being scientific, and which has made it so useful in conciliating minds which those previous
expositions had repelled. This tone consisted
chiefly in making the proper distinction between
the laws of the Production of Wealth, which are
real laws of nature, dependent on the properties
of objects, and the modes of its Distribution,
which, subject to certain conditions, depend on
human will. The common run of political economists confuse these together, under the designation of economic laws, which they deem incapable
of being defeated or modified by human effort ;
ascribing the same necessity to things dependent
on the unchangeable conditions of our earthly
existence, and to those which, being but the
necessary consequences of particular social arrangements, are merely co-extensive with these : given
certain institutions and customs, wages, profits,
and rent will be determined by certain causes ;
but this class of political economists drop the
indispensable presupposition, and argue that
these causes must, by an inherent necessity,
against which no human means can avail, determine the shares which fall, in the division of the
produce, to labourers, capitalists, and landlords.
The ' Principles of Political Economy ' yielded
to none of its predecessors in aiming at the
scientific appreciation of the action of these
causes, under the conditions which they presuppose ; but it set the example of not treating
those conditions as final. The economic generalizations which depend, not on necessities of nature
but on those combined with the existing arrangements of society, it deals with only as provisional,
and as liable to be much altered by the progress

of social improvement. I had indeed partially learnt this view of things from the thoughts awakened in me by the speculations of the St. Simonians; but it was made a living principle pervading and animating the book by my wife's promptings. This example illustrates well the general character of what she contributed to my writings. What was abstract and purely scientific was generally mine; the properly human element came from her: in all that concerned the application of philosophy to the exigencies of human society and progress, I was her pupil, alike in boldness of speculation and cautiousness of practical judgment. For, on the one hand, she was much more courageous and far-sighted than without her I should have been, in anticipations of an order of things to come, in which many of the limited generalizations now so often confounded with universal principles will cease to be applicable. Those parts of my writings, and especially of the Political Economy, which contemplate possibilities in the future such as, when affirmed by socialists, have in general been fiercely denied by political economists, would, but for her, either have been absent, or the suggestions would have been made much more timidly and in a more qualified form. But while she thus rendered me bolder in speculation on human affairs, her practical turn of mind, and her almost unerring estimate of practical obstacles, repressed in me all tendencies that were really visionary. Her mind invested all ideas in a concrete shape, and formed to itself a conception of how they would actually work: and her knowledge of the existing feelings and conduct of mankind was so seldom at fault, that the weak point in any unworkable suggestion seldom escaped her.[1]

During the years which intervened between the commencement of my married life and the catastrophe which closed it, the principal occurrences of my outward existence (unless I count as such a first attack of the family disease, and a consequent journey of more than six months for the recovery of health, in Italy, Sicily, and Greece) had reference to my position in the India House. In 1856 I was promoted to the rank of chief of the office in which I had served for upwards of thirty-three years. The appointment, that of Examiner of India Correspondence, was the highest, next to that of Secretary, in the East India Company's home service, involving the general superintendence of all the correspondence with the Indian Governments, except the military, naval, and financial. I held this office as long as it continued to exist, being a little more than two years; after which it pleased Parliament, in other words Lord Palmerston, to put an end to the East India Company as a branch of the Government of India under the Crown, and convert the administration of that country into a thing to be scrambled for by the second and third class of English parliamentary politicians. I was the chief manager of the resistance which the Company made to their own political extinction, and to the letters and petitions I wrote for them,

---

[1] A few dedicatory lines acknowledging what the book owed to her, were prefixed to some of the presentation copies of the Political Economy on its first publication. Her dislike of publicity alone prevented their insertion in the other copies of the work.

and the concluding chapter of my treatise on Representative Government, I must refer for my opinions on the folly and mischief of this ill-considered change. Personally I considered myself a gainer by it, as I had given enough of my life to India, and was not unwilling to retire on the liberal compensation granted. After the change was consummated, Lord Stanley, the First Secretary of State for India, made me the honourable offer of a seat in the Council, and the proposal was subsequently renewed by the Council itself, on the first occasion of its having to supply a vacancy in its own body. But the conditions of Indian Government under the new system made me anticipate nothing but useless vexation and waste of effort from any participation in it: and nothing that has since happened has had any tendency to make me regret my refusal.

During the two years which immediately preceded the cessation of my official life, my wife and I were working together at the ' Liberty.' I had first planned and written it as a short essay in 1854. It was in mounting the steps of the Capitol, in January, 1855, that the thought first arose of converting it into a volume. None of my writings have been either so carefully composed, or so sedulously corrected as this. After it had been written as usual twice over, we kept it by us, bringing it out from time to time, and going through it *de novo*, reading, weighing, and criticising every sentence. Its final revision was to have been a work of the winter of 1858-9, the first after my retirement, which we had arranged to pass in the South of Europe. That hope and every other were frustrated by the most unexpected and bitter calamity of her death—at Avignon, on our way to Montpellier, from a sudden attack of pulmonary congestion.

Since then I have sought for such alleviation as my state admitted of, by the mode of life which most enabled me to feel her still near me. I bought a cottage as close as possible to the place where she is buried, and there her daughter (my fellow-sufferer and now my chief comfort) and I, live constantly during a great portion of the year. My objects in life are solely those which were hers; my pursuits and occupations those in which she shared, or sympathized, and which are indissolubly associated with her. Her memory is to me a religion, and her approbation the standard by which, summing up as it does all worthiness, I endeavour to regulate my life.[1]

After my irreparable loss, one of my earliest cares was to print and publish the treatise, so much of which was the work of her whom I had lost, and consecrate it to her memory. I have made no alteration or addition to it, nor shall I ever. Though it wants the last touch of her hand, no substitute for that touch shall ever be attempted by mine.

The 'Liberty' was more directly and literally our joint production than anything else which bears my name, for there was not a sentence of it which was not several times gone through by us together, turned over in many ways, and carefully weeded of any faults, either in thought

---

[1] What precedes was written or revised previous to, or during the year 1861. What follows was written in 1870.

or expression, that we detected in it. It is in
consequence of this that, although it never underwent her final revision, it far surpasses, as a mere
specimen of composition, anything which has
proceeded from me either before or since. With
regard to the thoughts, it is difficult to identify
any particular part or element as being more
hers than all the rest. The whole mode of thinking of which the book was the expression, was
emphatically hers. But I also was so thoroughly
imbued with it, that the same thoughts naturally
occurred to us both. That I was thus penetrated
with it, however, I owe in a great degree to her.
There was a moment in my mental progress when
I might easily have fallen into a tendency towards
over-government, both social and political; as
there was also a moment when, by reaction from
a contrary excess, I might have become a less
thorough radical and democrat than I am. In
both these points, as in many others, she benefited
me as much by keeping me right where I was
right, as by leading me to new truths, and ridding
me of errors. My great readiness and eagerness
to learn from everybody, and to make room in
my opinions for every new acquisition by adjust-
ing the old and the new to one another, might,
but for her steadying influence, have seduced
me into modifying my early opinions too much.
She was in nothing more valuable to my mental
development than by her just measure of the
relative importance of different considerations,
which often protected me from allowing to truths
I had only recently learnt to see, a more important
place in my thoughts than was properly their due.

The 'Liberty' is likely to survive longer than

anything else that I have written (with the possible exception of the 'Logic'), because the conjunction of her mind with mine has rendered it a kind of philosophic text-book of a single truth, which the changes progressively taking place in modern society tend to bring out into ever stronger relief: the importance, to man and society, of a large variety in types of character, and of giving full freedom to human nature to expand itself in innumerable and conflicting directions. Nothing can better show how deep are the foundations of this truth, than the great impression made by the exposition of it at a time which, to superficial observation, did not seem to stand much in need of such a lesson. The fears we expressed, lest the inevitable growth of social equality and of the government of public opinion, should impose on mankind an oppressive yoke of uniformity in opinion and practice, might easily have appeared chimerical to those who looked more at present facts than at tendencies; for the gradual revolution that is taking place in society and institutions has, thus far, been decidedly favourable to the development of new opinions, and has procured for them a much more unprejudiced hearing than they previously met with. But this is a feature belonging to periods of transition, when old notions and feelings have been unsettled, and no new doctrines have yet succeeded to their ascendancy. At such times people of any mental activity, having given up their old beliefs, and not feeling quite sure that those they still retain can stand unmodified, listen eagerly to new opinions. But this state of things is necessarily transitory: some particular body of doctrine in time rallies the majority round it, organizes social institutions and modes of action conformably to itself, education impresses this new creed upon the new generations without the mental processes that have led to it, and by degrees it acquires the very same power of compression, so long exercised by the creeds of which it had taken the place. Whether this noxious power will be exercised, depends on whether mankind have by that time become aware that it cannot be exercised without stunting and dwarfing human nature. It is then that the teachings of the 'Liberty' will have their greatest value. And it is to be feared that they will retain that value a long time.

As regards originality, it has of course no other than that which every thoughtful mind gives to its own mode of conceiving and expressing truths which are common property. The leading thought of the book is one which though in many ages confined to insulated thinkers, mankind have probably at no time since the beginning of civilization been entirely without. To speak only of the last few generations, it is distinctly contained in the vein of important thought respecting education and culture, spread through the European mind by the labours and genius of Pestalozzi. The unqualified championship of it by Wilhelm von Humboldt is referred to in the book; but he by no means stood alone in his own country. During the early part of the present century the doctrine of the rights of individuality, and the claim of the moral nature to develope itself in its own way, was pushed by a whole school of German authors even to exaggeration; and the

writings of Goethe, the most celebrated of all
German authors, though not belonging to that
or to any other school, are penetrated throughout
by views of morals and of conduct in life, often
in my opinion not defensible, but which are
incessantly seeking whatever defence they admit
of in the theory of the right and duty of self-
development. In our own country, before the
book 'On Liberty' was written, the doctrine
of Individuality had been enthusiastically asserted,
in a style of vigorous declamation sometimes
reminding one of Fichte, by Mr. William Maccall,
in a series of writings of which the most elaborate
is entitled 'Elements of Individualism:' and
a remarkable American, Mr. Warren, had formed
a System of Society, on the foundation of the
'Sovereignty of the Individual,' had obtained a
number of followers, and had actually commenced the formation of a Village Community
(whether it now exists I know not), which, though
bearing a superficial resemblance to some of the
projects of Socialists, is diametrically opposite to
them in principle, since it recognises no authority
whatever in Society over the individual, except
to enforce equal freedom of development for all in-
dividualities. As the book which bears my name
claimed no originality for any of its doctrines,
and was not intended to write their history, the
only author who had preceded me in their assertion,
of whom I thought it appropriate to say anything,
was Humboldt, who furnished the motto to the
work; although in one passage I borrowed from
the Warrenites their phrase, the sovereignty of
the individual. It is hardly necessary here to
remark that there are abundant differences in

detail, between the conception of the doctrine
by any of the predecessors I have mentioned,
and that set forth in the book.

The political circumstances of the time induced
me, shortly after, to complete and publish a
pamphlet (' Thoughts on Parliamentary Reform '),
part of which had been written some years
previously, on the occasion of one of the abortive
Reform Bills, and had at the time been approved
and revised by her. Its principal features were,
hostility to the Ballot (a change of opinion in
both of us, in which she rather preceded me),
and a claim of representation for minorities;
not, however, at that time going beyond the
cumulative vote proposed by Mr. Garth Marshall.
In finishing the pamphlet for publication, with
a view to the discussions on the Reform Bill of
Lord Derby's and Mr. Disraeli's government in
1859, I added a third feature, a plurality of votes,
to be given, not to property, but to proved
superiority of education. This recommended
itself to me as a means of reconciling the irresistible claim of every man or woman to be con-
sulted, and to be allowed a voice, in the regulation
of affairs which vitally concern them, with the
superiority of weight justly due to opinions
grounded on superiority of knowledge. The
suggestion, however, was one which I had never
discussed with my almost infallible counsellor,
and I have no evidence that she would have
concurred in it. As far as I have been able to
observe, it has found favour with nobody; all
who desire any sort of inequality in the electoral
vote, desiring it in favour of property and not
of intelligence or knowledge. If it ever overcomes

the strong feeling which exists against it, this will only be after the establishment of a systematic National Education by which the various grades of politically valuable acquirement may be accurately defined and authenticated. Without this it will always remain liable to strong, possibly conclusive, objections; and with this, it would perhaps not be needed.

It was soon after the publication of 'Thoughts on Parliamentary Reform,' that I became acquainted with Mr. Hare's admirable system of Personal Representation, which, in its present shape, was then for the first time published. I saw in this great practical and philosophical idea, the greatest improvement of which the system of representative government is susceptible; an improvement which, in the most felicitous manner, exactly meets and cures the grand, and what before seemed the inherent, defect of the representative system; that of giving to a numerical majority all power, instead of only a power proportional to its numbers, and enabling the strongest party to exclude all weaker parties from making their opinions heard in the assembly of the nation, except through such opportunity as may be given to them by the accidentally unequal distribution of opinions in different localities. To these great evils nothing more than very imperfect palliations had seemed possible; but Mr. Hare's system affords a radical cure. This great discovery, for it is no less, in the political art, inspired me, as I believe it has inspired all thoughtful persons who have adopted it, with new and more sanguine hopes respecting the prospects of human society; by freeing the form of political institutions towards which the whole civilized world is manifestly and irresistibly tending, from the chief part of what seemed to qualify, or render doubtful, its ultimate benefits. Minorities, so long as they remain minorities, are, and ought to be, outvoted; but under arrangements which enable any assemblage of voters, amounting to a certain number, to place in the legislature a representative of its own choice, minorities cannot be suppressed. Independent opinions will force their way into the council of the nation and make themselves heard there, a thing which often cannot happen in the existing forms of representative democracy; and the legislature, instead of being weeded of individual peculiarities and entirely made up of men who simply represent the creed of great political or religious parties, will comprise a large proportion of the most eminent individual minds in the country, placed there, without reference to party, by voters who appreciate their individual eminence. I can understand that persons, otherwise intelligent, should, for want of sufficient examination, be repelled from Mr. Hare's plan by what they think the complex nature of its machinery. But any one who does not feel the want which the scheme is intended to supply; any one who throws it over as a mere theoretical subtlety or crotchet, tending to no valuable purpose, and unworthy of the attention of practical men, may be pronounced an incompetent statesman, unequal to the politics of the future. I mean, unless he is a minister or aspires to become one: for we are quite accustomed to a minister continuing to profess unqualified hostility to an improvement almost to the very day when his conscience, or his interest, induces him to take it up as a public measure, and carry it.

Had I met with Mr. Hare's system before the publication of my pamphlet, I should have given an account of it there. Not having done so, I wrote an article in Fraser's Magazine (reprinted in my miscellaneous writings) principally for that purpose, though I included in it, along with Mr. Hare's book, a review of two other productions on the question of the day; one of them a pamphlet by my early friend, Mr. John Austin, who had in his old age become an enemy to all further Parliamentary reform; the other an able and vigorous, though partially erroneous work by Mr. Lorimer.

In the course of the same summer I fulfilled a duty particularly incumbent upon me, that of helping (by an article in the Edinburgh Review) to make known Mr. Bain's profound treatise on the Mind, just then completed by the publication of its second volume. And I carried through the press a selection of my minor writings, forming the first two volumes of 'Dissertations and Discussions.' The selection had been made during my wife's lifetime, but the revision, in concert with her, with a view to republication, had been barely commenced; and when I had no longer the guidance of her judgment I despaired of pursuing it further, and republished the papers as they were, with the exception of striking out such passages as were no longer in accordance with my opinions. My literary work of the year was terminated with an essay in Fraser's Magazine (afterwards republished in the third volume of

' Dissertations and Discussions,') entitled ' A Few Words on Non-Intervention.' I was prompted to write this paper by a desire, while vindicating England from the imputations commonly brought against her on the Continent, of a peculiar selfishness in matters of foreign policy, to warn Englishmen of the colour given to this imputation by the low tone in which English statesmen are accustomed to speak of English policy as concerned only with English interests, and by the conduct of Lord Palmerston at that particular time in opposing the Suez Canal : and I took the opportunity of expressing ideas which had long been in my mind (some of them generated by my Indian experience, and others by the international questions which then greatly occupied the European public), respecting the true principles of international morality, and the legitimate modifications made in it by difference of times and circumstances; a subject I had already, to some extent, discussed in the vindication of the French Provisional Government of 1848 against the attacks of Lord Brougham and others, which I published at the time in the Westminster Review, and which is reprinted in the ' Dissertations.'

I had now settled, as I believed, for the remainder of my existence into a purely literary life ; if that can be called literary which continued to be occupied in a pre-eminent degree with politics, and not merely with theoretical, but practical politics, although a great part of the year was spent at a distance of many hundred miles from the chief seat of the politics of my own country, to which, and primarily for which, I wrote. But, in truth, the modern facilities of communication have not only removed all the disadvantages, to a political writer in tolerably easy circumstances, of distance from the scene of political action, but have converted them into advantages. The immediate and regular receipt of newspapers and periodicals keeps him *au courant* of even the most temporary politics, and gives him a much more correct view of the state and progress of opinion than he could acquire by personal contact with individuals : for every one's social intercourse is more or less limited to particular sets or classes, whose impressions and no others reach him through that channel ; and experience has taught me that those who give their time to the absorbing claims of what is called society, not having leisure to keep up a large acquaintance with the organs of opinion, remain much more ignorant of the general state either of the public mind, or of the active and instructed part of it, than a recluse who reads the newpapers need be. There are, no doubt, disadvantages in too long a separation from one's country—in not occasionally renewing one's impressions of the light in which men and things appear when seen from a position in the midst of them ; but the deliberate judgment formed at a distance, and undisturbed by inequalities of perspective, is the most to be depended on, even for application to practice. Alternating between the two positions, I combined the advantages of both. And, though the inspirer of my best thoughts was no longer with me, I was not alone : she had left a daughter, my step-daughter, *   *

*   *   *   *   *   *

*   *   * whose ever growing and

ripening talents from that day to this have been devoted to the same great purposes.　　*　　*

*　　*　　*　　*　　*　　*
Surely no one ever before was so fortunate, as, after such a loss as mine, to draw another prize in the lottery of life.　　*　　*　　*　　*

*　　*　　*　　Whoever, either now or here-after may think of me and of the work I have done, must never forget that it is the product not of one intellect and conscience, but of three.　　*　　*

*　　*　　*　　*　　*　　*

*　　*　　*　　*　　*　　*

The work of the years 1860 and 1861 consisted chiefly of two treatises, only one of which was intended for immediate publication. This was the ' Considerations on Representative Government; ' a connected exposition of what, by the thoughts of many years, I had come to regard as the best form of a popular constitution. Along with as much of the general theory of government as is necessary to support this particular portion of its practice, the volume contains my matured views of the principal questions which occupy the present age, within the province of purely organic institutions, and raises, by anticipation, some other questions to which growing necessities will sooner or later compel the attention both of theoretical and of practical politicians. The chief of these last, is the distinction between the function of making laws, for which a numerous popular assembly is radically unfit, and that of getting good laws made, which is its proper duty and cannot be satisfactorily fulfilled by any other authority : and the consequent need of a Legislative Commission, as a permanent part of the constitution of a free country; consisting of a small number of highly trained political minds, on whom, when Parliament has determined that a law shall be made, the task of making it should be devolved; Parliament retaining the power of passing or rejecting the bill when drawn up, but not of altering it otherwise than by sending proposed amendments to be dealt with by the Commission. The question here raised respecting the most important of all public functions, that of legislation, is a particular case of the great problem of modern political organization, stated, I believe, for the first time in its full extent by Bentham, though in my opinion not always satisfactorily resolved by him; the combination of complete popular control over public affairs, with the greatest attainable perfection of skilled agency.

The other treatise written at this time is the one which was published some years later [1] under the title of 'The Subjection of Women.' It was written　＊　＊　＊　＊　that there might, in any event, be in existence a written exposition of my opinions on that great question, as full and conclusive as I could make it. The intention was to keep this among other unpublished papers, improving it from time to time if I was able, and to publish it at the time when it should seem likely to be most useful. As ultimately published　＊　＊　＊　＊　＊　＊　＊　in what was of my own composition, all that is most striking and profound belongs to my wife; coming from the fund of thought which had been made common to us both, by

[1] In 1869.

I

our innumerable conversations and discussions on a topic which filled so large a place in our minds.

Soon after this time I took from their repository a portion of the unpublished papers which I had written during the last years of our married life, and shaped them, with some additional matter, into the little work entitled 'Utilitarianism;' which was first published, in three parts, in successive numbers of Fraser's Magazine, and afterwards reprinted in a volume.

Before this, however, the state of public affairs had become extremely critical, by the commencement of the American civil war. My strongest feelings were engaged in this struggle, which, I felt from the beginning, was destined to be a turning point, for good or evil, of the course of human affairs for an indefinite duration. Having been a deeply interested observer of the slavery quarrel in America, during the many years that preceded the open breach, I knew that it was in all its stages an aggressive enterprise of the slave-owners to extend the territory of slavery; under the combined influences of pecuniary interest, domineering temper, and the fanaticism of a class for its class privileges, influences so fully and powerfully depicted in the admirable work of my friend Professor Cairnes, 'The Slave Power.' Their success, if they succeeded, would be a victory of the powers of evil which would give courage to the enemies of progress and damp the spirits of its friends all over the civilized world, while it would create a formidable military power, grounded on the worst and most anti-social form of the tyranny of men over men, and, by destroying for a long time the prestige of the great democratic republic, would give to all the privileged classes of Europe a false confidence, probably only to be extinguished in blood. On the other hand, if the spirit of the North was sufficiently roused to carry the war to a successful termination, and if that termination did not come too soon and too easily, I foresaw, from the laws of human nature, and the experience of revolutions, that when it did come it would in all probability be thorough : that the bulk of the Northern population, whose conscience had as yet been awakened only to the point of resisting the further extension of slavery, but whose fidelity to the Constitution of the United States made them disapprove of any attempt by the Federal Government to interfere with slavery in the States where it already existed, would acquire feelings of another kind when the Constitution had been shaken off by armed rebellion, would determine to have done for ever with the accursed thing, and would join their banner with that of the noble body of Abolitionists, of whom Garrison was the courageous and single-minded apostle, Wendell Phillips the eloquent orator, and John Brown the voluntary martyr.[1] Then, too, the whole mind of the United States would be let loose from its bonds, no longer corrupted by the supposed necessity of apologizing to foreigners for the most flagrant of all possible violations of the free principles of

---

[1] The saying of this true hero, after his capture, that he was worth more for hanging than for any other purpose, reminds one, by its combination of wit, wisdom, and self-devotion, of Sir Thomas More.

their Constitution; while the tendency of a
fixed state of society to stereotype a set of national
opinions would be at least temporarily checked,
and the national mind would become more open
to the recognition of whatever was bad in either
the institutions or the customs of the people.
These hopes, so far as related to slavery, have
been completely, and in other respects are in
course of being progressively realized. Foreseeing
from the first this double set of consequences
from the success or failure of the rebellion, it
may be imagined with what feelings I contemplated the rush of nearly the whole upper and
middle classes of my own country, even those
who passed for Liberals, into a furious pro-
Southern partisanship: the working classes, and
some of the literary and scientific men, being
almost the sole exceptions to the general frenzy.
I never before felt so keenly how little permanent
improvement had reached the minds of our
influential classes, and of what small value were
the Liberal opinions they had got into the habit
of professing. None of the Continental Liberals
committed the same frightful mistake. But the
generation which had extorted negro emancipation from our West India planters had passed
away; another had succeeded which had not
learnt by many years of discussion and exposure
to feel strongly the enormities of slavery; and
the inattention habitual with Englishmen to
whatever is going on in the world outside their
own island, made them profoundly ignorant of
all the antecedents of the struggle, insomuch
that it was not generally believed in England,
for the first year or two of the war, that the

quarrel was one of slavery. There were men of high principle and unquestionable liberality of opinion, who thought it a dispute about tariffs, or assimilated it to the cases in which they were accustomed to sympathize, of a people struggling for independence.

It was my obvious duty to be one of the small minority who protested against this perverted state of public opinion. I was not the first to protest. It ought to be remembered to the honour of Mr. Hughes and of Mr. Ludlow, that they, by writings published at the very beginning of the struggle, began the protestation. Mr. Bright followed in one of the most powerful of his speeches, followed by others not less striking. I was on the point of adding my word to theirs, when there occurred, towards the end of 1861, the seizure of the Southern envoys on board a British vessel, by an officer of the United States. Even English forgetfulness has not yet had time to lose all remembrance of the explosion of feeling in England which then burst forth, the expectation, which prevailed for some weeks, of war with the United States, and the warlike preparations actually commenced on this side. While this state of things lasted, there was no chance of a hearing for anything favourable to the American cause ; and, moreover, I agreed with those who thought the act unjustifiable, and such as to require that England should demand its disavowal. When the disavowal came, and the alarm of war was over, I wrote, in January, 1862, the paper, in Fraser's Magazine, entitled ' The Contest in America.'   *   *   *   *
*   *   *   Written and published

when it was, this paper helped to encourage those Liberals who had felt overborne by the tide of illiberal opinion, and to form in favour of the good cause a nucleus of opinion which increased gradually, and, after the success of the North began to seem probable, rapidly. When we returned from our journey I wrote a second article, a review of Professor Cairnes' book, published in the Westminster Review. England is paying the penalty, in many uncomfortable ways, of the durable resentment which her ruling classes stirred up in the United States by their ostentatious wishes for the ruin of America as a nation : they have reason to be thankful that a few, if only a few, known writers and speakers, standing firmly by the Americans in the time of their greatest difficulty, effected a partial diversion of these bitter feelings, and made Great Britain not altogether odious to the Americans.

This duty having been performed, my principal occupation for the next two years was on subjects not political. The publication of Mr. Austin's Lectures on Jurisprudence after his decease, gave me an opportunity of paying a deserved tribute to his memory, and at the same time expressing some thoughts on a subject on which, in my old days of Benthamism, I had bestowed much study. But the chief product of those years was the Examination of Sir William Hamilton's Philosophy. His Lectures, published in 1860 and 1861, I had read towards the end of the latter year, with a half-formed intention of giving an account of them in a Review, but I soon found that this would be idle, and that justice could not be done to the subject in less than a volume. I had then to consider whether it would be advisable that I myself should attempt such a performance. On consideration, there seemed to be strong reason for doing so. I was greatly disappointed with the Lectures. I read them, certainly, with no prejudice against Sir William Hamilton. I had up to that time deferred the study of his Notes to Reid on account of their unfinished state, but I had not neglected his ' Discussions in Philosophy ; ' and though I knew that his general mode of treating the facts of mental philosophy differed from that of which I most approved, yet his vigorous polemic against the later Transcendentalists, and his strenuous assertion of some important principles, especially the Relativity of human knowledge, gave me many points of sympathy with his opinions, and made me think that genuine psychology had considerably more to gain than to lose by his authority and reputation. His Lectures and the Dissertations on Reid dispelled this illusion : and even the Discussions, read by the light which these throw on them, lose much of their value. I found that the points of apparent agreement between his opinions and mine were more verbal than real ; that the important philosophical principles which I had thought he recognised, were so explained away by him as to mean little or nothing, or were continually lost sight of, and doctrines entirely inconsistent with them were taught in nearly every part of his philosophical writings. My estimation of him was therefore so far altered, that instead of regarding him as occupying a kind of intermediate position between the two rival philosophies, holding some of the principles of both, and supplying to both powerful weapons of attack and defence, I now looked upon him as one of the pillars, and in this country from his high philosophical reputation the chief pillar, of that one of the two which seemed to me to be erroneous.

Now, the difference between these two schools of philosophy, that of Intuition, and that of Experience and Association, is not a mere matter of abstract speculation; it is full of practical consequences, and lies at the foundation of all the greatest differences of practical opinion in an age of progress. The practical reformer has continually to demand that changes be made in things which are supported by powerful and widely-spread feelings, or to question the apparent necessity and indefeasibleness of established facts; and it is often an indispensable part of his argument to show, how those powerful feelings had their origin, and how those facts came to seem necessary and indefeasible. There is therefore a natural hostility between him and a philosophy which discourages the explanation of feelings and moral facts by circumstances and association, and prefers to treat them as ultimate elements of human nature; a philosophy which is addicted to holding up favourite doctrines as intuitive truths, and deems intuition to be the voice of Nature and of God, speaking with an authority higher than that of our reason. In particular, I have long felt that the prevailing tendency to regard all the marked distinctions of human character as innate, and in the main indelible, and to ignore the irresistible proofs that by far the greater part of those differences, whether between individuals, races, or sexes, are such as not only might but naturally would be produced by differences in circumstances, is one of the chief hindrances to the rational treatment of great social questions, and one of the greatest stumbling blocks to human improvement. This tendency has its source in the intuitional metaphysics which characterized the reaction of the nineteenth century against the eighteenth, and it is a tendency so agreeable to human indolence, as well as to conservative interests generally, that unless attacked at the very root, it is sure to be carried to even a greater length than is really justified by the more moderate forms of the intuitional philosophy. That philosophy, not always in its moderate forms, had ruled the thought of Europe for the greater part of a century. My father's Analysis of the Mind, my own Logic, and Professor Bain's great treatise, had attempted to re-introduce a better mode of philosophizing, latterly with quite as much success as could be expected; but I had for some time felt that the mere contrast of the two philosophies was not enough, that there ought to be a hand-to-hand fight between them, that controversial as well as expository writings were needed, and that the time was come when such controversy would be useful. Considering then the writings and fame of Sir W. Hamilton as the great fortress of the intuitional philosophy in this country, a fortress the more formidable from the imposing character, and the in many respects great personal merits and mental endowments, of the man, I thought it might be a real service to philosophy to attempt a thorough examination of all his most important doctrines, and an estimate of his general claims to eminence as a philosopher, and I was confirmed in this resolution by observing that in the writings of at least one, and him one of the ablest, of Sir W. Hamilton's followers, his peculiar doctrines were made the justification of a view of religion which I hold to be profoundly immoral—that it is our duty to bow down in worship before a Being whose moral attributes are affirmed to be unknowable by us, and to be perhaps extremely different from those which, when we are speaking of our fellow creatures, we call by the same names.

As I advanced in my task, the damage to Sir W. Hamilton's reputation became greater than I at first expected, through the almost incredible multitude of inconsistencies which showed themselves on comparing different passages with one another. It was my business, however, to show things exactly as they were, and I did not flinch from it. I endeavoured always to treat the philosopher whom I criticised with the most scrupulous fairness; and I knew that he had abundance of disciples and admirers to correct me if I ever unintentionally did him injustice. Many of them accordingly have answered me, more or less elaborately; and they have pointed out oversights and misunderstandings, though few in number, and mostly very unimportant in substance. Such of those as had (to my knowledge) been pointed out before the publication of the latest edition (at present the third) have been corrected there, and the remainder of the criticisms have been, as far as seemed necessary, replied to. On the whole, the book has done its work: it has shown the weak side of Sir William Hamilton, and has reduced his too great philosophical reputation within more moderate bounds; and by some of its discussions, as well as by two expository chapters, on the notions of Matter and of Mind, it has perhaps thrown additional light on some of the disputed questions in the domain of psychology and metaphysics.

After the completion of the book on Hamilton, I applied myself to a task which a variety of reasons seemed to render specially incumbent upon me; that of giving an account, and forming an estimate, of the doctrines of Auguste Comte. I had contributed more than any one else to make his speculations known in England, and, in consequence chiefly of what I had said of him in my Logic, he had readers and admirers among thoughtful men on this side of the Channel at a time when his name had not yet in France emerged from obscurity. So unknown and unappreciated was he at the time when my Logic was written and published, that to criticise his weak points might well appear superfluous, while it was a duty to give as much publicity as one could to the important contributions he had made to philosophic thought. At the time, however, at which I have now arrived, this state of affairs had entirely changed. His name, at least, was known almost universally, and the general character of his doctrines very widely. He had taken his place in the estimation both of friends and opponents, as one of the conspicuous figures in the thought of the age. The better parts of his speculations had made great progress in working their way into those minds, which, by their previous culture and tendencies, were fitted to receive them : under cover of those better parts those of a worse character, greatly developed and added to in his later writings, had also made some way, having obtained active and enthusiastic adherents, some of them of no inconsiderable personal merit, in England, France, and other countries. These causes not only made it desirable that some one should undertake the task of sifting what is good from what is bad in M. Comte's speculations, but seemed to impose on myself in particular a special obligation to make the attempt. This I accordingly did in two Essays, published in successive numbers of the Westminster Review, and reprinted in a small volume under the title ' Auguste Comte and Positivism.'

The writings which I have now mentioned, together with a small number of papers in periodicals which I have not deemed worth preserving, were the whole of the products of my activity as a writer during the years from 1859 to 1865. In the early part of the last-mentioned year, in compliance with a wish frequently expressed to me by working men, I published cheap People's Editions of those of my writings which seemed the most likely to find readers among the working classes ; viz., Principles of Political Economy, Liberty, and Representative Government. This was a considerable sacrifice of my pecuniary interest, especially as I resigned all idea of deriving profit from the cheap editions, and after ascertaining from my publishers the lowest price which they thought would remunerate them on the usual terms of an equal division of profits, I gave up my half share to enable the price to be fixed still lower. To the credit of Messrs. Longman they fixed, unasked, a certain number of years after which the copyright and stereotype plates were to revert to me, and a certain number of copies after the sale of which I should receive half of any further profit. This number of copies (which in the case of the Political Economy was 10,000) has for some time been exceeded, and the People's Editions have begun to yield me a small but unexpected pecuniary return, though very far from an equivalent for the diminution of profit from the Library Editions.

In this summary of my outward life I have now arrived at the period at which my tranquil and retired existence as a writer of books was to be exchanged for the less congenial occupation of a member of the House of Commons. The proposal made to me early in 1865, by some electors of Westminster, did not present the idea to me for the first time. It was not even the first offer I had received, for, more than ten years previous, in consequence of my opinions on the Irish Land Question, Mr. Lucas and Mr. Duffy, in the name of the popular party in Ireland, offered to bring me into Parliament for an Irish county, which they could easily have done : but the incompatibility of a seat in Parliament with the office I then held in the India House, precluded even consideration of the proposal. After I had quitted the India House, several of my friends would gladly have seen me a member of Parliament; but there seemed no probability that the idea would ever take any practical shape. I was convinced that no numerous or influential portion of any electoral body, really wished to be represented by a person of my opinions ; and that one who possessed no local connexion or popularity, and who did not choose to stand as the mere organ of a party, had small chance of being elected anywhere unless through the expenditure of money. Now it was, and is, my fixed conviction, that a candidate ought not to incur one farthing of expense for undertaking a public duty. Such of the lawful expenses of an election as have no special reference to any particular candidate, ought to be borne as a public charge, either by the State or by the locality. What has to be done by the supporters of each candidate in order to bring his claims properly before the constituency, should be done by unpaid agency, or by voluntary subscription. If members of the electoral body, or others, are willing to subscribe money of their own for the purpose of bringing, by lawful means, into Parliament some one who they think would be useful there, no one is entitled to object : but that the expense, or any part of it, should fall on the candidate, is fundamentally wrong ; because it amounts in reality to buying his seat. Even on the most favourable supposition as to the mode in which the money is expended, there is a legitimate suspicion that any one who gives money for leave to undertake a public trust, has other than public ends to promote by it ; and (a consideration of the greatest importance) the cost of elections, when borne by the candidates, deprives the nation of the services, as members of Parliament, of all who cannot or will not afford to incur a heavy expense. I do not say that, so long as there is scarcely a chance for an independent candidate to come into Parliament without complying with this vicious practice, it must always be morally wrong in him to spend money, provided that no part of it is either directly or indirectly employed in corruption. But, to

justify it, he ought to be very certain that he can
be of more use to his country as a member of
Parliament than in any other mode which is open
to him ; and this assurance, in my own case, I did
not feel. It was by no means clear to me that
I could do more to advance the public objects
which had a claim on my exertions, from the
benches of the House of Commons, than from the
simple position of a writer. I felt, therefore, that
I ought not to seek election to Parliament, much
less to expend any money in procuring it.

But the conditions of the question were considerably altered when a body of electors sought
me out, and spontaneously offered to bring me
forward as their candidate. If it should appear,
on explanation, that they persisted in this wish,
knowing my opinions, and accepting the only
conditions on which I could conscientiously serve,
it was questionable whether this was not one of
those calls upon a member of the community by
his fellow-citizens, which he was scarcely justified
in rejecting. I therefore put their disposition to
the proof by one of the frankest explanations ever
tendered, I should think, to an electoral body by
a candidate. I wrote, in reply to the offer, a letter
for publication, saying that I had no personal wish
to be a member of Parliament, that I thought
a candidate ought neither to canvass nor to incur
any expense, and that I could not consent to do
either. I said further, that if elected, I could not
undertake to give any of my time and labour to
their local interests. With respect to general
politics, I told them without reserve, what I
thought on a number of important subjects on
which they had asked my opinion ; and one of

these being the suffrage, I made known to them, among other things, my conviction (as I was bound to do, since I intended, if elected, to act on it), that women were entitled to representation in Parliament on the same terms with men. It was the first time, doubtless, that such a doctrine had ever been mentioned to English electors; and the fact that I was elected after proposing it, gave the start to the movement which has since become so vigorous, in favour of women's suffrage. Nothing, at the time, appeared more unlikely than that a candidate (if candidate I could be called) whose professions and conduct set so completely at defiance all ordinary notions of electioneering, should nevertheless be elected. A well-known literary man was heard to say that the Almighty himself would have no chance of being elected on such a programme. I strictly adhered to it, neither spending money nor canvassing, nor did I take any personal part in the election, until about a week preceding the day of nomination, when I attended a few public meetings to state my principles and give answers to any questions which the electors might exercise their just right of putting to me for their own guidance; answers as plain and unreserved as my address. On one subject only, my religious opinions, I announced from the beginning that I would answer no questions; a determination which appeared to be completely approved by those who attended the meetings. My frankness on all other subjects on which I was interrogated, evidently did me far more good than my answers, whatever they might be, did harm. Among the proofs I received of this, one is too remarkable not to be recorded. In the pamphlet, 'Thoughts on

Parliamentary Reform,' I had said, rather bluntly, that the working classes, though differing from those of some other countries, in being ashamed of lying, are yet generally liars. This passage some opponent got printed in a placard, which was handed to me at a meeting, chiefly composed of the working classes, and I was asked whether I had written and published it. I at once answered ' I did.' Scarcely were these two words out of my mouth, when vehement applause resounded through the whole meeting. It was evident that the working people were so accustomed to expect equivocation and evasion from those who sought their suffrages, that when they found, instead of that, a direct avowal of what was likely to be disagreeable to them, instead of being affronted, they concluded at once that this was a person whom they could trust. A more striking instance never came under my notice of what, I believe, is the experience of those who best know the working classes, that the most essential of all recommendations to their favour is that of complete straight-forwardness ; its presence outweighs in their minds very strong objections, while no amount of other qualities will make amends for its apparent absence. The first working man who spoke after the incident I have mentioned (it was Mr. Odger) said, that the working classes had no desire not to be told of their faults ; they wanted friends, not flatterers, and felt under obligation to any one who told them anything in themselves which he sincerely believed to require amendment. And to this the meeting heartily responded.

Had I been defeated in the election, I should still have had no reason to regret the contact it had

brought me into with large bodies of my country-
men ; which not only gave me much new experience, but enabled me to scatter my political
opinions more widely, and, by making me known
in many quarters where I had never before been
heard of, increased the number of my readers, and
the presumable influence of my writings. These
latter effects were of course produced in a still
greater degree, when, as much to my surprise as
to that of any one, I was returned to Parliament
by a majority of some hundreds over my Conservative competitor.

I was a member of the House during the three
sessions of the Parliament which passed the Reform
Bill ; during which time Parliament was necessarily
my main occupation, except during the recess.
I was a tolerably frequent speaker, sometimes of
prepared speeches, sometimes extemporaneously.
But my choice of occasions was not such as I should
have made if my leading object had been Parliamentary influence. When I had gained the ear
of the House, which I did by a successful speech
on Mr. Gladstone's Reform Bill, the idea I proceeded on was that when anything was likely to
be as well done, or sufficiently well done, by other
people, there was no necessity for me to meddle
with it. As I, therefore, in general reserved myself
for work which no others were likely to do, a great
proportion of my appearances were on points on
which the bulk of the Liberal party, even the
advanced portion of it, either were of a different
opinion from mine, or were comparatively indifferent. Several of my speeches, especially one
against the motion for the abolition of capital
punishment, and another in favour of resuming the

right of seizing enemies' goods in neutral vessels, were opposed to what then was, and probably still is, regarded as the advanced Liberal opinion. My advocacy of women's suffrage and of Personal Representation, were at the time looked upon by many as whims of my own; but the great progress since made by those opinions, and especially the response made from almost all parts of the kingdom to the demand for women's suffrage, fully justified the timeliness of those movements, and have made what was undertaken as a moral and social duty, a personal success. Another duty which was particularly incumbent on me as one of the metropolitan members, was the attempt to obtain a Municipal Government for the Metropolis: but on that subject the indifference of the House of Commons was such that I found hardly any help or support within its walls. On this subject, however, I was the organ of an active and intelligent body of persons outside, with whom and not with me, the scheme originated, and who carried on all the agitation on the subject and drew up the Bills. My part was to bring in Bills already prepared, and to sustain the discussion of them during the short time they were allowed to remain before the House; after having taken an active part in the work of a Committee presided over by Mr. Ayrton, which sat through the greater part of the session of 1866, to take evidence on the subject. The very different position in which the question now stands (1870) may justly be attributed to the preparation which went on during those years, and which produced but little visible effect at the time; but all questions on which there are strong private interests on one side, and only the public good on the other, have a similar period of incubation to go through.

The same idea, that the use of my being in Parliament was to do work which others were not able or not willing to do, made me think it my duty to come to the front in defence of advanced Liberalism on occasions when the obloquy to be encountered was such as most of the advanced Liberals in the House, preferred not to incur. My first vote in the House was in support of an amendment in favour of Ireland, moved by an Irish member, and for which only five English and Scotch votes were given, including my own: the other four were Mr. Bright, Mr M'Laren, Mr. T. B. Potter, and Mr. Hadfield. And the second speech I delivered [1] was on the Bill to prolong the suspension of the Habeas Corpus in Ireland. In denouncing, on this occasion, the English mode of governing Ireland, I did no more than the general opinion of England now admits to have been just; but the anger against Fenianism was then in all its freshness; any attack on what Fenians attacked was looked upon as an apology for them; and I was so unfavourably received by the House, that more than one of my friends advised me (and my own judgment agreed with the advice) to wait, before speaking again, for the favourable opportunity that would be given by the first great debate on the Reform Bill. During this silence, many

---

[1] The first was in answer to Mr. Lowe's reply to Mr. Bright on the Cattle Plague Bill, and was thought at the time to have helped to get rid of a provision in the Government measure which would have given to landholders a second indemnity, after they had already been once indemnified for the loss of some of their cattle by the increased selling price of the remainder.

flattered themselves that I had turned out a failure, and that they should not be troubled with me any more. Perhaps their uncomplimentary comments may, by the force of reaction, have helped to make my speech on the Reform Bill the success it was. My position in the House was further improved by a speech in which I insisted on the duty of paying off the National Debt before our coal supplies are exhausted, and by an ironical reply to some of the Tory leaders who had quoted against me certain passages of my writings, and called me to account for others, especially for one in my ' Considerations on Representative Government,' which said that the Conservative party was, by the law of its composition, the stupidest party. They gained nothing by drawing attention to the passage, which up to that time had not excited any notice, but the *sobriquet* of ' the stupid party ' stuck to them for a considerable time afterwards. Having now no longer any apprehension of not being listened to, I confined myself, as I have since thought too much, to occasions on which my services seemed specially needed, and abstained more than enough from speaking on the great party questions. With the exception of Irish questions, and those which concerned the working classes, a single speech on Mr. Disraeli's Reform Bill was nearly all that I contributed to the great decisive debates of the last two of my three sessions.

I have, however, much satisfaction in looking back to the part I took on the two classes of subjects just mentioned. With regard to the working classes, the chief topic of my speech on Mr. Gladstone's Reform Bill was the assertion of their claims to the suffrage. A little later, after the resignation of Lord Russell's Ministry and the succession of a Tory Government, came the attempt of the working classes to hold a meeting in Hyde Park, their exclusion by the police, and the breaking down of the park railing by the crowd. Though Mr. Beales and the leaders of the working men had retired under protest when this took place, a scuffle ensued in which many innocent persons were maltreated by the police, and the exasperation of the working men was extreme. They showed a determination to make another attempt at a meeting in the Park, to which many of them would probably have come armed; the Government made military preparations to resist the attempt, and something very serious seemed impending. At this crisis I really believe that I was the means of preventing much mischief. I had in my place in Parliament taken the side of the working men, and strongly censured the conduct of the Government. I was invited, with several other Radical members, to a conference with the leading members of the Council of the Reform League; and the task fell chiefly upon myself, of persuading them to give up the Hyde Park project, and hold their meeting elsewhere. It was not Mr. Beales and Colonel Dickson who needed persuading; on the contrary, it was evident that these gentlemen had already exerted their influence in the same direction, thus far without success. It was the working men who held out, and so bent were they on their original scheme, that I was obliged to have recourse to *les grands moyens*. I told them that a proceeding which would certainly produce a collision with the military, could only be justifiable on two conditions : if the position of affairs had become such that a revolution was desirable, and if they thought themselves able to accomplish one. To this argument, after considerable discussion, they at last yielded : and I was able to inform Mr. Walpole that their intention was given up. I shall never forget the depth of his relief or the warmth of his expressions of gratitude. After the working men had conceded so much to me, I felt bound to comply with their request that I would attend and speak at their meeting at the Agricultural Hall ; the only meeting called by the Reform League which I ever attended. I had always declined being a member of the League, on the avowed ground that I did not agree in its programme of manhood suffrage and the ballot : from the ballot I dissented entirely ; and I could not consent to hoist the flag of manhood suffrage, even on the assurance that the exclusion of women was not intended to be implied ; since if one goes beyond what can be immediately carried, and professes to take one's stand on a principle, one should go the whole length of the principle. I have entered thus particularly into this matter because my conduct on this occasion gave great displeasure to the Tory and Tory-Liberal press, who have charged me ever since with having shown myself, in the trials of public life, intemperate and passionate. I do not know what they expected from me ; but they had reason to be thankful to me if they knew from what I had, in all probability, preserved them. And I do not believe it could have been done, at that particular juncture, by any one else. No other person, I believe, had at that moment the necessary influence for restraining the working classes, except Mr. Gladstone and Mr. Bright, neither of whom was available : Mr. Gladstone for obvious reasons ; Mr. Bright because he was out of town.

When, some time later, the Tory Government brought in a Bill to prevent public meetings in the Parks, I not only spoke strongly in opposition to it, but formed one of a number of advanced Liberals, who, aided by the very late period of the session, succeeded in defeating [1] the Bill by what is called talking it out. It has not since been renewed.

On Irish affairs also I felt bound to take a decided part. I was one of the foremost in the deputation of members of Parliament who prevailed on Lord Derby to spare the life of the condemned Fenian insurgent, General Burke. The Church question was so vigorously handled by the leaders of the party, in the session of 1868, as to require no more from me than an emphatic adhesion : but the land question was by no means in so advanced a position : the superstitions of landlordism had up to that time been little challenged, especially in Parliament, and the backward state of the question, so far as concerned the Parliamentary mind, was evidenced by the extremely mild measure brought in by Lord Russell's Government in 1866, which nevertheless could not be carried. On that Bill I delivered one of my most careful speeches, in which I attempted to lay down some of the principles of the subject, in a manner calculated less to stimulate friends, than to conciliate and convince opponents. The engrossing subject of Parliamentary Reform

[1] defending *1873* : misprint.

prevented either this Bill, or one of a similar
character brought in by Lord Derby's Government, from being carried through. They never
got beyond the second reading. Meanwhile the
signs of Irish disaffection had become much more
decided; the demand for complete separation
between the two countries had assumed a menacing
aspect, and there were few who did not feel that if
there was still any chance of reconciling Ireland to
the British connexion, it could only be by the
adoption of much more thorough reforms in the
territorial and social relations of the country, than
had yet been contemplated. The time seemed to
me to have come when it would be useful to speak
out my whole mind; and the result was my
pamphlet 'England and Ireland,' which was
written in the winter of 1867, and published
shortly before the commencement of the session
of 1868. The leading features of the pamphlet
were, on the one hand, an argument to show the
undesirableness, for Ireland as well as for England,
of separation between the countries, and on the
other, a proposal for settling the land question by
giving to the existing tenants a permanent tenure,
at a fixed rent, to be assessed after due inquiry by
the State.

The pamphlet was not popular, except in
Ireland, as I did not expect it to be. But, if no
measure short of that which I proposed would do
full justice to Ireland, or afford a prospect of
conciliating the mass of the Irish people, the duty
of proposing it was imperative; while if, on the
other hand, there was any intermediate course
which had a claim to a trial, I well know that to
propose something which would be called extreme,

was the true way not to impede but to facilitate a more moderate experiment. It is most improbable that a measure conceding so much to the tenantry as Mr. Gladstone's Irish Land Bill, would have been proposed by a Government, or could have been carried through Parliament, unless the British public had been led to perceive that a case might be made, and perhaps a party formed, for a measure considerably stronger. It is the character of the British people, or at least of the higher and middle classes who pass muster for the British people, that to induce them to approve of any change, it is necessary that they should look upon it as a middle course : they think every proposal extreme and violent unless they hear of some other proposal going still farther, upon which their antipathy to extreme views may discharge itself. So it proved in the present instance ; my proposal was condemned, but any scheme for Irish Land reform, short of mine, came to be thought moderate by comparison. I may observe that the attacks made on my plan usually gave a very incorrect idea of its nature. It was usually discussed as a proposal that the State should buy up the land and become the universal landlord ; though in fact it only offered to each individual landlord this as an alternative, if he liked better to sell his estate than to retain it on the new conditions ; and I fully anticipated that most landlords would continue to prefer the position of landowners to that of Government annuitants, and would retain their existing relation to their tenants, often on more indulgent terms than the full rents on which the compensation to be given them by Government would have been based. This and many other explanations I gave in a speech on Ireland, in the debate on Mr. Maguire's resolution, early in the session of 1868. A corrected report of this speech, together with my speech on Mr. Fortescue's Bill, has been published (not by me, but with my permission) in Ireland.

Another public duty, of a most serious kind, it was my lot to have to perform, both in and out of Parliament, during these years. A disturbance in Jamaica, provoked in the first instance by injustice, and exaggerated by rage and panic into a premeditated rebellion, had been the motive or excuse for taking hundreds of innocent lives by military violence, or by sentence of what were called courts-martial, continuing for weeks after the brief disturbance had been put down; with many atrocities of destruction of property, flogging women as well as men, and a general display of the brutal recklessness which usually prevails when fire and sword are let loose. The perpetrators of those deeds were defended and applauded in England by the same kind of people who had so long upheld negro slavery: and it seemed at first as if the British nation was about to incur the disgrace of letting pass without even a protest, excesses of authority as revolting as any of those for which, when perpetrated by the instruments of other Governments, Englishmen can hardly find terms sufficient to express their abhorrence. After a short time, however, an indignant feeling was roused: a voluntary Association formed itself under the name of the Jamaica Committee, to take such deliberation and action as the case might admit of, and adhesions poured in from all parts of the country. I was abroad at the time, but I sent in my name to the Committee as soon as I heard of it, and took an active part in the proceedings from the time of my return. There was much more at stake than only justice to the Negroes, imperative as was that consideration. The question was, whether the British dependencies, and eventually, perhaps, Great Britain itself, were to be under the government of law, or of military licence; whether the lives and persons of British subjects are at the mercy of any two or three officers however raw and inexperienced or reckless and brutal, whom a panic-stricken Governor, or other functionary, may assume the right to constitute into a so-called court-martial. This question could only be decided by an appeal to the tribunals; and such an appeal the Committee determined to make. Their determination led to a change in the chairmanship of the Committee, as the chairman, Mr. Charles Buxton, thought it not unjust indeed, but inexpedient, to prosecute Governor Eyre and his principal subordinates in a criminal court: but a numerously attended general meeting of the Association having decided this point against him, Mr. Buxton withdrew from the Committee, though continuing to work in the cause, and I was, quite unexpectedly on my own part, proposed and elected chairman. It became, in consequence, my duty to represent the Committee in the House of Commons, sometimes by putting questions to the Government, sometimes as the recipient of questions, more or less provocative, addressed by individual members to myself; but especially as speaker in the important debate originated in the session of 1866, by

Mr. Buxton: and the speech I then delivered is that which I should probably select as the best of my speeches in Parliament.[1] For more than two years we carried on the combat, trying every avenue legally open to us, to the Courts of Criminal Justice. A bench of magistrates in one of the most Tory counties in England dismissed our case: we were more successful before the magistrates at Bow Street; which gave an opportunity to the Lord Chief Justice of the Queen's Bench, Sir Alexander Cockburn, for delivering his celebrated charge, which settled the law of the question in favour of liberty, as far as it is in the power of a judge's charge to settle it. There, however, our success ended, for the Old Bailey Grand Jury by throwing out our Bill prevented the case from coming to trial. It was clear that to bring English functionaries to the bar of a criminal court for abuses of power committed against negroes and mulattoes was not a popular proceeding with the English middle classes. We had, however, redeemed, so far as lay in us, the character of our country, by showing that there was at any rate a body of persons determined to use all the means which the law afforded to obtain justice for the injured. We had elicited from the highest criminal judge in the nation an authoritative declaration that the law was what we maintained it to be; and we had given an emphatic warning to those

---

[1] Among the most active members of the Committee were Mr. P. A. Taylor, M.P., always faithful and energetic in every assertion of the principles of liberty; Mr. Goldwin Smith, Mr. Frederick Harrison, Mr. Slack, Mr. Chamerovzow, Mr. Shaen, and Mr. Chesson, the Honorary Secretary of the Association.

who might be tempted to similar guilt hereafter, that, though they might escape the actual sentence of a criminal tribunal, they were not safe against being put to some trouble and expense in order to avoid it. Colonial governors and other persons in authority, will have a considerable motive to stop short of such extremities in future.

As a matter of curiosity I kept some specimens of the abusive letters, almost all of them anonymous, which I received while these proceedings were going on. They are evidence of the sympathy felt with the brutalities in Jamaica by the brutal part of the population at home. They graduated from coarse jokes, verbal and pictorial, up to threats of assassination.

Among other matters of importance in which I took an active part, but which excited little interest in the public, two deserve particular mention. I joined with several other independent Liberals in defeating an Extradition Bill introduced at the very end of the session of 1866, and by which, though surrender avowedly for political offences was not authorized, political refugees, if charged by a foreign Government with acts which are necessarily incident to all attempts at insurrection, would have been surrendered to be dealt with by the criminal courts of the Government against which they had rebelled : thus making the British Government an accomplice in the vengeance of foreign despotisms. The defeat of this proposal led to the appointment of a Select Committee (in which I was included), to examine and report on the whole subject of Extradition Treaties ; and the result was, that in the Extradition Act which passed through Parliament after I had ceased to be a member, opportunity is given to any one whose extradition is demanded, of being heard before an English court of justice to prove that the offence with which he is charged, is really political. The cause of European freedom has thus been saved from a serious misfortune, and our own country from a great iniquity. The other subject to be mentioned is the fight kept up by a body of advanced Liberals in the session of 1868, on the Bribery Bill of Mr. Disraeli's Government, in which I took a very active part. I had taken counsel with several of those who had applied their minds most carefully to the details of the subject—Mr. W. D. Christie, Serjeant Pulling, Mr. Chadwick—as well as bestowed much thought of my own, for the purpose of framing such amendments and additional clauses as might make the Bill really effective against the numerous modes of corruption, direct and indirect, which might otherwise, as there was much reason to fear, be increased instead of diminished by the Reform Act. We also aimed at engrafting on the Bill, measures for diminishing the mischievous burden of what are called the legitimate expenses of elections. Among our many amendments, was that of Mr. Fawcett for making the returning officer's expenses a charge on the rates, instead of on the candidates ; another was the prohibition of paid canvassers, and the limitation of paid agents to one for each candidate ; a third was the extension of the precautions and penalties against bribery, to municipal elections, which are well known to be not only a preparatory school for bribery at Parliamentary elections, but an habitual cover for it. The Conservative Government, however, when once they had carried the leading provision of their Bill (for which I voted and spoke), the transfer of the jurisdiction in elections from the House of Commons to the Judges, made a determined resistance to all other improvements; and after one of the most important proposals, that of Mr. Fawcett, had actually obtained a majority, they summoned the strength of their party and threw out the clause in a subsequent stage. The Liberal party in the House was greatly dishonoured by the conduct of many of its members in giving no help whatever to this attempt to secure the necessary conditions of an honest representation of the people. With their large majority in the House they could have carried all the amendments, or better ones if they had better to propose. But it was late in the session; members were eager to set about their preparations for the impending General Election: and while some (such as Sir Robert Anstruther) honourably remained at their post, though rival candidates were already canvassing their constituency, a much greater number placed their electioneering interests before their public duty. Many Liberals also looked with indifference on legislation against bribery, thinking that it merely diverted public interest from the Ballot, which they considered, very mistakenly as I expect it will turn out, to be a sufficient, and the only, remedy. From these causes our fight, though kept up with great vigour for several nights, was wholly unsuccessful, and the practices which we sought to render more difficult, prevailed more widely than ever in the first General Election held under the new electoral law.

In the general debates on Mr. Disraeli's Reform

Bill, my participation was limited to the one speech already mentioned; but I made the Bill an occasion for bringing the two greatest improvements which remain to be made in Representative Government, formally before the House and the nation. One of them was Personal, or, as it is called with equal propriety, Proportional Representation. I brought this under the consideration of the House, by an expository and argumentative speech on Mr. Hare's plan; and subsequently I was active in support of the very imperfect substitute for that plan, which, in a small number of constituencies, Parliament was induced to adopt. This poor makeshift had scarcely any recommendation, except that it was a partial recognition of the evil which it did so little to remedy. As such, however, it was attacked by the same fallacies, and required to be defended on the same principles, as a really good measure; and its adoption in a few Parliamentary elections, as well as the subsequent introduction of what is called the Cumulative Vote in the elections for the London School Board, have had the good effect of converting the equal claim of all electors to a proportional share in the representation, from a subject of merely speculative discussion, into a question of practical politics, much sooner than would otherwise have been the case.

This assertion of my opinions on Personal Representation cannot be credited with any considerable or visible amount of practical result. It was otherwise with the other motion which I made in the form of an amendment to the Reform Bill, and which was by far the most important, perhaps the only really important, public service

I performed in the capacity of a member of Parliament: a motion to strike out the words which were understood to limit the electoral franchise to males, and thereby to admit to the suffrage all women who, as householders or otherwise, possessed the qualification required of male electors. For women not to make their claim to the suffrage, at the time when the elective franchise was being largely extended, would have been to abjure the claim altogether; and a movement on the subject was begun in 1866, when I presented a petition for the suffrage, signed by a considerable number of distinguished women. But it was as yet uncertain whether the proposal would obtain more than a few stray votes in the House: and when, after a debate in which the speakers on the contrary side were conspicuous by their feebleness, the votes recorded in favour of the motion amounted to 73—made up by pairs and tellers to above 80—the surprise was general, and the encouragement great: the greater, too, because one of those who voted for the motion was Mr. Bright, a fact which could only be attributed to the impression made on him by the debate, as he had previously made no secret of his non-concurrence in the proposal.   *   *   *   *   *

I believe I have mentioned all that is worth remembering of my proceedings in the House. But their enumeration, even if complete, would give but an inadequate idea of my occupations during that period, and especially of the time taken up by correspondence. For many years before my election to Parliament, I had been continually receiving letters from strangers, mostly addressed to me as a writer on philosophy, and either propounding difficulties or communicating thoughts on subjects connected with logic or political economy. In common, I suppose, with all who are known as political economists, I was a recipient of all the shallow theories and absurd proposals by which people are perpetually endeavouring to show the way to universal wealth and happiness by some artful reorganization of the currency. When there were signs of sufficient intelligence in the writers to make it worth while attempting to put them right, I took the trouble to point out their errors, until the growth of my correspondence made it necessary to dismiss such persons with very brief answers. Many, however, of the communications I received were more worthy of attention than these, and in some, over-sights of detail were pointed out in my writings, which I was thus enabled to correct. Correspondence of this sort naturally multiplied with the multiplication of the subjects on which I wrote, especially those of a metaphysical character. But when I became a member of Parliament, I began to receive letters on private grievances and on every imaginable subject that related to any kind of public affairs, however remote from my knowledge or pursuits. It was not my constituents in Westminster who laid this burden on me: they kept with remarkable fidelity to the understanding on which I had consented to serve. I received, indeed, now and then an application from some ingenuous youth to procure for him a small Government appointment; but these were few, and how simple and ignorant the writers were, was shown by the fact that the applications came in about equally whichever party was in power. My invariable answer was, that it was contrary to the principles on which I was elected to ask favours of any Government. But, on the whole, hardly any part of the country gave me less trouble than my own constituents. The general mass of correspondence, however, swelled into an oppressive burden.   *   *   *   *   *

*   *   *   *   *   *

*   *   *   *   *   *   *

While I remained in Parliament my work as an author was unavoidably limited to the recess. During that time I wrote (besides the pamphlet on Ireland, already mentioned), the Essay on Plato, published in the Edinburgh Review, and reprinted in the third volume of ' Dissertations and Discussions ; ' and the address which, conformably to custom, I delivered to the University of St. Andrew's, whose students had done me the honour of electing me to the office of Rector.   In this Discourse I gave expression to many thoughts and opinions which had been accumulating in me through life, respecting the various studies which belong to a liberal education, their uses and influences, and the mode in which they should be pursued to render their influences most beneficial. The position taken up, vindicating the high educational value alike of the old classic and the new scientific studies, on even stronger grounds than are urged by most of their advocates, and insisting that it is only the stupid inefficiency of the usual teaching which makes those studies be regarded as competitors instead of allies, was, I think, calculated, not only to aid and stimulate the improvement which has happily commenced in the national institutions for higher education, but to diffuse juster ideas than we often find, even in highly educated men, on the conditions of the highest mental cultivation.

During this period also I commenced (and completed soon after I had left Parliament) the performance of a duty to philosophy and to the memory of my father, by preparing and publishing an edition of the ' Analysis of the Phenomena of the Human Mind,' with notes bringing up the doctrines of that admirable book to the latest improvements in science and in speculation. This was a joint undertaking: the psychological notes being furnished in about equal proportions by Mr. Bain and myself, while Mr. Grote supplied some valuable contributions on points in the history of philosophy incidentally raised, and Dr. Andrew Findlater supplied the deficiencies in the book which had been occasioned by the imperfect philological knowledge of the time when it was written. Having been originally published at a time when the current of metaphysical speculation ran in a quite opposite direction to the psychology of Experience and Association, the ' Analysis ' had not obtained the amount of immediate success which it deserved, though it had made a deep impression on many individual minds, and had largely contributed, through those minds, to create that more favourable atmosphere for the Association Psychology of which we now have the benefit. Admirably adapted for a class-book of the Experience Metaphysics, it only required to be enriched, and in some cases corrected, by the results of more recent labours in the same school of thought, to stand, as it now does, in

company with Mr. Bain's treatises, at the head of
the systematic works on Analytic Psychology.

In the autumn of 1868 the Parliament which
passed the Reform Act was dissolved, and at the
new election for Westminster I was thrown out;
not to my surprise, nor, I believe, to that of my
principal supporters, though in the few days
preceding the election they had become more
sanguine than before. That I should not have
been elected at all would not have required any
explanation; what excites curiosity is that I
should have been elected the first time, or, having
been elected then, should have been defeated
afterwards. But the efforts made to defeat me
were far greater on the second occasion than on
the first. For one thing, the Tory Government
was now struggling for existence, and success in
any contest was of more importance to them.
Then, too, all persons of Tory feelings were far
more embittered against me individually than
on the previous occasion; many who had at
first been either favourable or indifferent, were
vehemently opposed to my re-election. As I had
shown in my political writings that I was aware
of the weak points in democratic opinions, some
Conservatives, it seems, had not been without
hopes of finding me an opponent of democracy:
as I was able to see the Conservative side of the
question, they presumed that, like them, I could
not see any other side. Yet if they had really
read my writings, they would have known that
after giving full weight to all that appeared to me
well grounded in the arguments against democracy,
I unhesitatingly decided in its favour, while
recommending that it should be accompanied by

such institutions as were consistent with its
principle and calculated to ward off its incon-
veniences : one of the chief of these remedies being
Proportional Representation, on which scarcely
any of the Conservatives gave me any support.
Some Tory expectations appear to have been
founded on the approbation I had expressed of
plural voting, under certain conditions : and it
has been surmised that the suggestion of this sort
made in one of the resolutions which Mr. Disraeli
introduced into the House preparatory to his
Reform Bill (a suggestion which meeting with
no favour he did not press), may have been
occasioned by what I had written on the point :
but if so, it was forgotten that I had made it an
express condition that the privilege of a plurality
of votes should be annexed to education, not to
property, and even so, had approved of it only on
the supposition of universal suffrage. How utterly
inadmissible such plural voting would be under
the suffrage given by the present Reform Act, is
proved, to any who could otherwise doubt it, by
the very small weight which the working classes
are found to possess in elections, even under the
law which gives no more votes to any one elector
than to any other.

While I thus was far more obnoxious to the
Tory interest, and to many Conservative Liberals
than I had formerly been, the course I pursued in
Parliament had by no means been such as to make
Liberals generally at all enthusiastic in my support.
It has already been mentioned, how large a pro-
portion of my prominent appearances had been on
questions on which I differed from most of the
Liberal party, or about which they cared little, and

how few occasions there had been on which the
line I took was such as could lead them to attach
any great value to me as an organ of their opinions.
I had moreover done things which had excited,
in many minds, a personal prejudice against me.
Many were offended by what they called the
persecution of Mr. Eyre : and still greater offence
was taken at my sending a subscription to the
election expenses of Mr. Bradlaugh. Having
refused to be at any expense for my own election,
and having had all its expenses defrayed by
others, I felt under a peculiar obligation to
subscribe in my turn where funds were deficient
for candidates whose election was desirable.
I accordingly sent subscriptions to nearly all the
working class candidates, and among others to
Mr. Bradlaugh. He had the support of the working
classes ; having heard him speak, I knew him to
be a man of ability, and he had proved that he was
the reverse of a demagogue, by placing himself in
strong opposition to the prevailing opinion of the
democratic party on two such important subjects
as Malthusianism and Personal Representation.
Men of this sort, who, while sharing the democratic feelings of the working classes, judged
political questions for themselves, and had
courage to assert their individual convictions
against popular opposition, were needed, as it
seemed to me, in Parliament, and I did not think
that Mr. Bradlaugh's anti-religious opinions (even
though he had been intemperate in the expression
of them) ought to exclude him. In subscribing,
however, to his election, I did what would have
been highly imprudent if I had been at liberty to

consider only the interests of my own re-election; and, as might be expected, the utmost possible use, both fair and unfair, was made of this act of mine to stir up the electors of Westminster against me. To these various causes, combined with an unscrupulous use of the usual pecuniary and other influences on the side of my Tory competitor, while none were used on my side, it is to be ascribed that I failed at my second election after having succeeded at the first. No sooner was the result of the election known than I received three or four invitations to become a candidate for other constituencies, chiefly counties; but even if success could have been expected, and this without expense, I was not disposed to deny myself the relief of returning to private life. I had no cause to feel humiliated at my rejection by the electors; and if I had, the feeling would have been far outweighed by the numerous expressions of regret which I received from all sorts of persons and places, and in a most marked degree from those members of the Liberal party in Parliament, with whom I had been accustomed to act.

Since that time little has occurred which there is need to commemorate in this place. I returned to my old pursuits and to the enjoyment of a country life in the south of Europe, alternating twice a year with a residence of some few weeks or months in the neighbourhood of London. I have written various articles in periodicals (chiefly in my friend Mr. Morley's Fortnightly Review), have made a small number of speeches on public occasions, have published the 'Subjection of Women,' written some years before, with some

additions   *   *   *   *   and
have commenced the preparation of matter for
future books, of which it will be time to speak
more particularly if I live to finish them. Here
therefore, for the present, this memoir may close.

SPEECH ON
THE UTILITY OF KNOWLEDGE

Spoken at the Mutual Improvement Society in 1823

THE beneficial effects produced upon the human mind and upon the structure of society by the revival of science and by the cessation of feudal darkness have been so obvious that there is scarcely room for the smallest discussion. No one, I apprehend, would insult the understanding of this Society by reviving the ascetic sophistry of the fanatic Rousseau by maintaining that what are called the comforts and conveniences of life are in fact neither comforts nor conveniences, and add not the smallest particle to human happiness; that the progress of civilization is in fact the progress of barbarism, and that the Hurons and the Iroquois are the happiest and the most enlightened of mankind. Were such a reasoner to arise I should ask him by what authority he claims to know better than A, B, and C what constitutes the happiness of A, B, and C. I should maintain that what all men have uniformly considered as comforts and conveniences cannot be otherwise than comforts and conveniences, and I should require him who considers knowledge as standing in the way of happiness to go and legislate for those savages upon whose blissful state of ignorance he would have an opportunity of trying his skill without those obstacles which he finds in the knowledge of this comparatively enlightened country.

Such doctrines are scarcely worthy of a serious reply, but as the refutation may be made remarkably pointed and concise, it may be better to give it. In reasoning on these general questions a want of precision in the use of language is the principal engine of sophistry. Here the confusion lies in the word *knowledge*, a word so vague and indefinite as to be an easy instrument in the hands of *mala fide* arguers, being capable of signifying just as much or as little as they please. It is not this kind of knowledge which is of such extensive importance. The only useful knowledge is that which teaches us how to seek what is good and avoid what is evil ; in short, how to increase the sum of human happiness. This is the great end : it may be well or ill pursued, but to say that knowledge can be an enemy to happiness is to say that men will enjoy less happiness, when they know how to seek it, than when they do not. This reasoning is on a par with that of any one who should refuse when asked to point out the road to York, saying that his inquirer would have a much better chance of reaching York without direction than with it. It is impossible then to suppose that any one should get up in this Society and maintain that knowledge in the abstract is mischievous. Arguments may indeed be directed against much of what passes current under the name of knowledge to show that it is not really knowledge but prejudice, and is therefore not favourable but unfavourable to happiness. But this is one of those cases where the reason of the exception proves the truth of the general rule. It is precisely because knowledge is useful that prejudice is mischievous.

The question, simple in itself, is in some degree confused by the manner in which it is worded, and which, with deference to the worthy proposer, might, I conceive, have been made more clearly expressive of his meaning. If asked whether the revival of letters has tended to promote happiness I know what to say, and by what arguments to support it; but if I am asked whether it tends to refine or to corrupt manners I confess myself at a stand. The three words, manners, corrupt, and refine, are to me in the sense here bestowed upon them equally enigmatical. If by refinement of manners is meant that ceremonious politeness in intercourse between the higher orders, and that assiduous gallantry towards the fair sex which were the distinguishing characteristics of the old feudal aristocracy, then I should say that manners had not gained but lost by the revival of letters: but far from lamenting I should rejoice in the change, as I do in everything which turns the attention of mankind from the frivolous details of a petty and ceremonious trifling to the concerns which interest their real and substantial welfare. But if the intention of the proposer was to inquire into the effect of increased civilization in promoting genuine morality, then although on a general view of the question all will probably agree with me that this effect has been highly beneficial, it will be no loss of time to examine in detail from how dreadful a state of misery the human race has been elevated by knowledge into a state where they have at least the hope, the speedy hope, of establishing a better state of things.

The revival of art and science has contributed to promote morality in two ways : by the increase of wealth and by the diffusion of information. The discoveries in chemical and mechanical philosophy—should I not rather say the creation of these branches of knowledge ?—has enabled the human race to provide themselves abundantly at little expense of labour with those necessaries and comforts which formerly they either could not procure at all, or if at all, only in a very small amount and with very great labour. This increase of wealth must have contributed greatly to the improvement of morality. I would not be understood as affirming that the rich are more moral than the poor. As far as general reasoning and my own particular experience can lead me I should rather adopt the contrary conclusion. But when the augmentation of wealth is not, by being confined in the hands of a few, reduced to be but one expedient more for the oppression of the many ; when, I say, instead of being exclusively devoted to the enjoyment of a few, the increase of wealth is generally and equally diffused throughout the whole community ; then by conferring upon the working classes the inestimable benefit of leisure, it forces them to seek society, it forces them to seek education. Each working man becomes himself better qualified to distinguish right from wrong, while each knows that he is under the constant surveillance of hundreds and thousands equally instructed with himself. Thus does the improvement of the physical sciences, by increasing and diffusing wealth, indirectly tend to promote morality.

But the evils which man is doomed to suffer

from the hands of nature are nothing when compared to those which man frequently suffers from man. Communities have been known to flourish in spots which Nature seems to have selected for the sepulchre of the universe; but there is no country, however favoured by nature, which superstition and misgovernment do not suffice to ruin. Let us therefore take a general view of the situation of our ancestors with respect to these two main points, religion and government.

And first as to their government: he must be an adept in the art of rendering mankind miserable who could devise anything more destructive of all happiness. It was not here the common vice of a rude government, where each man has not yet learned to trust his neighbour, and where no one will as yet renounce the privilege of protecting himself. These are imperfect governments, for they afford imperfect securities for happiness, but they are not in every sense as execrable as the feudal system. Imagine a tribe with a government such as that to which I have alluded spreading itself by conquest over a large portion of the globe, and reducing the native population to the state of domestic cattle! Each chief absolute master of thousands of human beings, and himself acknowledging no regular government, but striving to retain his pristine independency! Not only is no one secure from the arbitrary will of a master; even that master cannot afford him protection against other despots and slaves! It has frequently been made a question whether despotism or anarchy is worst; but this is not the question here, for the feudal system united the evils of both. The laws were openly and flagrantly violated, and the violations remained unpunished. Judge of the security which the administration of justice could afford when the trial by battle was the best expedient which could be devised to ensure the purity of judicature, and where it was usual for the party who was cast in a lawsuit to challenge his judge to mortal combat.

The religion of our ancestors is next to be considered, and here I shall begin by laying down a principle of which the ordinary reasoners on these subjects have usually lost sight. It is not indeed extremely recondite, for it is no other than this, that priests are men. They are usually considered as partaking of that perfect goodness and wisdom which they verbally attribute to the Great Master whom they profess to serve, although the actions and precepts which they ascribe to Him partake but too often of a contrary character.

From the principle that priests are men I draw the inference that in those cases which very frequently occur, and in which their individual interest is opposed to the interest of mankind, they will act as other men would act in similar circumstances; they would pursue their own interest to the detriment of mankind. Now if all men agree to believe whatever they say, they have a decided interest in making them believe everything which is likely to make them venerate and worship their spiritual guides; and if true opinions on the subject of religion are not of a nature calculated to inspire the requisite degree of veneration, it would be unfair to expect that these irresponsible directors of the public mind should confine themselves strictly to what is true; and we might indeed predict with tolerable certainty that they

would not fail to intermingle much of what is
utterly false, the more so as they may do this
without the slightest insincerity. There is no fact
better ascertained than the facility with which
men are persuaded to believe what they wish. It
is only necessary that there should be some one,
who may be either a knave or a madman, to start
a falsehood ; if it is unfavourable to the clergy he
will be hunted down as a heretic, but if it is
favourable to them it will not be long before he
finds many sincere disciples among the clergy
themselves, who of course propagate it among the
laity. It is in this way that the Catholic priesthood
added to their religion the profitable doctrine of
purgatory and masses for the dead, the crime-
promoting doctrine of indulgences, and above all
the terrific engines of auricular confession and
absolution, the concentration of which, and
particularly of the former, in the hands of the
clergy, make it astonishing that mankind should
ever have emancipated themselves from the terrific
sway of priests and their coadjutors, aristocracies
and kings. If at this day we rarely hear of murders
perpetrated in the name of religion, still more
rarely of those terrible persecutions which once
disgraced every nation in Europe, we owe this to
the revival of letters and the consequent diffusion
of knowledge.

Such a government and such a religion as our
ancestors had the happiness to enjoy afford us
in some degree the means of appreciating that
ancestorial[1] wisdom which is even now held up to us
as a model for imitation. In the nineteenth century
we are not infrequently called upon to pursue

[1] *Sic.*

the course which was followed by those sages, our ancestors, in the eleventh and twelfth. But this appeal from the age of civilization to the age of barbarism is made, we may observe, by those and by those alone who now, as then, would wish to see the great mass of mankind subject to the despotic sway of nobles, priests, and kings. But although it is in one respect true that the aristocracy of wealth and rank has given place to the democracy of intellect, I would not insinuate that the evils of feudal despotism and superstition are altogether eradicated even from this enlightened country. Knowledge has done much, but it has not yet done all. We are still subject to a constitution which is at best a shattered fragment of the feudal system; we are still subject to a priesthood who do whatever is yet in their power to excite a spirit of religious intolerance and to support the domination of a despotic aristocracy. We cannot therefore be surprised that those who are interested in misgovernment should raise a cry against the diffusion of knowledge on the ground that it renders the people dissatisfied with their institutions. When despotism and superstition were in their greatest vigour the same cry was raised, and for the same reason. Knowledge has triumphed. It has worked the downfall of much that is mischievous. It is in vain to suppose that it will pass by and spare any institution the existence of which is pernicious to mankind.

SPEECH ON
THE BRITISH CONSTITUTION

By the word Constitution, Sir, I understand the
institutions which exist for the purpose, or with
the supposed effect, of affording securities for good
government. The question, therefore, concerning
the goodness of our Constitution is the question
whether in so far as depends upon institutions,
good government is practically attained. It will,
I think, be allowed that as long as we suffer under
any evil of which government is the cause, good
government in the practical sense of the word is
not attained. The first question, therefore, is, do
any evils exist? the second, are any of them to be
imputed to our government?

To most persons it would appear very un-
necessary to prove that evils of some sort or
another do exist, and impossible to suppose the
contrary opinion capable of being entertained by
any rational being. So much language has however been held, which if it has not this meaning
has none at all, that I am compelled to regard even
this point as not out of the reach of controversy.
If we believe some gentlemen, England is a perfect
Utopia. The happiness of the golden age was
nothing to that we enjoy. Luxury pervades the
upper classes; comfort and knowledge diffuse
themselves among the middle; competence and
contentment among the lower. We are great in
war, honoured and powerful in peace: no man in
his senses *could* hope for anything better, and no
honest man *would*. If this be true, it certainly puts

an end to the question. If no evils exist, none, it is evident, can be occasioned by our practical Constitution. If we are already enjoying the whole of the happiness which we are to look for in this world, it is very obvious that we have nothing better to do than just to remain as we are. I must confess, however, that my aspirations do not stop at that degree of felicity to which we have at present attained, and that rather a higher standard of competence and contentment than six shillings a week will afford seems to me greatly to be desired for our agricultural population. Prosperity, Sir, is the test of good government, but the prosperity must first be proved.

We have flourished under the Constitution. Who has flourished under the Constitution? These gentlemen are apt to fall into the mistake, a very natural one I admit, of supposing that all the world has flourished because they have. Do they mean to allege that the great body of the people has flourished? But the people is not a word in their vocabulary. Instead of the people they talk of the country, the wealth, power and glory of the country, by which is to be understood the wealth, power, and glory of one man in a hundred, and the misery of the remaining ninety-nine. By this word country, they always mean the aristocracy. Whenever they talk of the prosperity of the country it is the prosperity of the aristocracy that is meant. When they say country, read aristocracy, and you will never be far from the truth. They tell you that the Constitution has worked well: you ask them particulars, and they answer that it has brought us a great deal of money and a great deal of glory. So much the better for those who have got it : I am sure we have got none. They may talk as they please about our being the richest nation in the world. The richest nation in one sense of the word we certainly are, but then it is like Mr. Alexander Baring and me, between us we certainly have a very handsome fortune. But what illustrates more than anything else the peculiar view which they take of national prosperity is their talk about military and naval renown. They have particularly selected as a proof of good government exactly what I should have chosen as a specimen of bad. I have as little respect, Sir, for a fighting nation as I have for a fighting individual, and I am by no means anxious that my country should be considered the ' Tom Cribb ' of Europe.

They talk of the last war and seem to think it highly honourable to our Constitution that having first got us into what they call ' an arduous struggle ', it afterwards at the expense of many myriads of lives got us out again. But let me ask what was gained by the last war, and who gained it ? We knocked down one despot and set up a score ; this was their concern, not ours. Then as to the substantial part of the gain, the money and glory—the generals, and admirals, and colonels, and lieutenant-colonels, and all the rest of them, got money, and most of them a little glory, some a great deal. The poor privates who took the disagreeable part of the business, and who were sent home when it was over to loiter about Chelsea Hospital with one leg or follow the plough with two, they got no glory ; any more than those at home who paid the piper. The contractors who had the fingering of the loans got no glory, but they got what was much better, many millions of pounds sterling which made them very comfortable at our expense. Sir, I grudge nobody his glory if he would pay for it himself. I have a great respect for Sir Arthur Wellesley, and *ceteris paribus*, I would much rather that he should be, as he is, a hero and a duke, than not: but when I consider that every feather in his cap has cost the nation more than he and his whole lineage would fetch if they were sold for lumber, I own that I much regret the solid pudding which we threw away in order that he might obtain empty praise.

Those who have called in question the goodness of our Constitution never thought of denying that it was good for some persons. The British Constitution is the Constitution of the rich. It has made this country the paradise of the wealthy. It has annexed to wealth a greater share of political power, and a greater command over the minds of men, than were ever possessed by it elsewhere. It has given to those who have money already great facilities for making it more. It has produced a fine breed of country gentlemen, and to support the breed it has charged us with an additional threepence on the quartern loaf. All this, Sir, is very fine, but I cannot help reflecting that the peasant of Languedoc eats his three meals of meat a day, and cultivates his vineyard; he has cheap justice at his doors; he may go where he pleases, engage in any trade that he pleases, and tread upon as many partridge eggs as he pleases, and need not fear to find himself next day on the treadmill, a victim of the unpaid patriotism of a game-eating squire. We are a free country, Sir, but it is as Sparta was free; the Helots are over-looked.

Whenever the hon. opener sees so much as a scrap of good he gives the credit of it to the Constitution. By this rule we ought to impute to it our evils. I might say that our manufacturers are starving by reason of the Constitution. I might say that our peasantry is the poorest in Europe because our Constitution is the worst. I believe a greater number of individuals suffer capital punishment in this country than in all the rest of Europe put together, and I might thence infer that our Constitution is a complication of all the vices of all the governments in Europe. But I do not think myself justified in reasoning unfairly because the hon. opener has set me the example. I impute to the Constitution no evils which do not naturally follow from the interests to which it has given birth. But when there is an obvious connexion between the evil suffered and the interests of the governors, I think it reasonable to place the evil to the account of the Constitution, because it is the Constitution which suffers the interests of the governors to be paramount to those of the governed. Such is the case with those evils which were depicted in perhaps more unmeasured language than was necessary by my hon. friend opposite on a former evening, and if I were to swell the list, as I might do, I should perhaps be betrayed into language still more intemperate than his. But as this part of our case has already been well stated, I shall allow it to rest upon his statements and proceed to another.

I thought, Sir, that the question related to the practice of the Constitution, but the defenders of the Constitution have thought otherwise; they seem determined to prove *a priori* the goodness of the Constitution, finding themselves unable to prove it *a posteriori*, and they have been good enough to reveal to us their several theories of the Constitution with the view, as I suppose, of convincing us that if we are not very well off, yet upon correct principles we ought to be. Now though I myself care very little by what machinery my pocket is picked, the beauty of the machinery has sometimes the effect of persuading people that their pocket is not picked when in fact it is. It may therefore conduce somewhat to the understanding of the question if their theories be cleared away. The commonplace theories have all had their supporters in the Society. We are told by one that our Constitution is a balance; by another that it is a representation of classes; by others that it is an aristocratical republic efficiently checked by public opinion. To this I will add my theory that it is an aristocratical republic insufficiently checked by public opinion. If I seem to dismiss these theories in a summary manner, want of time must be my apology.

The class-representation theory requires several words as it is the most modern and the most plausible. It has been very fully, though not very distinctly, stated this evening, and amounts to this, that if the landed interest, the mercantile interest, the army, the law, the manufacturing interest, and all the other great interests are represented, and the people represented, enough is done for good government, and that under our Constitution this is actually the case.

Now it seems to be forgotten in this view of the

subject that every one of these classes has two interests—its separate interest and its share of the general interest. That which ought to be represented is the latter. What really is represented is the former. Most true it is that the separate interests of a great number of classes are represented in the House of Commons, and so perfectly is the system adapted to ensure the predominance of these interests that there is hardly any class of plunderers (pickpockets and highwaymen excepted), which has not a greater number of representatives in the House of Commons than the whole body of the plundered. The consequence is that there is hardly ever a job proposed for the benefit of any set of persons at the expense of the community which does not find in that assembly somebody or other who is interested in supporting it ; and as there is a natural alliance among jobs of every description, one interest plays into the hands of another—*hodie mihi, cras tibi* is the word —and the upshot of it is that taking the great jobs with the little ones there is not on the face of God's earth such another jobbing assembly as the House of Commons. Sir, this is the very thing we complain of. The amount of misrule is not diminished by the multitude of the sharers. According to our notions the House of Commons should represent only one interest, the general interest. As for these particular interests which are opposed to the general one, as nobody ought to attend to them, I suppose nobody need represent them.

Fable, Sir, as we are taught by the ancients sometimes throws light upon truth. I will tell you a fable and you shall judge for yourself whether or not it is in point.

Once upon a time there happened an insurrection among the beasts. The little beasts grew tired of being eaten by the great ones. The swinish, goatish, and sheepish multitude grew weary of the sway of the intellectual and virtuous. They demanded to be governed by just and equal laws, and as a security for these laws, to be subject to a representative government. The Lion, finding himself hard-pressed, called together the aristocracy of the forest, and they jointly offered a rich reward to whoever could devise a scheme for extricating them from their embarrassment. The Fox offered himself, and his offer being accepted, went forth to the assembled multitude and addressed them thus : ' Surely, my friends, you would not deny to others the advantage which you seek to partake of yourselves. The only true representation is representation by classes. The tigrish [1] interest should be represented, the wolfish interest should be represented, all the other interests should be represented, and the great body of the beasts should be represented. My royal master has an objection to anarchy, but he is no enemy to a rational and well-regulated freedom : any other sort of representation he never will agree to, but a class representation he consents to grant.' The people, delighted to have got the name of a representation, quietly dispersed, and writs were issued to the different interests to choose their representatives. The tigers chose six tigers, the panthers six panthers, the hyaenas six hyaenas, and the wolves six wolves. The remaining beasts, who were only allowed to choose six, chose by common consent six dogs. The parliament was opened by a speech

[1] *Sic.*

from the Lion recommending unanimity. When this was concluded the Jackal, who was Chancellor of the Exchequer, introduced the subject of the Civil List, and after a long panegyric on the royal virtues proposed a grant for the support of those virtues of 1,000 sheep a year. The proposition was received with acclamations from the ministerial benches. The Tiger happening to be in the opposition made an eloquent speech in which he enlarged much upon the necessity of economy, inveighed bitterly against the profusion of ministers, and ended by moving that His Majesty must be humbly requested to content himself with 999. The dogs declared that as kings must eat, they had no objection to His Majesty devouring as many dead sheep as he pleased, but solemnly protested against his consuming any of their constituents alive. This remonstrance had its natural effect. The first impulse of the representatives of the aristocracy was to fall tooth and nail upon the representatives of the people. The Lion, however, representing that such conduct would be dishonourable, and the Fox that it might provoke a renewal of the insurrection, they abandoned the intention of worrying these demagogues and contented themselves with always outvoting them. The sequel may be guessed. The Lion got his thousand sheep, the Fox his pension of 100 ducks a year, and the panthers, wolves, and the other members of the aristocracy got as many kids and lambs in a quiet way as they could devour.

With this allegory, which is worth a thousand syllogisms, I shall dismiss the subject of the class representation.

The gentleman who first propounded to us the

theory of the balance will forgive me saying that he seems to have studied the Constitution chiefly in the writings of its panegyrists. The balance of King, Lords, and Commons I have met with in books, and it has a very pretty appearance upon paper; but even those who maintain that it existed once acknowledge that it has no existence now: the Commons, it is allowed, have complete possession of the Government, and the only balance now contended for is a balance in the House of Commons itself. That there is such a balance I do not deny, since a balance is still a balance although the weights may be unequal. But if anybody maintains that the weights are equal he should first find means of explaining away the fact that the aristocracy alone commands twice as many members of parliament as the King and the people together. The parliament is just as effectual an instrument of the aristocracy if they have a majority of the votes as it would be if they had the whole. With the fact that the parliament is made by the aristocracy staring us in the face, it would be useless to enter into the speculative question whether the balance is possible, or whether, if possible, it would be good. Possible or not, at any rate it does not exist. If there be any counterpoise to the power of the aristocracy it cannot come from within the House of Commons; it must come from without.

With that class of the defenders of our Constitution who consider public opinion as expressed by petitions, public meetings, and a free press as the one and sufficient check, I am less widely at issue. The question between us is merely a question of degree. We both allow that the House

of Commons requires a check ; we both agree that
public opinion is the proper check. They think
that the check is sufficient if the public are allowed
to speak freely ; I think that it is not sufficient
unless they are allowed to act as well as speak.
Now I do not see how the question between us
can be tried except by looking about us and seeing
what this free speaking has done. That it has
done much, I allow. It is probably the cause that
we are not at this moment the slaves of a military
despotism. But has it abolished the Corn Laws ?
Has it abolished the Game Laws ? Did it prevent
the Six Acts ? Did it prevent the Manchester
Massacre, or did it prevent the House of Commons
from approving of it ? Has it cut down our civil,
and military, and naval establishments ? Has it
reformed the Magistracy, the Church, and the
Law ? It has been said by the gentleman who
started this theory that the laws of England are
deserving of absolute condemnation. If this be true,
what a satire is it upon the Constitution which
he applauded ! For my part I do not think the laws
of England deserving of absolute condemnation,
but I think that they require many and great
ameliorations, ameliorations which I am persuaded
that none but a reformed parliament will have
the courage, I will not say the inclination, to make.

What is the influence of public opinion ?
Nothing at bottom but the influence of *fear*. Of
what consequence is it to a minister what the
public say, so long as they content themselves
with saying ? but when it comes to blows it
becomes a serious matter. I do not deny the
influence of character, of the opinion of others,
even independently of fear. The opinion of others

is a peaceful check upon every man, but then it
must be the opinion of his own class. Experience
has shown that there is no action so wicked that
even an honest man will not do it if he is borne out
by the opinion of those with whom he habitually
associates. Was there ever a more unpopular
minister than Lord Castlereagh ? Was there ever
a minister who cared so little about it ? The
reason was that although he had the people against
him, the predominant portion of the aristocracy
was for him, and all his concern about public dissatisfaction was to keep it below the point of
a general insurrection. Things are a little better
now because we accidentally have a ministry who,
knowing themselves to be no favourites with the
bulk of the aristocracy, and feeling that, to use
a homely expression, it is touch and go with their
places, count the people as a sort of makeweight,
though an inconsiderable one, to that portion of
the aristocracy who are on their side. But should
they be turned out, and should we for our sins
be visited with another Castlereagh, we shall be
governed by the new one exactly as we were
governed by the old, in spite of the public opinion
check, the dread of insurrection which it seems we
have, and which the Turks have likewise. The
Constitution of Turkey may be defined to be the
fear of the bowstring, and the Constitution of
Great Britain it seems, according to this view of it,
may be defined to be the fear of the guillotine.
Let who will be satisfied with this check, I for one
have a most decided objection to it.

I fear that my observations on the theories of
the Constitution have been dull, but I must crave
the indulgence of the Society for a short time
longer. There is another subject which must not

be altogether passed over. Gentlemen have not merely enlarged upon the goodness of our Constitution, they have expatiated upon the exceeding badness of every other. More especially a popular government has been the theme of their invectives, nor have they by any means spared the people themselves. This, Sir, is the way with them. If we believe some people, the many who are interested in good government are the determined enemies of good government, and the only persons who are its friends are the few who are interested against it. They are always fearing evil to the many from the many, never from the few. Now I beg you to remark how many advantages these gentlemen have over me. We are always ready to believe what we fear. The orator who has the fear of his audience on his side has only to awaken the emotion by a few frightful words, and persuasion follows of itself. Very different is the task of him who has the fear of his audience against him. Having to work conviction by means of evidence in minds ill-prepared to receive it, to have any chance of success he must heap proof upon proof, he must add argument to argument, his discourse lengthens into prolixity, he has wearied the patience of his audience before he has triumphed over their apprehensions, and to the misfortune of failing in his object he adds that of being voted a bore. Sir, it is among the disadvantages of my present situation that I am compelled to be prolix. Misrepresentation is always beautifully brief; refutation always tediously long. There are single sentences in the speech of the hon. opener each containing half a score of assumptions, each assumption requiring a long detail of facts or train of reasoning to refute it.

SPEECH ON PERFECTIBILITY

Spoken in 1828

MR. PRESIDENT, if I had much anxiety to save my credit as a wise and practical person I should not venture to stand forth in defence of the progressiveness of the human mind. I know that among all that class of persons who consider themselves to be *par excellence* the wise and the practical, it is esteemed a proof of consummate judgement to despair of doing good. I know that it is thought essential to a man who has any knowledge of the world to have an extremely bad opinion of it, and that whenever there are two ways of explaining any fact, wise and practical people always take that way which attributes most folly or most immorality to the mass of mankind. Sir, it is not for me to dispute the palm of practicality with these sage and cautious persons. Howsoever it may be with all other aberrations of the human intellect, there is one description of errors from which it would be uncandid to deny that they are wholly free, viz. all those which arise from immoderate benevolence or ill-regulated philanthropy. It behoves those who have discarded errors so pleasing, so encouraging, so ennobling to every virtuous mind, to be very certain that they have discarded them in favour of truth. Those who have stripped themselves so philosophically of every prejudice which acts as a stimulus to our duty should be very sure that they have left no other prejudices of a more discreditable description behind. They may be assured that the errors of benevolence are by no means those from which human prosperity has most to apprehend, and however desirable it may be for the good of mankind that the love of virtue should never rise above temperate, we must be careful not to go on cooling it till it sinks to the freezing point. Sir, I do not feel my virtue to be of so warm and impetuous a character as to need any cooling, neither have I that confidence in my own judgement which would induce me to set up my opinion of truth in opposition to hopes and feelings which at least serve as a counteracting force against hopes and feelings far less pure, and I cannot but think far more pernicious. If we must err, at least let our errors not be on the side of selfishness ; it is not that part, that element of the human constitution which needs strengthening ; there is not the slightest danger that it should ever be weaker than the good of human society requires.

But is it indeed an error to suppose mankind capable of great improvement ? And is it really a mark of wisdom to deride all grand schemes of human amelioration as visionary ? I can assure hon. gentlemen that, so far from being a proof of any wisdom, it is what any fool can do as well as themselves, and I believe it is the fools principally who have attached to that mode of proceeding the reputation of wisdom. For as I have observed that if there is a man in public or private life who is so impenetrably dull that reason and argument never make the slightest impression upon him, the dull people immediately set him down as a man of excellent judgement and strong sense ; as if because men of talent and genius are sometimes deficient in judgement it followed that it was only necessary to be without one spark of talent or genius in order to be a man of consummate judgement. In the same manner because people are sometimes deceived by rash hopes I think I have observed that not the man who hopes when others despair, but the man who despairs when others hope is admired by a large class of persons as a sage, and wisdom is supposed to consist not in seeing further than other people, but in not seeing so far. I mean no disrespect to some highly estimable persons who are of a different opinion from myself on this question, but I am persuaded that a vast majority of those who laugh at the hopes of those who think that man can be raised to any higher rank as a moral and intellectual being, do so from a principle very different from wisdom or knowledge of the world. I believe that the great majority of those who speak of perfectibility as a dream, do so because they feel that it is one which would afford them no pleasure if it were realized. I believe that they hold the progressiveness of the human mind to be chimerical because they are conscious that they themselves are doing nothing to forward it, and are anxious to believe that great work impossible in which, if it were possible, they know it would be their duty to assist. I believe that there is something else which powerfully helps many persons to the same conclusion—a consciousness that they do not wish to get rid of their own imperfections, and a consequent unwillingness to believe it practicable that others should throw off theirs. I believe that if persons ignorant of the world sometimes mis-

calculate from expecting to find mankind wiser
and better than they are, those persons who most
affect to know the world are incessantly miscal-
culating the opposite way, and confidently reckoning upon a greater degree of knavery and folly
among mankind than really exists. These last
indeed differ from the others in not being so ready
to correct their error, since the same utter incapacity of taking any generous and enlarged views
which caused their mistake prevents them from
discovering it, and makes them impute those
effects of the better part of man's nature which
they did not calculate upon only to a different
species of selfishness. I will even say that so far
from its being a mark of wisdom to despair of
human improvement there is no more certain
indication of narrow views and a limited understanding, and that the wisest men of all political
and religious opinions, from Condorcet to Mr.
Coleridge, have been something nearly approaching to perfectibilians. Nay, further, that the anti-
perfectibility doctrine, far from having the
sanction of experience, is brought forward in
opposition to one of the clearest cases of experience
which human affairs present, and that by all just
rules of induction we ought to conclude that an
extremely high degree of moral and intellectual
excellence may be made to prevail among mankind
at large, since causes exist which have confessedly
been proved adequate to produce it in many
particular instances.

In the little which I intend to say I shall attempt
little more than to expand and develop this last
remark. There are others in this Society far more
competent than myself to discuss in detail the past

progress of the human mind, and the stages
through which it is likely to pass in the road to
further improvements. I leave it to them to
point out how the difficulties are to be struggled
with ; it is enough for me if I can establish on the
ground of solid experience that these difficulties
may be overcome.

I shall confine myself in the first instance to the
question of moral improvement. I shall not ask
you, Sir, to expect among mankind any degree of
moral excellence that is without parallel. My
standard shall be one which we all know, which we
all believe in, with which we are all familiar in our
own experience. I suppose it will not be denied
that there are, and have been, persons who have
possessed a very high degree of virtue. Now here
I take my stand ; there have been such persons.
I do not care how many nor who they were. If I
were to name any person, any historical character
to whom I think the designation applicable, without doubt that person might be cavilled at and
something raked up to throw a doubt upon his
virtue, for it is difficult to adduce evidence on such
a point that shall leave no possibility of cavil : but
will those persons who say that this man or that
man was not virtuous go farther and say that
nobody was ever virtuous ? I should think not.
All they can say is that in the most virtuous there
has been some frailty, some fault, a weakness
which has rendered even the best of them less than
perfect. Certainly all this may be safely admitted.
I shall not affirm that men in general can be made
better than the best men whom the human race
has hitherto produced.

Well then, here is a fact ; there have been

virtuous men. Now what made them virtuous ?
I call upon the gentlemen on the other side to
answer this question, for if it should turn out that
those who are virtuous are so from causes, which
though they now act only upon a few, can be made
to act upon all mankind, or the greater part, it is
within the power of human exertion to make all
or most men as virtuous as those are. I therefore
challenge the hon. gentlemen to say to what they
attribute the superior moral excellence of some
persons. If they do not answer, I will. It is to
the original influence of good moral education in
their early years, and the insensible influence of the
world, of society, and public opinion upon their
habits and associations in after life. Here then
is specific experience. It is distinctly proved that
these two forces, education and public opinion,
when they are both of them brought fairly into
play and made to act in harmony with one another,
are capable of producing high moral excellence ;
and yet the greater part of the arguments which
have been advanced against us this evening are
intended to prove that moral education and public
opinion are *not* capable of producing these effects.

Why then have these causes not produced the
same effects upon all which they have upon some ?
Because they have not acted upon all. No pains
have been taken with the moral education of
mankind in general. The great business of moral
education, to form virtuous habits of mind, is
I may say entirely neglected : the child is indeed
punished for certain immoral acts, but as for going
to the root of the evil and correcting the dis-
positions in which these acts originate, the thing
is never thought of, or if it is thought of, nothing

can be more ridiculously inefficacious than the means which are taken to effect it. And all this from sheer ignorance, for it is not that people do not set a sufficient value upon those habits of mind which lead to good habits of conduct; it is that they really do not know how such habits are generated, what they depend upon and what mode of education favours or counteracts them. While that education which is called education is in this deplorable state, that insensible education which is not called education is still worse, for almost everywhere the great objects of ambition, those which ought to be the rewards of high intellectual and moral excellence, are the rewards either of wealth, as in this country, or of private favour, as in most others; and it is an established fact in the nature of man that whatever are the means by which the great recompenses of ambition are to be obtained, the person who possesses these means and can therefore pretend to these recompenses, is the person who exercises influence over the public mind; he is the person whose favour is courted, whose actions are imitated, whose opinions are adopted, and the contagion of whose failings is caught by the mass of mankind.

It is a very poor and ill-divided public opinion which can be formed out of an aggregate so ill-composed, and yet that public opinion which is the result of so bad a moral education is sufficient, whenever it is combined with a better moral education, to produce all the virtue which we see realized in some individuals of mankind as they now are.

It will of course be said that although good moral education and the operation of public opinion produce so much excellence in some persons, it

does not follow that they can in all. I maintain
on the contrary that there is much less difficulty
in producing it in all than there has been to
produce it in some. Whatever of moral excellence
now exists has been produced in spite of a thousand
obstacles ; in spite of systems of education which
if the names were altered, and they were reported
to us as existing in some far distant country,
would be considered incredible from the absolute
fatuity, the utter abnegation of intellect which
they exhibit ; in spite of laws which in a hundred
ways inflict evil upon one man for the benefit of
another, and generate a spirit of domination and
oppression on one side, of cringing and servility,
mixed with bitter and vindictive resentment, on
the other ; in spite of systems of judicial procedure
which seem devised on purpose to give right and
wrong an equal chance, and in which every
possible encouragement is held out to the vice of
insincerity ; in spite of political institutions which
in this at least the most civilized country in the
world, render wealth the only acquisition which
is desired, poverty almost the only evil that is
dreaded. All these evils might be remedied by the
hand of God. If notwithstanding all these things
the best moral education which the present circumstances of mankind admit of has produced in
those to whom it is given so much excellence, what
may not be expected if we remove these obstacles,
and when they are taken away, give even as good
a moral education to the greater portion of mankind—why not to all mankind, for moral excellence does not suppose a high order of intellectual cultivation, since it is often found in
greatest perfection in the rudest minds ?

With respect to such doctrines as have been advanced this evening on the other side, some of them, I must confess, have surprised me. We have been told that it is impossible to diminish the amount of vice because vice arises from the passions, and it is impossible to vanquish the passions. Now, Sir, I demur to this : first, that it is taking a very narrow view of the principles of morals and the nature of the human mind to suppose that it is necessary for any good purpose to vanquish the passions. There is not one of the passions which by a well-regulated education may not be converted into an auxiliary of the moral principle ; there is not one of the passions which may not be as fully and much more permanently gratified by a course of virtuous conduct than by vice. And if this be the case, surely it would be the worst of policy even looking to moral excellence without regarding happiness in the least, to eradicate the passions, because it is they which furnish the active principle, the moving force ; the passions are the spring, the moral principle only the regulator of human life.

But further, this very assertion that the passions cannot be vanquished may be taken as a specimen of the shallow philosophy of these gentlemen and their very superficial experience of mankind. They who profess to know human nature so well seem to be very little aware what it is capable of. Have we not seen that men have lain for their whole lives upon beds of spikes ; that they have stood all their lives upon the tops of pillars ; that they have remained all their lives without stirring for one moment from a certain posture because they have willed it ? Have they not swung by hooks drawn through their backs, and suffered themselves to be crushed by chariot wheels, and laid themselves voluntarily on funeral piles to be burned ? Have not these things been done, not by heroes and philosophers, but thousands and millions of common men, commonly educated ; and then these gentlemen come and give us arguments which, if they prove anything, prove the impossibility of all this. We could do none of these things : why ? Because we have never been accustomed to fix our imaginations on these things long enough for our first horror of them to wear off. But what caused these surprising achievements ? It must have been either religion, conscience, or public opinion. Gentlemen may choose ; it shall be any one of the three. We have heard the force of each of the three separately explained away, and very plausible arguments adduced to prove that no one of them is strong enough to produce these effects, and yet let me ask these gentlemen the reason why the effects are produced. I will give up any two of the forces to them, but they must grant me the third. If they ask my own opinion it is that all helped, but that the proximate motive had most influence, that derived from public opinion ; and some hon. gentlemen who have sometimes wondered at hearing public opinion spoken of in this Society as the immense force that it is, may perhaps now see from these instances why it is so spoken of. (Introduce a passage from Combe.) [1]

But if such is the force of public opinion, what is wanting to produce that high state of general

[1] [George Combe (1788–1858), phrenologist. The reference is probably to his *Constitution of Man*.]

morality which we aspire to ? Simply that public
opinion should be well directed in respect of
morality ; that such a system of education should
exist as will give to the mass of mankind not
learning but common-sense practical judgement
in ordinary affairs, and shall enable them to see
that a thing is wrong when it is wrong, as shall
make them despise humbug, see through casuistry
and imposture, not to accept a subterfuge and
excuses for neglecting a duty, and not think the
same thing laudable under a fine name and
blamable under a vulgar one ; for instance, not to
think, like some persons in this room, that giving
a man money, or money's worth, for voting against
his conviction is criminal when called bribery, but
laudable when called legitimate influence of
property ; to judge of men by the manner in
which they act, not by the manner in which they
talk ; not to estimate a man's moral excellence by
the quantity of grimace which he exhibits in his
own person, or by the quantity of hypocrisy which
he exacts from his family and dependents ; not to
give men any credit for making great sacrifices at
other people's expense, or for being philanthropic
at a distance and prudent at home ; not to think
that charity consists in making laws to take away
bread from the poor and subscribing a few pounds
annually to some institution for giving it to them ;
and in short not see a great many other nice
distinctions which the refined and cultivated people
of the present day are able to see and very ready
to act upon. And there is another thing that is
requisite : to take men out of the sphere of the
opinion of their separate and private coteries and
make them amenable to the general tribunal of

the public at large ; to leave no class possessed of power sufficient to protect one another in defying public opinion, and to manufacture a separate code of morality for their private guidance ; and so to organize the political institutions of a country that no one could possess any power save what might be given to him by the favourable sentiments, not of any separate class with a separate interest, but of the people.

NOTES OF MY SPEECH AGAINST STERLING, 1829[1]

BEFORE I commence it is proper to explain to those who were not present at the last debate the reasons which will induce me to occupy their attention with other topics and in another manner than what the terms of the question would suggest, or perhaps in most cases justify.

An hon. gentleman who spoke towards the conclusion of the previous debate and whose speech I imagine most of those who heard it will not easily forget, has thought proper to ground his defence of the merits of Montesquieu chiefly upon the demerits of those who have adopted a method of philosophising opposite to that of Montesquieu in politics and legislation. Whether this be the proper basis to rest the discussion upon is a question which will probably be answered differently by different persons; at all events I do not mean to contend that it is not, as it is my intention to imitate the hon. gentleman in making this, whether it be a branch of the subject or a digression from it, the principal topic of my speech. I am impelled to this by what indeed forms my only motive for troubling the Society at all on this question, and especially for undertaking the task, for which I feel myself wholly unfit, of opening the debate. I mean the desire of taking with as little

[1] [John Sterling (1806–44), the friend of Coleridge and Carlyle, the latter being the author of his biography.]

delay as possible what appears to me the proper
notice of the fierce attack which the hon. gentleman was pleased to make upon the principles and
practice of those who think as I do on this question.
The hon. gentleman was not content with stigma-
tizing their opinions as false, he ascribed to those
opinions all manner of demoralizing effects : there
was no end to the expressions which he heaped,
indicative of the odious or disagreeable habits of
mind which were connected with those opinions,
and of which, as he told us, the character and lives
of the persons who held them were a practical
illustration. The persons of whom these things
were alleged were generally all those the current
of whose speculations on government and laws
runs in a different channel from that in which he
tells us Montesquieu's did, but more particularly
those who profess the principles of Mr. Bentham.
Sir, I do not profess to be a follower of Mr. Bentham, partly because no person who thinks for
himself will ever call himself the follower of any
one, and partly because I altogether dissent from
many of the opinions which those who are ignorant
enough to fancy that there is a Benthamite sect
are also ignorant enough to suppose to be the
opinions of that sect. And I believe that of the
far too great numbers of speeches which the indulgence of this Society has permitted me to make
during this and the last two years, a majority would
be found to have been made in opposition to some
one or other of what are vulgarly considered to be
the Benthamite doctrines. In those opinions of
Mr. Bentham, however, which have been the object
of the hon. gentleman's invective, as in most of the
opinions really professed by that great man, I have

the misfortune to agree ; and I consequently feel myself a party concerned in the hon. gentleman's denunciations, and as such I do not feel disposed to sit down quietly under them. I am far from denying that among the countless aberrations of the human understanding it is possible that a person might think all which the hon. gentleman has said, and might think that it was his duty to say it. I take it, however, for granted that in resorting to this mode of controversy the hon. gentleman did not reckon upon having the use of it entirely to himself. I conclude that in dealing with his opponents after this fashion he was alive to the possibility that those whom he attacked might one day come to the conclusion that the employment of this description of weapons on his part justified a recourse to it on theirs. They have indeed hitherto remained tolerably passive under the animadversions which the hon. gentleman is in the habit of pouring forth against them for various reasons, and among others probably because they did not consider it very dignified to evince an over-anxiety to stand forth in defence of themselves on slight occasions. But they have entered into no compact with the hon. gentleman that he shall fight with daggers and they with foils, and they will probably think that it is now time for the hon. gentleman to be reminded that the censorial authority which he has assumed over us is one to which he has no title but by his own election of himself to that office. On the contrary I believe that the sense of the Society will go along with me when I say that while we do justice to the hon. gentleman's talents, and are ready to submit to any moderate pretensions which he may set up to authority among us on that ground, we yet do not recognize in him any such vast and immeasurable superiority to ourselves as should entitle him to pronounce dictatorially upon the moral tendency of our principles and of our minds : above all we do not discern in him that calmness of temperament, that impartiality in collecting and care in weighing evidence, that power of representing to himself the feelings and the ideas of other men, or that accurate knowledge of the systems and opinions that he condemns which are necessary for executing so high a judicial office faithfully.

I believe the hon. gentleman does not seek to conceal that he once held the opinions which he now so strongly censures. Now I by no means wish to insinuate that these opinions as they existed in his mind may not have been attended with every absurd and every immoral consequence which he deduces from them. From the apparent incapacity of the hon. gentleman to rest anywhere but in extremes that was probably the case. But I would beg the hon. gentleman to remember that if in his mind these opinions were really as absurd and as immoral as he represents them, the case is far otherwise in ours, and that we do not think it absolutely necessary that we should be bound by his inferences from our opinions ; nay more, that we think ourselves fully as well qualified to judge what are the legitimate consequences deducible from our principles as he is, having probably considered them much more ; and that we do not precisely see why our morality should be made responsible for the errors of his logic.

With respect to the merits of Montesquieu the hon. gentleman has told us very little about them.

But it appeared that the historical school of jurists, of which he told us that Montesquieu was the founder, stood very high in his estimation, not so much however for anything which they did but for something which they have not done; they did not fall into the error, which he says has been committed by Mr. Bentham, of imagining that there is a universal science of politics applicable with certain modifications to all countries. They think on the contrary that every country ought to have its separate science of politics founded on an attentive consideration of its history, and in which the conservation of all the principal institutions of that country and of all the habits and feelings of its people should be received as a fundamental axiom.

Now, Sir, these may be the hon. gentleman's opinions, but it is altogether a mistake to suppose that they were Montesquieu's. Montesquieu did not undertake to treat of the science of politics or of legislation. It is only incidentally that we learn from his book any of his opinions on these subjects. Montesquieu's book is essentially a treatise on a branch of the philosophy of history : he treated of assigned duties, i. e. the pervading principle of the laws of any country : his object was to inquire what are the circumstances which give to the whole body of the institutions of any country that peculiar character which distinguishes them from the institutions of other countries. In doing this he of course had frequent occasion to show not only why an institution had been established, but why it should be, by adducing the reasons of expediency which had led to its establishment in different states. But what I wish to point out is that by the very nature of his design he was confined to the circumstances of difference in the situation of different nations, from which it by no means follows that he was insensible to the more numerous and far more important circumstances of agreement. Although his notions unquestionably were very often obscure and confused on various topics of what may be termed the metaphysics of law, I believe him to have been altogether guiltless of the absurdities to which the hon. gentleman, his defender, lays claim on his behalf : doctrines which, when we come to analyse them, amount to this, that there are no tendencies which are common to all mankind ; for if there are any tendencies common to all mankind, and in particular if all the stronger tendencies of human nature are such, both those which require to be regulated and those whose agency you must employ to regulate them, it surely is not an irrational subject of inquiry what are the laws and other social arrangements which would be desirable if no other tendencies than these universal tendencies of human nature existed. And this when ascertained merely constitutes *pro tanto* a universal science of politics, although before we apply it to any particular nation we must also ascertain what are the tendencies peculiar to that nation, and correct the abstract principles of the science by the modifications which those tendencies introduce.

I was surprised at first to find that the hon. gentleman, professing to discuss the merits of two opposite schools of law, one of which was that of Mr. Bentham's, should have adverted only to Mr. Bentham's opinions on constitutional legislation, omitting his much more original and valuable labours in other branches of the field of law. But the fact is that if the hon. gentleman had not acted in that manner he would not have found anything to differ from Mr. Bentham upon. Nobody ever supposed that the detailed provisions of the civil and penal code were to be the same for any two countries, or for the same country at different periods of its history. What is universal in this branch of the science consist chiefly in what I have already termed the metaphysics of law which belongs equally to all nations because it is in truth nothing more than the explication of the fundamental ideas which are involved in the very conception of a law or a body of laws of whatever description. And this of which Montesquieu was absolutely ignorant, to which the Roman jurists made but a very distant approximation, and which by the way it would do the hon. gentleman no harm to study, is a branch of science which we owe entirely to Mr. Bentham and to those who have followed in his footsteps.

The hon. gentleman, however, confined his animadversions to Mr. Bentham's opinions on constitutional law, of which he seems to have formed rather a curious idea. He says that a tribe of North American Indians is the exact type and representation of Mr. Bentham's republic, for there we may see universal suffrage, daily parliaments, and the total absence of all such pernicious institutions as a church or an aristocracy, to which Mr. Bentham ascribes all the evils which exist. Now I really do not know that the hon. gentleman in the days of his radicalism may not have had the egregious folly to think that a good government might be constructed out of negatives, but of this he may perfectly assure himself, that Mr. Bentham does not ; that in Mr. Bentham's estimation there go some positive conditions to the making up of a good state of society as well as some negative ones, and that the negative conditions are only required in order to give to the positive conditions full effect. In order that the hon. gentleman may be enabled better to comprehend the nature of the blunder which he has been committing I will beg him to suppose that he were a writer on medicine, of which I dare say that he knows a great deal more than he does of Mr. Bentham's philosophy, and that in this character he had composed and given to the world a treatise on poisons ; and suppose that having read this book I were to walk up to the hon. gentleman, present him with a bag of sawdust and to say, 'Look here : behold the type, the *beau idéal* of your system of diet : observe this sawdust ; there is no arsenic in it, no verdigris, not one particle of corrosive sublimate is here ; you are bound to give this to all your patients and make it their daily food.' Let the hon. gentleman consider what answer he would give to a person who should thus address him, and suppose himself answered in the same way.

With respect to universal suffrage and short parliaments which the hon. gentleman has most unaccountably found among a people who have no parliaments and no representative system at all, I will tell the hon. gentleman that he has himself done precisely what, when it is done by any other person, makes him so excessively indignant. He has taken the mere *accidents* of Mr. Bentham's system, those very parts of it which Mr. Bentham himself would allow ought to vary with difference of circumstances, and has insisted upon judging of the whole system by those accidents, keeping its great and leading principle wholly out of view. Universal suffrage and annual parliaments, let me tell the hon. gentleman, are in Mr. Bentham's apprehension nothing more than a particular set of means for giving effect to his system. The one great principle of Mr. Bentham's system is, that that body which, like the House of Commons in this country, holds substantially in its own hands the governing power should be chosen by, and accountable to, some portion or other of the people whose interest is not materially different from that of the whole. Now this, I am ready to maintain in the face of the hon. gentleman, is a universal principle in politics, a principle which he may add if he pleases to the two other principles respecting slavery and Christianity, which he says are not inconsistent with any form of government which ought to exist ; and Mr. Bentham, of whose pretended universal science of politics the hon. gentleman has such a horror, gives so moderate an extent to that science that he does not require the hon. gentleman to do more than add a third universal proposition to the two which he has already conceded, for wherever this one principle is in operation, there is Mr. Bentham's system, and in all the other parts of the social system the hon. gentleman is at perfect liberty as far as Mr. Bentham is concerned to determine himself by circumstances. Whether this principle is or is not in operation among the North American Indians I am not sufficiently conversant with that people to know. The hon. gentleman, however, might have found another people in North America, on the banks of the Ohio, and likewise a people on the other side of the British Channel in both of which by various means, and among others by the miserable contrivance of a ballot box, this sole principle of Mr. Bentham's system has been brought happily into operation ; and either of which I can assure the hon. gentleman, is a much nearer approximation to the *beau idéal* of Mr. Bentham's republic than the example which he suggested to us. And I am perfectly willing that the merits of Mr. Bentham's system should be tried by the effects with which it is attended in either of these cases, being persuaded that these two nations considered as entire nations are by many degrees the happiest and the most virtuous nations on the face of the earth ; and that although the form of their government would not of itself have sufficed to make them so, yet if it had not been for the form of their government those other circumstances which have co-operated in producing the effect would many of them never have had existence, and such as did exist being entirely curtailed and stripped of their beneficial effect might as well, for the happiness and virtue of the people, have likewise been non-existent.[1]

[1] [Cf. the letter to Sterling of 15 April 1829 in Elliot, *Letters of John Stuart Mill*, vol. i. p. 1, which seems to arise out of this speech.]

SPEECH ON THE CHURCH

My hon. friend, the proposer of the question, has observed in his speech that it is difficult to speak against the church because men will not listen to the evidence. The experience of the preceding evening has shown that there is another difficulty, viz. that when they do listen to it, they are very much disposed to fritter it away. It would indeed be difficult to compose a speech on any subject that would stand the test which these gentlemen seemed disposed to apply to it. If you rest your case upon the universal principles of human nature and show that from the situation in which the Church of England is placed certain actions are the natural consequences, this is called declamation and assumption, and you are asked for facts. When, in obedience to this demand, you bring forward facts drawn from different periods of church history, these facts are exhibited singly, and you are triumphantly informed that each one, if there were only that one, might be a singular instance and was no proof of a general rule. If you allude to persecuting statutes enacted long ago you are told that they were evidence of a spirit which no longer exists; if to show that the spirit survives you observe that the laws still subsist, even although it is not possible to execute them, you are told by way of reply that as the spirit is not strong enough to surmount an impossibility no such spirit exists. If you cite a flagrant instance of direct persecution in what are considered by churchmen to be the best times of the church, you are told with much indignation that the church

has changed. If you quote a modern instance
which fortunately happens to be universally
known, they then at last stand at bay, drop all
artifice and evasion, turn round upon the man
who dares to condemn the persecution, and accuse
him of sympathizing with the impious. And here,
Sir, I cannot help blaming my hon. friend, not
indeed for the warmth with which he repelled this
accusation, for most assuredly if it was a charge
to be repelled at all it was a charge to be repelled
warmly ; but I blame him because the accusation,
coming from the quarter it did and on the occasion
on which it did, was one which he had reason to be
proud of. I am thankful to the hon. gentleman
for the term. I invite the hon. gentleman to
apply it to me. I should blush to be that which
the hon. gentleman would not call a friend of the
impious. I thank heaven that my heart is not so
hardened by bigotry, nor my understanding so
perverted by lawyercraft but that I can sympathize
with an oppressed man. The man, be he Christian
or atheist, who endures torture and ignominy
because he will not swerve from his convictions is
to me a martyr, and I should detest myself if
I could not venerate him as he deserves. What
is it to me if Mr. Carlile [1] is not a good reasoner ?
I never thought him a good reasoner, but he is
what I respect infinitely more, he is a man of
principle and a man who will stand to his principles
though he should stand alone ; and though to be
merely supposed to sympathize with him is
tantamount to an admission of impiety, shall

---

[1] [Richard Carlile (1790–1843), freethinker and book-
seller, was several times imprisoned for the publication
of radical works in politics and theology.]

I because this man is not a good logician, a man who is as ready to die at the stake for what he thinks the truth as any clergyman of the Church of England can be ready for what he thinks the truth to conduct him thither, shall I knowing how few such men there are and how much is due to those few when they arise, be deterred from expressing my disapprobation of their persecutors by a cry of impiety ? Let the hon. gentleman keep such stuff for the House of Commons ; there he will find in hundreds of bosoms a chord which will respond to that which vibrates in his own ; but I much mistake the tone of feeling in this Society if it contains one man, Tory or churchman though he be, to whom such feelings as the hon. gentleman gave utterance to on the preceding evening are not entirely unknown.

With regard to the question in hand, it would certainly be a waste of words to discuss whether or not the Church of England is a persecuting church with a gentleman who thinks that to immure Mr. Carlile and about twenty of his co-adjutors in dungeons for terms of two, three, and five years is not persecution. If a man squares his conscience by what the church does to him, of course the church can never be in the wrong ; and if the good old practice of burning heretics were revived, no doubt some persons would be still found who would maintain that even this was not persecution. But my hon. friend who spoke fourth on the preceding evening is not of this stamp, and to him a somewhat different answer is due. He had discretion enough to admit the iniquity of these persecutions but affirmed that they are not imputable to the clergy of the Church

of England. I am glad, Sir, that this is the line
of defence now resorted to by the more able
advocates of the Church of England, because in
the first place it shows that in their opinion the
time is now come when such proceedings as those
which have taken place against Mr. Carlile no
longer admit of being openly defended : but
further I rejoice to learn that these are the sentiments of my hon. friend, because as he seems on
this occasion to exculpate the church, not because
such proceedings are defensible, but because the
church has no share in them, I am led to conclude
that if it could be proved to his satisfaction that
these persecutions are in any degree imputable
to the church he would no longer consider the
church capable of being defended on this ground.
Now I shall easily be able to adduce evidence which
will satisfy even my hon. friend's scepticism on
this point. I do not pretend that the church alone
is to blame ; there is enough of religious bigotry,
God knows, both in other professions and in other
sects, although the existence of a powerful body
who are bound by interest to work up that baneful
spirit to the highest pitch cannot have much tendency to mitigate it at least. But there is a good
deal to be said in respect to the part which the
Church of England has actually taken in the
persecution. My hon. friend in speaking on this
subject has shown (to parody an expression of
Mr. Sheridan) a very pious ignorance on some
topics : he has buried all transactions of this
description anterior to the late prosecution of the
Rev. R. F. Tayler in discreet oblivion. In that
proceeding he says that Dissenters were the chief
agents, and seems not to be aware that the prime

mover in the affair, Mr. Alderman Atkins, is no
Dissenter but a most orthodox high churchman.
Although, however, my hon. friend cannot carry
his recollection any further back, I can, and I can
state for the benefit of his rather short memory
that more than one-half of the prosecutions of
Mr. Carlile, his family and his coadjutors, were
at the prosecution of the Society for the Suppression of Vice. Now although I give my hon. friend
credit for a very considerable degree of ingenuity,
I do not suppose him to possess so great a share of
it as to be able to explain away the list of sub-
scribers to that Society, a list comprising nearly
as great a number of bishops and dignitaries of
the church as subscribed to that other creditable
establishment, the Bridge Street Association, which
last attempt to revive the execrable tyranny over
political opinion the good sense and virtue of this
country crushed in the bud. As I have alluded to
this final ebullition of feelings, which though as far
as ever from being extinguished, no man now
dares avow, I cannot help saying that I find it
difficult to decide which aspect of the affair tells
most against the reverend gentleman, the odious-
ness of the design or the contemptible imbecility
of the execution. The whole funds of that Association sufficed only for, I believe, nine prosecutions, and these in every or almost every instance
directed against mere accessories, and not princi-
pals, in what they pretended to call an offence.
But the Association is gone where all such Associations ought to go ; gone, I should say, for ever
were it not that clergymen who, according to the
well-known remark of Lord Clarendon, understand
the least and take the worst measure of human

affairs, of all men who can read or write are likely
enough to suffer themselves to be hoaxed out of
a little more of their money by some cunning
attorney who, if he can succeed in persuading them
that his object in asking for it is to make use of it
for the purpose of helping to degrade the human
mind, can make himself sure of raising among
a large portion of them at least enough to make
his own fortune by law expenses, which is generally
the purpose of the more prominent agents in such
transactions.

But if this institution is now no more, the Vice
Society still exists, and by this Society were most
of the prosecutions against Carlile and his followers
instituted. (Here introduce the record.) The very
fact that such proceedings could emanate from
a Society so named is a pregnant proof of the
spirit which prevails among its lay and clerical
members. Suppression of opinions they term
suppression of vice; the honest promulgation of
doctrines different from what they consider right
they have the audacity to term a vice, an act of
immorality. I do not affect surprise at this; it is
far better to say plainly that he who does not
believe as they do is *ipso facto* a vicious and
profligate man than to impute all manner of other
vices to him, as they have almost invariably done.
The common vice of partisans, that of heaping
calumnies upon the head of an opponent, is one
by which it is matter of common observation that
priests of all religions, whether from blind cre-
dulity or from a still worse principle, have been
distinguished beyond all other men. The clergy
of the Church of England have not, it is true,
come quite up to the mark of the Roman Catholic

clergy in this respect, because they have never had
so much power of making false statements un-
contradicted, but they have carried the practice
of defamation as far as it could with safety be
carried, and have by their calumnies embittered
the lives of men among the brightest ornaments of
human nature.

If my hon. friend has made so lame a defence of
the church on the subject of religious prosecutions,
his coadjutor has made a still more feeble one on
the subject of those badges of a more widely
spreading spirit of persecution which exist on our
statute book under the name of the Test and
Corporation Acts. The hon. gentleman says that
these Acts were not intended for the support of
the church. The hon. gentleman is a good lawyer,
but Blackstone was a better; and if the hon.
gentleman is right, Blackstone is wrong, for
Blackstone says expressly that these Acts exist for
the support of the church. But when I find the
hon. gentleman ignorant of the tricks by which
the Protestant Dissenters were persuaded not to
oppose these Acts under the pretence that they
would not be enforced against them, tricks which
are wittily typified by Arbuthnot under the
emblem of Don Diego persuading Jack to hang
himself under pretence that Sir Roger would cut
him down ; when I likewise find the hon. gentleman ignorant, at least apparently so, of the too
celebrated Act of Uniformity ; when I find him
equally ignorant of the equally celebrated statute
termed the Occasional Conformity Act passed to
keep out those who, although Dissenters, yet not
considering the service of the Church of England
to be profane or idolatrous thought that they could

conscientiously attend it occasionally and thereby escape the disabilities of the law; when I see all this, and when I find him absolutely astonished that Hume should be considered a good witness against the church, a man who sold his conscience for them, a writer who violated every law of historical veracity in order to screen the church, I am tempted to ask under what high church power, in what obscure corner of the Kingdom, remote from all access of books and converse of men, the hon. gentleman imbibed his knowledge of history.

The battle of the church really is not to be thus fought. We all know how great allowances ought to be made for an extemporaneous effusion, but it really is a fact that some knowledge of the subject is necessary even to make a defender of the church; and until the hon. gentleman shall have acquired such knowledge, or at least shall have it more under his command than he appeared to have on the former evening, it would be much wiser in him were he to leave the cause of the church in the hands of my hon. friend who so ably followed on the same side.

I have now concluded by far the greater part of what I intend to trouble the Society with on this evening. It was in fact only in order to support and vindicate my friend, the proposer of the question, that I felt desirous of taking any part whatever in the discussion, since I do not consider the question to be one which admits of being discussed with much prospect of advantage in a debate, at least if the end in view be mutual persuasion. The difference between us is too deeply rooted, and is connected on both sides with too great a number of extensive and important principles, each of them far more than sufficient to form in itself the subject of an animated and protracted discussion. How, for instance, can we agree in our estimation of the church in respect of the support which it lends to the aristocratic institutions of this country, so long as there is one portion among us who disapprove of these institutions, and think that every support which they possess is one too many; while the remainder, so far from thinking that any support should be taken away, are of opinion that these institutions require, and ought to have, still stronger supports than it possesses? Or how again can two of the ablest speakers on the last evening agree in their estimate of Hume's argument in favour of a church establishment, that it diminishes the activity of the clergy, when the one is a warm admirer and partaker of religious enthusiasm, and the other condemns it under the name of fanaticism? There is a great deal more involved in this question than can be stated in a debate, and I should despise the man who, having previously been of a different opinion, could be convinced in an evening by my hon. friend's arguments or by mine. I believe it is perfectly well understood between my other hon. friend and me that his opinion is the legitimate consequence of his principles, and my opinion of mine. I do not, however, think that a discussion of this sort is wholly useless. Though it does not enable us to compare our several views, it enables all of us to know what they are, which I cannot but consider as a point gained in favour of truth and fair dealing, since I think I have observed that much of the misrepresentation and misunderstanding which take place both in public and in private life, and are a very serious impediment to the fair and legitimate collision of opinion, arises from real bona fide ignorance on one side of the views and principles of the other. It is so important that a perfect mutual understanding should exist on this point that I think I shall be justified in occupying five minutes more of the Society's time for that purpose. As my object is only that gentlemen should know the reasons, not that they should be convinced by them, five minutes will suffice for that purpose as well as an hour.

My hon. friend has given us an able statement of his reasons, and I freely admit that several of them are deserving of grave consideration. I do not at present intend to contest these reasons; I have only to state my own, and I shall be satisfied with one grand one, but that indeed may be said in a certain sense to include all the rest. I am an enemy to church establishments because an established clergy must be enemies to the progressiveness of the human mind. I hold that it is of the nature of the human mind to be progressive. But stop! I must not forget that there are persons in this country, and for aught I know in this Society, to whom the march of intellect, which is another word for the progressiveness of the human mind, is a subject of laughter and derision. I know indeed that this feigned laughter is in reality a cloak for the most abject fear, and that it would be a most delightful relief to the minds of many of these laughers if they could really feel towards the march of intellect all the contempt they express. Still, however, since there are such persons I think it advisable not to use any expression at which they are likely to cavil. I hold then that it is of the nature of the human mind to profit by experience. As the aggregate of our experience is every day increasing, this of itself has a tendency to render the species progressive, but besides this we become better qualified to profit by experience in proportion to the culture of our intellectual faculties; and of that culture there are two great instruments, education and discussion. I hold that wherever mankind have been qualified to profit by experience by possessing even in a moderate degree these two great instruments, they have as the mass of experience has increased, constantly grown wiser and better; and that this progressive advancement has never been interrupted but when these two means of instruction have been prevented from existing by despotism, as in the Roman Empire, by anarchy, as in feudal Europe, or by superstition and priestcraft, as in Spain and Portugal. I further hold that from the present state and future prospects of Great Britain, France, and North America, there is humanly speaking no probability that these causes of retrogression should ever again recur; and that from the increasing diffusion and growing power of the two great instruments, education and discussion, it is to be expected that the human mind in these countries will continue to advance, not only with an unretarded, but as it has done during the last twenty years, with a rapidly increasing pace.

Now it is to this great tendency of the human mind, and to education and discussion as the promoters of it, that in my view of the matter an established clergy by a sort of moral necessity must be, and at any rate always is, the bitter enemy. When I say an established clergy I mean any clergy which is paid on condition of teaching a particular creed, but more especially a clergy connected with the governing powers of the State, and bound by that connexion to the support of certain political tenets as well as religious ones.

If there were a corporate body of physicians or a corporate body of engineers paid by the State, rewarded with honours and wealth on condition that they should always teach a certain set of doctrines in physic or mechanics, it can scarcely be doubted that such a body would be interested in preventing all improvement in physic or mechanics, lest the public should get beyond their particular tenets, and having done so should cease to regard them, their teachers, with due veneration. Happily this is not the case. Neither the physician nor the engineer is bound down to a particular set of opinions in their respective sciences; the clergyman is. Wherever there is a hierarchy, wherever there is such a thing as church government, adherence to certain tenets is the condition on which he holds both his emoluments and his power. If there be not only a hierarchy but a hierarchy connected with the ruling powers in the State, it becomes the interest of its members to uphold the existing government with all the political and moral, as well as religious, prejudices which may conduce to their holding that government in veneration. It will perhaps be said that these opinions are the right opinions. This may be true, but it likewise may be false. It would be a considerable stretch of arrogance in mankind to suppose that they had already attained

the pinnacle of knowledge either in religion or
politics ; it is highly probable that there is still
room for improvement in both : I am sure there
is much need, at least so long as our perfect
government finds it very difficult to prevent half
our population from dying of hunger ; and our
perfect religion has not yet found the means of
preventing our jails from being constantly full.
I shall not, however, choose to rest my case upon
any argument which implies that it is possible for
an established opinion to be wrong. I will suppose
that our clergy teach no opinions but such as are
right, either in religion or politics. It is not the
less true that in the progress of human improvement every one of these opinions comes to be
questioned. The good of mankind requires that
it should be so. The good of mankind requires
that nothing should be believed until the question
be first asked, what evidence there is for it. The
very idea of progressiveness implies not indeed the
rejection but the questioning of all established
opinions. The human intellect is then only in its
right state when it has searched all things in order
that it may hold fast by that which is good. Now
when this spirit of universal inquiry arises it must
extend to those two most important subjects ;
the experience of all ages warrants the assertion
that when the human mind once begins to improve,
men will discuss religion and politics, and no force
which does not go the length of crushing the
spirit of improvement altogether can prevent it.
In consequence of this discussion persons are sure
to arise who dispute the established opinions ;
these persons are listened to, they are allowed at
least a patient hearing. This the clergy will never

voluntarily allow. It is of no use to say that the clergy may defend their opinions; so they may; and if the opinions be true and be defended with as much ability as they are attacked, they will be defended successfully. But this would give an immensity of trouble. It is well known that richly endowed bodies are never very fond of trouble; it is allowed both by the friends and the enemies of opulent church establishments that the love of ease is always their predominant infirmity. Besides the trouble there is moreover always a lurking apprehension lest, after all, their endeavours to keep the people in the right path should not succeed, or if it should, people should no longer duly venerate their parties for communicating to them truths which as they had examined into the evidence they would seem to owe to their own understanding alone. How much easier and how much safer would it be if they could be prevented from inquiring at all, if they could be made to regard the very act of inquiry, nay the very thought of questioning an established opinion, as involving the deepest guilt. It is true that they will not then hold these opinions like rational creatures, but it is of no consequence to the clergy that they should hold them like rational beings provided they only hold them strongly enough, and no opinions are held so strongly as those which we are taught that it is impious even to demand a reason for.

Such are the motives which induce an endowed clergy to be the enemies of discussion, and as discussion always accompanies improvement, they are the enemies of improvement. In order to prevent discussion they have not scrupled, wherever they had the power, to debase the human mind down to the level of the brutes. In all countries where they could get the civil power to side with them, that is in almost all the Catholic countries of Europe, they have succeeded in their nefarious purpose, and mankind are still grovelling at their feet. It is very idle to say that these are Catholic priests, and therefore not to be quoted against the Church of England. That the Catholic priests perpetrated these things is not owing to any peculiar perversity in the nature of the men ; it is owing to their interests as priests, aided by a religion which gave them more power to effect their purposes, but did not give them a stronger motive. In England at the Reformation it became the interest of the civil power to raise public feeling against the church, and the latter consequently had no longer much power, either moral or political, of effecting its ends ; but as soon as under Charles I it found the civil power ready to renew the alliance, it recommenced its war against the progress of the human mind, and nearly succeeded in throwing us back to the condition of France and Spain. Fortunately the habit of free inquiry had in the preceding years been too strong to be checked, and we were saved by a revolution from the double consummation of civil and ecclesiastical tyranny. Though this grand conspiracy had failed, the Church of England has never ceased its resistance in the detail. Not one step has been made from persecution to religious liberty but in the teeth of their most strenuous opposition ; never have they suffered one particle of discussion in religion and politics which it was in their power to prevent ; not a step has been taken with their goodwill for the diffusion of education. I speak of them as a body. They have never originated any one plan for spreading or improving it, and whatever plans have been prepared by others, from the Lancastrian and Infant Schools up to the University of London, they have as a body most violently opposed; except that in most of these instances when they at last found that the thing would go on in spite of their opposition, they have as the next best thing to preventing the improvement altogether attempted to keep it in their own hands for sectarian purposes. As people would read, they might read the Bible and the Prayer Book; but as for reading the Bible without the Prayer Book, no, no; that was not to be endured. Their only doubt was whether the persons who proposed it were atheists, Deists, or Dissenters. The word of God was not fit to be read unless that of man was administered along with it, and their account of what God said, or what in their opinion He should have said, was to be forced down the throats of babes and sucklings avowedly on the ground that unless a belief in it were firmly fixed in the mind at an age previous to that at which the reasoning faculty begins to operate, in all probability the habit would never establish itself at all. But I have exceeded the time which I allowed myself for stating the grounds of my disapprobation of the church. I have stated them sufficiently for purposes of information. It was not my object to state them for purposes of argument. Here, therefore, I shall stop.

SPEECH ON
SECULAR EDUCATION

SIR, the commencement at Manchester of a movement for a national education not under the control or management of either established or non-established clergy has already, it would seem, made no inconsiderable impression on the public, or else *The Times* has made a false move and miscalculated the signs of the coming public opinion ; for already at the very beginning of the agitation that journal has discovered, what it did not find out in the case of the Corn Law League until the fourth or fifth year of its existence, that the thing is not merely a good thing, but what is so much better in the estimation of *The Times*, a thing destined to succeed. The promoters doubtless thought no less, but they probably did not expect so early a recognition of their prospects. How much then it is to be lamented that an enterprise of so much promise should have been inaugurated by an act of truckling and compromise ; that for the sake of conciliating people who are not to be conciliated and whom it ought not to have been an object to conciliate, the Association should have let itself be persuaded by Mr. Cobden, aided by some dissenting ministers, to sacrifice its distinctive flag, and instead of calling itself an Association for secular education should have sheltered its timidity under the ambiguous designation of unsectarian.

If this is only a change in words and means

nothing it deserves no better name than that of deception; if it does mean anything, if by un-sectarian is to be understood something different from secular education, the broad principle of religious freedom which was to be the foundation of this great educational movement is abandoned.

In the debates of the Conference there was a good deal of misunderstanding, some of it I fear rather wilful on the part of Mr. Cobden and his supporters respecting the import of the word secular. There is no uncertainty about it. There is not a better defined word in the English language. Secular is whatever has reference to this life. Secular instruction is instruction respecting the concerns of this life. Secular subjects therefore are all subjects except religion. All the arts and sciences are secular knowledge. To say that secular means irreligious implies that all the arts and sciences are irreligious, and is very like saying that all professions except that of the law are illegal. There is a difference between irreligious and not religious, however it may suit the pur-poses of many persons to confound it. Now on the principles of religious freedom which we were led to believe that it was the purpose of this Association to accept, instruction on subjects not religious is as much the right of those who will not accept religious instruction as of those who will. To know the laws of the physical world, the properties of their own bodies and minds, the past history of their species, is as much a benefit to the Jew, the Mussulman, the Deist, the Atheist, as to the orthodox churchman; and it is as iniquitous to withhold it from them. Education provided by the public must be education for all, and to be

education for all it must be purely secular education.

When, then, the Association refuses to say that
their education is secular but are willing to say
that it shall be unsectarian, what do they mean ?
Doubtless that it is still to be exclusive, though in
a minor degree. That religion is to be taught, but
not sectarian religion. That they are not to have
Church of England teaching, or Catholic teaching,
or Baptist, or Methodist, or Unitarian teaching,
but I suppose Christian teaching ; that is, whatever common elements of Christianity are supposed to be found in all these sects alike. How
far this is likely to conciliate the various classes of
sectarians the Association will probably hear
loudly enough from the sectarians themselves.
I am much mistaken if they will be at all thankful
for any religious teaching which expresses no
opinion on a subject on which Christians differ in
opinion, or if the substratum of universal Christianity which it is proposed to teach will appear
to them at all different from Deism. But this is
their concern. I take higher ground. I maintain
that if you could carry all the sects with you by
your compromise you would have effected nothing
but a compact among the more powerful bodies
to cease fighting among themselves and join in
trampling on the weaker. You would have con-
trived a national education not for all, but for
believers in the New Testament. The Jew and the
unbeliever would be excluded from it though they
would not the less be required to pay for it. I do
not hear that their money is to be refused, that
they are to be exempted from the school rate.
Religious exclusion and inequality are as odious

when practised towards minorities as majorities. I thought the principle of the Association had been that of justice, but I find it is that of being unjust to those alone who are not numerous enough to resist.

I cannot help remarking how much less confidence professed Christians appear to have in the truth and power of their principles than infidels generally have in theirs. Disbelievers in Christianity almost always hail the advance of public intelligence as favourable to them; the more informed and exercised a mind is, the more likely they account it to adopt their opinions: but I cannot find a trace of similar confidence in most of the professedly religious. If they hold their belief with the same full assurance as the others their disbelief, surely infidels and the children of infidels are those to whom, even more than to any others, they would be eager to give all instruction which could render their minds more capable of pursuing and recognizing truth. A person is without religious belief, or in other words is in their estimation in a state of the most pitiable, the most calamitous ignorance by which any one can possibly be afflicted, and for this reason they refuse him instruction, they refuse him knowledge and the cultivation and discipline of the intellect, as if they thought that mental cultivation could not possibly be favourable to Christianity, unless the mind is first strongly prepossessed on its behalf. Such sentiments as these are not complimentary to Christianity nor to the sincerity of their belief in it. Its greatest enemy could say nothing worse of it than that either ignorance or early prejudice is the soil it must have to flourish in, and that to instruct unbelievers, to make them rational and thinking beings, is but to confirm them in unbelief. I hoped that the founders of the Lancaster Association had been persons who thought that mental cultivation opens the mind to all truth, whether expressly taught or not. Let us hope that this conviction is still theirs and will guide and animate their labours; but they have missed through pusillanimity a splendid opportunity for inscribing it on their banner and proclaiming it in the face of the world.

INDEX

PRINTED IN GREAT BRITAIN
AT THE UNIVERSITY PRESS, OXFORD
BY VIVIAN RIDLER
PRINTER TO THE UNIVERSITY